BUSINESS/SCIENCE/TECHNOLOGY DIVISION
CHICAGO PUBLIC LIBRARY
400 SOUTH STATE STREET
CHICAGO, ILLINOIS 60605

D0147262

DISCARD

Class, Power
& Austerity

Class, Power & Austerity
The New York City Fiscal Crisis

ERIC LICHTEN

Introduction by Stanley Aronowitz

CRITICAL STUDIES IN WORK & COMMUNITY SERIES

Bergin & Garvey Publishers, Inc.
Massachusetts

To my father, mother and Laureen

First published in 1986 by
Bergin & Garvey Publishers, Inc.
670 Amherst Road
South Hadley, Massachusetts 01075

Copyright © 1986 by Bergin & Garvey Publishers, Inc.
All rights reserved. No part of this publication may be reproduced or transmitted in any form or by any means, electronic or mechanical, including photocopy, recording of any information storage or retrieval system, without permission in writing from the publisher.

6789   987654321

Library of Congress Cataloging-in-Publication Data

Lichten, Eric.
  Class, power, and austerity.

  (Critical studies in work & Community series)
  Bibliography: p.
  Includes index.
  1. New York (N.Y.)—Economic conditions.   2. New York (N.Y.)—Social conditions.   3. Municipal finance—New York (N.Y.)   4. Tax and expenditure limitations—New York (N.Y.)   I. Title.   II. Series.
  HC108.N7L47   1986   336.747'1   85-22954
  ISBN 0-89789-090-6
  ISBN 0-89789-091-4 (pbk.)

Printed in the United States of America

Contents

Preface

"Reagan is a true capitalist and so am I . . . I really don't care about social programs. Reagan cares about strength, power, spending for the military, just like I do."

30-year-old stockbroker from
Forest Hills, N.Y., *New York Times*

"The President and his co-conspirators have been conducting undeclared war against blacks and Hispanics, welfare clients, women, children, and blue-collar workers. Under way is another episode of class conflict between rich and poor."

Robert Lekachman, in his *Greed Is Not Enough: Reaganomics*

This is a time of crisis and transformation in America's economic and political life. Equally profound are the transformations in American consciousness and the ideologies by which we understand and make sense of ourselves and society. It is a time for yuppies, glorification of the self, gentrification, corporate domination, individualism in ideology, authoritarian conformity into fact. In politics, it is a time when budget cutters happily wield sharp axes, motivated by ideological commitment and repressive pragmatism, turning back years of social progress made within the welfare state. It is a time for redirecting public monies from social to military programs, as military contractors and investors in the public debt grow richer, while the poor are told that they must be sacrificed to the politics of the budget deficit. Most of all, it is a time for militarism in politics and ideology, as national consciousness turns from altruism to barbarism, from a progressive social consciousness to reactionary Social Darwinism. This is the time of Reagan, corporate power over state and society, growing poverty, union weakness, fiscal crisis, and austerity.

This work addresses this crisis by studying, and using as the basis for theorizing further, the watershed moment in the transformation from the politics of growth to the politics of scarcity, from the social welfare to the austerity state: the fiscal crisis of New York City, circa 1974–77. During this crisis, the political accommodations and policies that characterized America's liberal consensus and welfare-state politics were dismantled, to the detriment of labor and the poor. Having reached these class accommodations during the years of economic affluence, state growth, and militance on the part of labor and the poor, these class relations could not survive under the weight of economic decline and fiscal crisis. New class relations based on the current conditions of crisis, selective scarcity, and corporate domination developed and were institutionalized as austerity. I have called these new class relations the "austerity state."

In the sense that this book explores the transformation of social and political policy, it is concerned with the relations of class and power, economy and state. Since C. Wright Mills wrote his seminal work on the structure of power in America, *The Power Elite,* America's social scientists have been concerned with these issues. Yet, after decades of debate and argument, of studies and counter-studies, the literature from elite and pluralist theorists of power had grown inconclusive and stale. However, with the appearance of the Marxist literature on the relations of the capitalist state, class, and power, the debate shifted to new terrain, with new problematics. In the works of James O'Connor, Nicos Poulantzas, Ralph Miliband, and Claus Offe, to name a prominent few, the empirical and theoretical work on this subject grew in importance and altered the directions of the debate.

To these theorists, what was critical was the structure, functions, and contradictions of the state as it exists within capitalist—hence, class—societies. Rather than closing inquiry, the questions raised by these theorists moved the debates in new directions. It is from within the problematics established by this tradition that this work began and grew.

With the critical appearance of the fiscal crisis of New York came an opportunity to view the relations of class and state within a situation of crisis. It seemed likely and, I hypothesized, quite correct, that crises provided the opportunity to study a given power structure even as it was being transformed during that crisis. I found that the fiscal crisis of the city indeed presented a unique opportunity for such a study.

Of greater significance, beyond the development of social science research and theory, was that the fiscal crisis provided the milieu for the transformation of the class politics of the city. As the fiscal crisis deepened, the city's banking and corporate community mobilized in an austerity movement. The politics and policies that had given the city its progressive reputation were viciously attacked. In the light of the austerity movement, the city's huge education, social welfare, hospital, health care, and service network found itself vulnerable and without adequate support to sustain its funding. Eventually, as the city faced repeated skirmishes with bankruptcy, drastic budget cuts were forced, reducing the level of services to the public and the city's indigent clients.

The city's workers, unions, and poor were savaged by the draconian sized budget cuts: 60,000 city jobs were lost; schools and health clinics were closed, day-care centers were defunded; for the first time tuition was imposed on the students at the City University; police, fire and sanitation services were reduced; and the subway fare was significantly raised. All of this was legitimized by the fiscal crisis and the ideology of scarcity that it caused. Since the city was forced out of the debt markets, where other municipalities borrowed money to provide services and meet expenses, the choice seemed to be either bankruptcy or austerity.

This book offers a new interpretation of this crisis. By focusing on the fiscal crisis of New York and the development of austerity, I have been able to draw upon a significant moment in the city's history to speak about the issues of class and power. I demonstrate that this city does not have a pluralist power structure; rather, its power structure must be understood to exclude the poor, the working class, and all but certain fractions of the capitalist class.

I interpret the history of the fiscal crisis as a demonstration of the power of capital against the weaknesses of labor and progressive forces as they are now constituted. As the fiscal crisis deepened, the power of the city's banks increased while the power of its labor unions decreased. As a consequence, the formal mechanisms of government were superseded by austerity boards (the Municipal Assistance Corporation and the Emergency Financial Control Board) and thereby removed from popular influence. In this way, through the institutionalization of austerity, the city's banks and corporate leaders were able to redirect the city's political and economic policies.

This work also speaks to the weakness of Labor in this moment of crisis. Without a doubt, the labor movement today finds itself losing ground in America's new class politics. During the post-war era, Labor tied its own hands by stressing class accommodation, cooperation, and economism over class struggle. During the years of economic growth this policy falsely promised the working class the achievement of the "American Dream." However, in these years of economic decline, the labor movement has found itself with few powerful friends, and little power of its own. As a consequence, these are years of labor concessions, and Labor hardly resembles a broadly based, effectively mobilized movement. In chapters 7, 8, and 9 I address the weakness of Labor through an analysis of the actions of the city's labor unions during the fiscal crisis. For Labor to reassert its strength politically and at the workplace, the old ideologies of class accommodation need to be replaced. A new emphasis on class struggle—at the workplace, in the community, and in the state—is necessary for Labor's resurgence. This requires new alliances among progressives, community activists, workers, and the poor, to confront the power of capital, its ideologies and its austerity.

Class, Power
& Austerity

Introduction

The American welfare state has always been more feeble than its European counterparts. Lacking a politically conscious working-class movement with sufficient strength to impose a broad range of state-supported social benefits, the United States Congress and successive administrations, beginning with Franklin Roosevelt's, only managed to establish a relatively minimalist welfare establishment. There is still no national health scheme, except for social security recipients and this was enacted for the first time in the 1980s; jobless benefits are time-bound, after which an unemployed worker is obliged to apply for welfare, a step which usually means being stripped of durable goods such as house and car. Moreover, the low income for the unemployed is designed to force the worker to accept a lower paying job than previously held. And the time constraints built into federal standards assume a normally healthy economy, even though unemployment from all sources has now reached almost one-fifth of the labor force.*

Nevertheless, until the early 1970s, the system which at the time was only about 35 years old was widely viewed as securely woven into our

*This figure of 20 percent may be startling to those who listen to the government's unemployment statistics, which today hover around 7.5 percent. It is an amazing but little-known fact that the U.S. Department of Labor uses a method of employment calculation almost unheard of in western countries. The DOL does *not count as unemployed* 1) unemployed welfare recipients; 2) first-time job seekers who have yet to find work (a vast number of young people); and 3) "discouraged" workers, that is, those who have been out of work so long they have stopped looking. Furthermore, the DOL *does count among the employed* the more than two million members of the military. If one adjusts the unemployment figures to account for the government's deceptive calculations, the U.S. economy has a tremendous unemployment problem.

social fabric; like baseball, it was virtually unchallengeable. The myriad complaints of business people and professionals—that the tax burden to support social spending was too high to pay for a gaggle of loafers and even delinquents from the proper circles of American society—were mostly the grumblings of a minority. Fueled by the Vietnam war, the 1960s was a time for welfare expansion and the post-New Deal Johnson administration made the most of it. As it turned out, the end of the war in 1973 spelled doom for the spirit of reform, for while Johnson's successor, Richard Nixon, deplored the apparently ceaseless growth of the federal bureaucracy, his first term was marked by efforts to end the war spurred by confrontations with a mass anti-war movement and, especially, the dramatic military defeat of American forces in southeast Asia.

However, wartime prosperity was already giving way to stagflation. The economy began to suffer from two closely related maladies: sharpening international competition, especially from Germany and Japan, that was cutting deeply not only into America's exports, but also into domestic production, as a trickle of imports turned into a flood by 1975; and an international energy and food crisis that resulted in double-digit inflation. The value of the dollar plummeted on world money markets in consequence of skyrocketing balance of payments and trade deficits and Wall Street (read: investors) became increasingly nervous about their own finances.

Since the 1930s Wall Street had been intimately involved in providing capital for cities. The money was needed because local taxes, derived principally from commercial and industrial real estate and personal income, were simply not sufficient to rebuild streets, water systems, and other infrastructures or to support the massive municipal school and welfare systems. Large investors made loans at high interest rates and most cities had been able, with federal support, to pay them back in a timely fashion in preparation for the next loans. But, by the mid-70s, most American cities were suffering from the effects of massive industrial disinvestment, a taxpayer revolt limiting their ability to raise money from real property, and a mounting welfare load, the product of both disinvestment and the continuing stream of migrants from an apparently depressed farm belt in the south and west. On top of all this, the second Nixon and then the Ford administrations felt strong enough to mount an attack on social spending, especially for the cities, regarded as bastions of Democratic political power, reflecting the still important labor movement and black and other minority communities. The cities were cut back under the rubric of revenue sharing which meant that grants from the federal government for programs they previously funded almost entirely, would now only match local spending.

As federal funds began to dry up, investors made more stringent conditions for making loans. And, as Eric Lichten shows, New York City became the harbinger of a new era in social policy, one that tied the fate of millions of urban dwellers closely to the international and national markets. Cities were only the first target in a still raging struggle over the size and scope of social expenditures, and it may be said that the politics and economics of what was known as the New York fiscal crisis set the pattern for the new austerity that marks current social policy.

Lichten's enormously valuable study is perhaps the best we have on the fiscal crisis. The narrative of the development of the crisis is clear and detailed and, most important, the cast of characters is larger than most accounts of the events leading up to near-bankruptcy. Lichten deals not only with the relation of the major banks, New York's chief creditors, to the city administration, but also with the response of the larger and powerful municipal unions, in whose hands a different solution to the crisis may have been possible. Lichten's concept of the austerity state is a truly original organizing principle for understanding our current social policy. Thus, this is much more than a case study; it is nothing less than a theory of the economic and political dynamics of contemporary domestic government programs. Lichten has transcended the limits of sociology and political science and offers a subtle political economy of the fiscal crisis without lapsing into reductionism. The book will be a valuable source for years to come.

This is the second volume in the series *Critical Studies in Work and Community,* designed to provide theoretically informed ethnographies, case studies, and other forms of research that illuminate some of the new social realities of our time.

Stanley Aronowitz

1

The Austerity State

"Can New York City balance its budget and make up millions of dollars of deficits without improving productivity?" he asked.

"Absolutely not," he answered.

"Who do you think runs government?"

"Perhaps no one."

> Major Edward I. Koch, in dialogue with
> himself, *New York Times*

"The demands of the lender become reasonable because the lender is the lender."

> Stephen Berger, *New York Times*

"What really determines what happens is power—pure, simple muscle and nothing else."

> Al Viani, AFSCME, personal interview

"There is no power on earth like the power of the free market place. And governments hate it, because they cannot control it."

> Walter B. Wriston, *New York Times*

Fiscal Crisis and the Austerity State

New York City's fiscal crisis was a harbinger of crises to come in post-affluent America. Even now, as the city celebrates its "fiscal health," fiscal crisis has reached beyond the borders to effect the politics of the federal government and, as a consequence, the policies possible in New York City. The characteristics of the city's crisis now appear in greater scope at the federal level, encouraging the attempt to dismantle the

1

welfare state. The failure of the city's revenues to cover increasingly large budget deficits, resulting in debt service increasing as a proportion of the total budget, the concomitant assault on the city's welfare and labor policies, and its ability to deliver essential services, have now been generalized to American society as a whole through the federal fiscal crisis.

In both cases, austerity developed as public policy with the fiscal crisis as its legitimator. Now, political conflicts emerge over how to distribute and institute austerity; not over its necessity. Clearly, austerity now dominates policy discourse within the political establishment.

If fiscal crisis is now a predominant concern for politicians across the country, austerity is now their solution. Austerity has become the policy of the 1980s, and no mainstream American politician has mounted a campaign against it. Instead, conventional political "wisdom" now asserts the historical inevitability and absolute necessity of an austere public sector. Austerity, with its underlying ideology of scarcity and Social Darwinism, goes unchallenged, and in the process the social welfare apparatus, for which so many have struggled during the past fifty years, is now endangered.

What we have here is nothing short of a full-scale assault on the liberal agenda that characterized and gave force to America's social welfare state. The class accommodations of the postwar growth years no longer carry the ideological and political force that is needed to move forward in the face of slow or negligible economic growth, mounting deficits in both international trade and federal budgets, and the decline of basic smokestack industries in America. Both austerity and austerity-minded politicians have become central features of political life and discourse in the 1980s, as a consequence of the same basic social process: the crisis of capitalism and capital's struggle against labor. Austerity is now the dominant strategy, asserting the domination of labor by capital—within the state and at the workplace.

The argument here is that the social welfare state—however underdeveloped it has been in America compared to the Northern European social welfare states—has lost its legitimacy in America. Fewer and fewer Americans consider themselves "liberals," and successful politicians today gain support by criticizing the welfare state. The welfare state is now identified in the public mind as wasteful and inefficient in its ability to sustain economic growth. Its policies toward the poor and disabled are perceived by much of the public as providing incentives for sloth and laziness. Given this public perception, the fiscal crisis of the state provides the ideological justification for an attack on the social programs of liberalism. The liberal consensus has been replaced by a conservative consensus, whose policy makers need austerity as the centerpiece of their program.

To understand the conservatives' need for austerity as the linchpin of their agenda, one has only to look at the failure of recent liberal policies to correct the tailspin of the American economy. As this decline of the American economy proceeded, so, too, did organized resistance, by Labor and community activists, to both productivity at the workplace and scarcity for the poor. The historically high federal and local budget deficits, as well as public debt, need to be understood as being the consequences of long-term class struggles over the production and distribution of society's collective wealth. The argument of this book is that fiscal crisis is not the result of a badly mismanaged macroeconomic policy. It is not merely a momentary aberration, which can be set right by balancing budgets according to business rationality. Instead, fiscal crisis is viewed as part of and the consequence of a class-based struggle over wealth, income, and economic security.

While the conceptualization of workplace struggles as class struggles is widely accepted, such analysis is extended here to the community struggles of the 1960s and 1970s, including the struggles of blacks and other minorities for more income and control over their communities. This conceptualization is valid, since the struggles by America's oppressed minorities for income and security had impact on the production and distribution of wealth in America. And although these struggles were explicitly organized as being based on racial and ethnic identity, their content was one of class. Certainly their success was dependent upon the extent to which they provided access for their members to the material rewards of society. In other words, these struggles were class struggles because they asserted the need for a redistribution of material rewards —whether in the form of jobs, income, government transfer payments and programs, housing, or education. And this redistribution was made within the framework of a zero-sum game: the gains were made at some other group's or class's expense. What was gained had to be paid for—in taxes or in wages. Hence, these were class struggles which expanded the welfare state. Eventually, the backlash to these and other working-class gains would lead to today's austerity politics.

The gains made by the working class during the 1960s and early 1970s are now in danger of being reversed by a policy engineered to meet the needs of another class—the capitalist class. This policy is austerity. In effect, as the past gains of workers and the poor are reversed by austerity, the social welfare state is replaced by the "austerity state." The main feature of such a state is the redesign of state budgetary policies to reduce the social expenditures that characterized the welfare policies of the past and to increase the influence of the private sector over public policy. The austerity state provides public policy with a more direct role in enhancing corporate power at the expense of the poor, the elderly, the workers, and the labor unions. Along with a redirection of budgetary priorities, the austerity state slashes the programs that enforce corporate accountability to workers and the community (such as workplace safety and environmental protection programs), while supporting the hypermobility of capital. In this way, the austerity state encourages the accumulation of capital by removing government obstacles to growth—even where these obstacles protect communities, jobs, and the health and safety of workers. The austerity state legitimizes policy through an ideological framework, which emphasizes government's incapacity and its lack of resources. In these two ways, through a critique of the public sector and through the notion that scarcity dominates public-sector decisions, the austerity state encourages the needs of capital over all other needs.

Along with these antilabor, procapital policies, the austerity state seeks to reestablish the connection between productivity and wages—a connection that was threatened by gains made within the social welfare state. The poor, as well as other clients of the welfare state, asserted their right to income without productivity. If capital could not provide stable employment for the poor, the state was pressured to sustain them with income and security. As the number of state clients grew, so too did the number and power of public-sector workers. And with the growth of public-sector unions, came a struggle within the public sector over income and productivity. Since productivity in the public sector cannot be so easily measured, and since the criterion of profit does not enter into collective bargaining, state workers demanded and often won wages and benefits that reduced their labor while increasing their compensation. The connection between productivity and wages was broken for these workers, as they demonstrated that wages are a consequence of class power. The market criteria for setting wages could not remain an ideological fetter on the organized struggles of public workers. Their workplace was politicized and was now subject to power struggles. The connection in fact and ideology between productivity and the value of labor power was broken to the advantage of these workers. The austerity state has reasserted the priorities of management for productivity, even while cutting wages and benefits. Labor is disciplined by the threat of layoffs, legitimized by the ideology of scarcity. The state's managers—whether they are Democrats or Republicans—cry that the state lacks the funds that are needed to provide both jobs and services. As a consequence, the ideological and structural terrain of class struggles vis-a-vis the state has been altered. The austerity state weakens the ability of workers, unions, and clients to redistribute wealth away from capital. Hence, the austerity state realigns the power relations between capital, labor, government, and clients. Capital gets tax incentives; labor gives concessions; state clients get budget cuts.

In terms of its own policies toward the poor, the austerity state reduces the funds supporting both the jobless poor and the working poor. Previously won programs, such as housing and aid to families with dependent children, are slashed, and, equally important, progressive reform aimed at assisting the poor is no longer on the political agenda. It is no longer part of political discourse. The discourse had been reversed. Previously, the discourse was a liberal one, and the policy debate was centered on the expansion of social programs. Now, however, the discourse is a conservative one, based on austerity, and with yearly federal deficits of $200 billion the policy debate centers on *how much* to cut from social programs. After one full Reagan administration, austerity has already severely eroded America's welfare state. As David Stockman, former Budget Director for the Reagan administration, told *Fortune Magazine:*

> We haven't thrown overboard the mainline programs like food stamps and aid to education, but their constant-dollar costs have shrunk. The Great Society programs started under Lyndon Johnson [job training, aid to elementary and secondary education, social service programs, and so forth] peaked out at a cost of $140 billion in 1984 dollars in 1979-80. The cost will be down to $110 billion this year, no matter what Congress does. We have not succeeded in challenging the premise of the Great Society, but the level has been adjusted downward by about 20%.
>
> Aside from defense, interest, and Social Security, we have shrunk the government by 15%. The domestic budget is not growing seriously in real terms. Means-tested entitlements have been capped off. Nobody is liberalizing entitlements anymore. After a period of unremitting expansion in domestic spending, we have had zero growth in real terms since 1980—leaving aside defense and interest. No new programs, no new entitlements, no new claims on the taxpayers' dollars.[1]

Yet, Stockman modestly assesses the change of direction that this budget process represents. During these austere Reagan years, budget cuts have hurt or crippled programs for mass transit, job training, child nutrition, housing rehabilitation in inner cities, and education, to name just a few. For the poor, austerity has further eroded what was already a meager existence. As reported by *Business Week:*

> The drive to cap welfare costs was a smashing success. Adjusted for inflation, spending for welfare programs was no higher in fiscal 1984 than in 1980, and excluding medicaid, was 5% lower: $24.9 billion in 1984 vs. $26.1 billion in 1980. For 1985, federal aid for the poor totals $78 billion—less than 8.5% of total government expenditures, compared with 10% five years ago . . .

As a result of this clean sweep, politicians and welfare experts generally agree that there is little room for additional cuts. Says Henry Aaron, former assistant secretary of the Health, Education & Welfare Dept.: "This closet has been cleaned."

The concern now is that the cuts already made have actually reduced the living standard of the average welfare family. . . . The Census Bureau estimates that between 1979 and 1982, the population living below the poverty line rose 44%, to 29 million—even after accounting for the value of government benefits. . . . But under the new eligibility standards, the government will pay less this year for welfare—in inflation-adjusted dollars—than it did in fiscal 1980.[2]

The conservative agenda is now on the table and the conservatives themselves are serving austerity. This is the austerity state. Its ideology is Corporatist, Social Darwinist, and anti-Labor. It seeks to return to the private sector many of the functions of government associated with the welfare state. It asks not what the state can do for the poor; rather, it returns to the notion that the private sector can best meet all our needs, without qualification. The austerity state is a return to a private sector unencumbered by an activist welfare state.

Austerity politics is a different type of politics than any that has been heretofore encountered. Its underlying basis involves a strong reliance on finance capital to underwrite government debt; yet, finance capital's needs are not fixed to the national debt. Whenever it is able, finance capital retains an independence from any national loyalty and an ability, as well as a need, to flow where it can prosper. Nevertheless, as the debtors increase their debt, finance capital is itself threatened. The very same process that allows finance capital to prosper also provides a threat to its security. Therein lies the contradiction as well as the impetus for instability. Since the flow of finance capital involves and necessitates large quantities of speculative investment, the potential for economic chaos and collapse is increased. Furthermore, the security of investments may depend on controlling the politicization of the investment process. As debts increase, governments are pushed toward austerity budgeting to insure their ability to secure the debt and leave open their access to finance capital. This process enhances the power of finance capital as investors negotiate with governments at all levels. In 1974, it was New York City; in 1984, Argentina and Mexico; soon, it may very well be the federal government of the United States. In this uncertain international financial milieu, the possibilities for financial chaos are endless. But within this realm of economic uncertainty, with speculative investment and the hypermobility of both finance and industrial capital characterizing the class politics of austerity, one thing seems certain. The capitalist state, in its national and local manifestations, has either moved or been moved toward austerity budgeting. And with this move, the budget has been politicized to the benefit of capital and to the detriment of the allies and clients of the social welfare state.

The austerity state finds fiscal crisis to be an ally—an ideological legitimator. Seizing fiscal crisis, Republicans and Democrats alike call for and institute a public policy—in the name of tax reform, business incentives and growth, real estate development, social welfare reform—which redistributes income upward. The fiscal crisis of the state has been used as the legitimator for reducing government spending for social programs to an austere level. These social programs had resulted from the struggles waged by poor and working-class people, by community activists and public sector employees alike, in the golden age of activism—the 1960s and early 1970s. Capital, in the workplaces and through its local and national power, has reasserted its initiative against the gains won by labor and by working-class and poor communities throughout the nation. We now witness the age of austerity legitimized by the discourse of scarcity—a language of limitations—replacing the previous discourse of affluence and the further development of the social welfare state. Make no mistake about this—what we now witness is a heightening of capital's power at society's expense; a strengthening of capital's command over the capitalist state—in personnel and in function.

Though austerity followed years of social activism by a large number of progressive groups and movements, no claim is being made here that a well-funded social welfare state had emerged in the United States. Clearly, in comparison to the social democracies of northern Europe, America's commitment to alleviating the poverty, inequality, and generally low level of economic security was, at most, minimal. Nevertheless, America then had a political discourse with affluence at its core, and with this came the legitimacy of a more socially responsive state apparatus, which accepted the necessity of alleviating some of the burdens of a capitalist society. That disource and its policies have now dissolved under the onslaught of economic and fiscal crisis and the rise of the right wing. The language of limitations and of corporate domination now characterizes political discourse. This discourse eschews social responsibility, while promoting corporate interests and a "trickle-down" philosophy of economy and state. The crisis of capitalism and the fiscal crisis of the state have been seized by capital as an opportunity to redirect government. Where is the opposition?

This book presents an analysis of fiscal crisis, austerity, and class power based on research that was done on the fiscal crisis of New York City. The fiscal crisis of the state has been analyzed and studied by many writers and researchers, as if it were independent of the broader social relations of advanced capitalism; especially the relations of production, class, and state. For some, fiscal crisis is merely an aggravated case of fiscal "strain," in which the main problem is resource management. According to this view, predominant in mainstream political science policy analysis, fiscal strain results from declining resources, which bring about an increase in interest-group politics. In a sense, the interest groups scurry after the meager morsels of revenues. The task of a city administration is to reassert its formal authority in the face of these declining revenues and hyperactive interest groups, perhaps by centralizing the decision-making process and thereby gaining the ability to manage retrenchment. Here, the budgetary process seems to be a technical one, requiring technocratic solutions. Increasing the productivity of some public-sector workers while laying off others and increasing administrative rationality have also been presented as possible solutions. Here the managerial perspective that is dominant in the private sector is brought to bear on the public sector and on public policy. [3] What is missing in this sort of analysis is a theory which views fiscal crisis as part of the transformation of the relations of class and state. Fiscal crisis, and the process by which it is resolved, does not merely happen as a result of pluralist politics. The crisis process itself reveals the weakness of pluralist theory, as the following pages will show.

In addition to the views described above, fiscal crisis is also sometimes seen as the result of "misguided" politics, inherent weaknesses of interest-group politics, the unresponsiveness of bureaucratic government to a changing external environment, and the failure of the politics of welfare. All of these views lay blame for the contemporary crisis of the state and the economy on one group or another, but rarely on the social relations of a capitalist society. Lacking here is the connection between class production, class power, and the state that underlies the fiscal crisis of the state. In these mainstream views, what has been lost is an equilibrium between revenues and expenditures; these analyses proceed from the consequences of broader contradictions. The fiscal crisis is the consequence, not the cause; it is the manifestation, and not the crisis itself. The present study places the crisis, and its uses, within a broader theoretical framework: within a theory of class struggle, crisis, and the capitalist state.

This book diverges from the more orthodox presentations of crisis. It presents the study of fiscal crisis as being also, and foremost, the study of class struggle as it impacts on the state and public sector. For most social scientists, American capitalism is not basically a contradictory system, with crisis tendencies. Crises, however deep, are viewed as momentary lapses within a basically well-integrated and socially stable system. The system's stability, according to these views, is best represented by the cooperation that is generally found among business, labor, and political leaders. Crises become vehicles which promote system integration as these leaders enter into a joint partnership to resolve the malignant crisis. Felix Rohatyn, the architect of New York City's escape from fiscal crisis, writes that "Business/Labor/Government cooperation coupled with courageous, interventionist political leadership saved New York City."[4] But the terms of cooperation may involve quite different levels of power and interest; one partner's cooperation may only indicate powerlessness. Such was the case with labor's cooperation during the fiscal crisis of New York City. Rohatyn's view obscures the recognition that the crisis itself and what may appear to be class cooperation may actually be the process of class struggle between irreconcilable interests; one group's gain and safety may be the other group's loss—of power, of income, of control. Crisis is struggle over the mode of production and distribution through which a society is organized. This book shows that crisis is struggle—and that there are winners and losers, even as leaders applaud their partnerships.

Pluralist, technocratic, and integration theories cannot but fail to understand the deep, underlying dimensions of the crisis of our age. For them, class and state operate as part of separate institutional processes; one does not overly influence the other. Class, production, and state hold no systemic contradictory processes; democracy and capitalism in America go hand in hand. The process of mediating a fiscal crisis, even where the mediation process isolates decision-making from representative government and electoral politics, necessitates "rational" solutions, based upon market criteria. One cannot provide services when one cannot afford them. And one dare not raise corporate taxes, since everyone recognizes the marketplace's domination over our lives. Yet, we call this democracy and pluralism. How odd this must seem to the unemployed and underemployed, the poor, the child who sees her school in shambles and who plays in dirty streets, the aged who depend on social security, students who depend on government-backed student loans, and workers who pay too much in taxes for too little in return, while the corporate sector pays proportionately lower taxes as austerity becomes government policy.

Having done away with the analysis of class and state, and therefore with the study of power, the analysts described above are left without a theory of crisis. Crisis is then the product of a history made by the errors of freely acting and independent human actors, who seem to react according to whim. Here, history evolves and moves accidentally, based only on the actions of individuals, without context, structures, or constraint. Lost is Marx's notion, made so forcefully and eloquently, that: "Men make their own history, but they do not make it as they please;

they do not make it under circumstances chosen by themselves, but under circumstances directly encountered, given and transmitted from the past. The tradition of all the dead generations weighs like a nightmare on the brain of the living.''[5] Lost is the analysis that makes sense of the historical subject in capitalism—a class being, acting, and creating change within a culture and social structure, within a history of struggle, exploitation, and oppression. The analysis of crisis gains insight only when it shows and understands the forces of change; whether they be progressive or reactionary, humane or guided by the cold and calculating rationality of capitalism.

The purpose of this book is to critique not only the society that produces the crises of this age, which in turn empower the austerity state, but also the social theories that seek to explain these crises. The book, therefore, is about both crisis and ideology. The dominant discourse, the hegemonic ideology of crisis that is now taken as fact, is challenged here. This hegemonic ideology of scarcity and the need for public austerity and corporate power negates the victories of the recent past. The argument advanced is that while the crisis is deep, the social theories are not. Nor do these social theories that seek to explain crisis challenge this hegemony. While the crisis is itself a failure of corporate capitalism to resolve its internal contradictions and to control class struggle, mainstream social science continues to fail to comprehend this struggle. In so doing, it has also failed to present a counterhegemony.

The failure to comprehend critically the limitations of this system as well as to fail to point to potentially progressive alternatives and counterhegemonic discourse constitute a single-minded dimensionality that pervades American economic, political, and sociological theory. Given these failures, social theory loses its critical content and instead interprets crisis by denying the prior gains of workers and the poor. By ignoring the fact that class struggle has produced the crises of our time, social analysts contribute to the ideological hegemony of austerity. Only if austerity is recognized as emerging from and representing a class struggle can the power of its ideology of scarcity be confronted. The problem of the fiscal crisis of the state is not that there is no money, no state revenues. The problem lies in the redirection of the state vis-a-vis capital and labor and in the weakness of progressive forces to alter the process of producing and allocating wealth in American capitalism. The fiscal crisis of the state is a measure of the power of contending class forces. The public policies that form in response to this fiscal crisis measure the viability of class organizations during the 1980s. By focusing on these relations of power and class, a counter-hegemonic ideology in opposition to austerity—and, by extension, to the capitalist class and its needs—is made possible. The history of austerity and the suffering it has brought to so many has already made such a focus necessary.

Crisis as Product and Process of Class Struggle

This book presents a history of the fiscal crisis of New York City that focuses on the resolution of that crisis into austerity. Such a focus exposes the crisis process and the solution of austerity as a nonobjective policy, by no means class-neutral, that is based on the relative power, or lack thereof, of class-based actors and forces. According to this view, the control and flow of finance capital, within the context of an international finance system, has enabled finance capital, as well as the rationale of corporate capitalism, to exert power within the context of the fiscal crisis. This process was accomplished in part because of two closely related factors: on the one hand, the ideological hegemony of capital's view of the fiscal crisis and, on the other hand, the ideological reluctance and structural inability of the municipal labor unions to challenge both finance capital and its ideological hegemony. As this book demonstrates, the social contract that unionism has adopted as the guiding ideology of the labor movement in the United States basically accepts capital's and management's legitimacy in the workplace and in the overall direction of the economy. Given this ideological allegiance, the notion that fiscal crisis is class struggle is one that could not be accepted by union leaders. Rather, their ideological conformity has led these leaders to accept austerity as a framework for the mediation of fiscal crisis. In other words, the labor unions' reformist contract ideology leads them to seek cooperation with capital and management, no matter whether they are private or public sector unions. America's unions do not seek class struggle and class confrontation; nor do they seek more power over the production and distribution of wealth. They do not seek control over investment policies. They do not seek class subordination of capital to labor. Ultimately, they seek class collaboration and cooperation for the benefit of an alleged "community," wherein the interests of labor and capital are mutually supportive. Given this ideology, labor unions have been cooperating with austerity. Having done so, this cooperation has rendered these unions powerless vis-a-vis capital within the state.

By now it is obvious that this study diverges from the more orthodox ways in which the fiscal crisis of New York City—and austerity throughout the United States, for that matter—have been presented and understood by politicians, by the popular press, and by mainstream social science. The study of fiscal crisis is also the study of class struggle as it impacts upon the state. The fiscal crisis of New York City developed as a consequence of struggle over the production and distribution of wealth, within a geographic boundary, which also constituted a political-economic boundary. Here I do not separate the fiscal crisis of government, i.e., New York City, from class struggles. Ultimately, the fiscal crisis results from the political and state response to the conflict over the quality of everyday life. This conflict has taken the form of struggles over wages, benefits, and the productivity of city workers. There have also been similar battles pitting manufacturing workers against their bosses, as well as an international division of labor, which encourages capital's flight to wage-saving havens. The conflict has been seen in struggles for day care, for free education, and, in the broadest sense, in the struggle by the working classes and the poor for liberation from want and scarcity. Class struggle here is intended to mean the struggle over the very manner in which the society provides for its daily existence. In that sense, it was class struggle, within the material framework of corporate capitalism facing decline, that created the pressures that resulted in fiscal strain and then in fiscal crisis.

Ultimately, the present argument offers a theory of crisis. Crisis, in its political-economic manifestation, is viewed as both *the product and the process* of struggle. As a product, crisis is the consequence of a history of production; with its own history of class struggle, and with the changing relations of state and economy, class, and power, within that history. However, crisis may also be viewed as a social process, and not the "natural" result of uncontrollable economic forces. Crisis is produced by human actors and is the consequence of human action within, in this case, a definite stage of class society, with very definite relations of state, economy, class, and power. This work shows how crisis emerges from the real, tangible struggles between antagonistic class forces and interests, how it emerges from the concrete history of struggle.

Furthermore, and equally important, crisis is also the act of, or process of, struggle. It is through the crisis process itself that the very relations of class and power, economy and state, are transformed. During crisis periods, the institutional arrangements by which we live, are governed, and produce, are open to change to both progressive and reactionary forces, though the extent to which opportunity exists for change are not necessarily the same for the right and the left at any given historical moment.

The theory I present here is that crises develop from particular struggles within a set of definite contradictory relations, themselves "grounded" and set within history. The argument is that crises are not the consequence of blind, uncontrollable forces of history. According to this view, then, crises are not inevitable in the social form that they concretely take; nor are crises resolved through inevitable, rational mechanisms or "solutions." Crises are produced, mediated, and resolved through human actions. These actions themselves are to be understood from within their historical character, grounded within their class context.

The theoretical perspective developed here returns the notion of crisis and social change to real living and acting human subjects—in this case, class beings—and removes the conceptualization of crisis from those who claim that crisis and history are inevitable and preordained. Simply stated: by conceptualizing crisis as both a product and a process, I show it both to be formed in struggle and also to be the process of struggle itself. Then, it can be shown that crisis as struggle has no "rational" solution that is separated from its class character or from its character as struggle. It can now be asserted that crisis is not a system dysfunction, which holds out its own logical, specific solution. The resolution of crisis, referred to as the crisis process, can now be seen to constitute struggle at the point of crisis; that is, struggle over solutions to crisis. Solutions are not neutral. Instead, they are political, since they represent the contradictory and conflicting needs of different classes, and other groups, within society. In this sense, crisis becomes a process of social change. To argue otherwise is to miss the significance of the political and ideological confrontations which occur as a crisis meets its "solutions."

As can readily be seen, this type of theorizing about crisis has become foreign to both mainstream and Marxist scholars. In both their paradigms, crisis seems to be inevitable, whether as a consequence of system dysfunctions, or of the failure to rationalize government, or of the inherent contradictions of capitalist production. In all these paradigms, crisis is inevitable and occurs without human subjectivity, without human-made history. If crisis is inevitable, so, too, is crisis resolution; its form, like the crisis itself, must be predetermined by a given set of social forces. According to this theory, there is little room for human maneuvering and human-made history. Here there are no alternatives to the way things are. Here there are no human actors capable of impacting on new directions in human history. Even within the Marxist paradigm, history seems preset by those who write about crisis. Although the members of the working class are seen by some as the "gravediggers" of capitalism, the work of such writers as Althusser, Wright, and Wallerstein loses its critical possibilities due to its mechanical character.[6]

This book redresses the error through an analysis of a specific crisis. The fiscal crisis of New York City is viewed from the assertion made above that crisis is both the *product of* and the actual *process of* struggle. We will see how the crisis developed and how it was resolved, that is was both real and produced. It was real as the consequence of changes in the material base of the city; it was used to effect class-based needs and aims. The crisis was resolved through austerity. Yet, its resolution weakened the city's public sector labor unions, hurt the power and influence of workers, and resulted in an increased government responsiveness to the needs of capital. To put it in plain and simple terms: the crisis resulted in austerity, due to the power of finance and corporate capital.

Yet, I do not view austerity as necessary. It is viewed as a class solution, designed by powerful members of the capitalist class and by state managers (politicians) who are ideologically tied to the needs of capital. Furthermore, the effective application of austerity demonstrates the failure of corporatist unions—themselves ideologically committed to capitalism—to oppose effectively the mobilization of finance and corporate capital. During crisis, the formal processes of government are open to change. Yet, the labor unions were not able to effect changes that reflected working-class power. Instead, finance capital was able to effect the kinds of changes, such as austerity, that exhibited its power and asserted its needs over all others. As austerity has moved from New York City to Washington, D.C., from the local level to the federal, its class character must be understood and discussed. In that sense, this book about class and power, economy and state, budgets and ideologies, corporatist unions, banks, and social change has much to tell about contemporary America.

Fiscal Crisis and the Debtor Government

Every day, newspaper headlines underline the public concern and uneasiness with the historically huge and rapidly increasing levels of public debt. The federal budget deficits, large as they are, merely constitute the tip of the iceberg, however. Each and every deficit dollar represents principal and interest that is being paid or will be paid to investors in the public debt. These debts mount as federal, state, and local governments borrow to meet expenses beyond their total revenue bases. And with the increased demand for investors and financing come historically high interest rates, which the public must pay as financiers and investors choose among the many willing government debtors.

This situation, of course, creates a public burden on the government treasuries, on its revenues, as increasingly high proportions of revenue go to retiring maturing notes and bonds. The cycle of increasing budget deficits—borrowing—and paying back creates the politics of the debtor government. As reported in the *New York Times,*

> One of the fastest-growing items in the Federal budget—faster even than military spending as a proportion of gross national product—is interest payments on the national debt. This year the Government will pay about $108 billion for debt service, more than five times as much as in 1974 and 13.5 times as much as twenty years ago.
> Moreover, this burden—accounting now for a peacetime record 14 cents of every dollar the Government spends—is almost certain to rise

even more because of the huge deficits that loom for several years.

"The net interest bill on the national debt will grow and grow," Rudolph G. Penner, director of the Congressional Budget Office, told Congress [*New York Times,* 30 January, 1984, p. D9].

The new class politics of austerity must be understood if one is to comprehend the new relation of class and power in contemporary America. As this new class power relation has developed, the politics of the debtor government has given rise to the policy of austerity. This is evident as all levels of government tighten the reins on public spending and cut back in the areas of least resistance: human resources and the income maintenance programs of the social welfare state. These programs affect nearly everyone, though in different ways. In addition to cutting back on funding to service the needs of the poor and the infirm, to educate the young, to house the homeless, or to reeducate and employ the under- and unemployed, the debtor government and its austerity politics stand by as America's infrastructure crumbles. All the while, the austerity state provides tax incentives and rebates to capital within a reactionary, antiworker, military Keynesianism.

To some analysts, this all seems necessary and inevitable. For them, history or some other blind force has led us into a bankrupt condition, which has forced our hand. In this, the commonly held mainstream view, austerity is a necessary evil, which will "put our house back in order." But "our house" has been decorated unevenly—some rooms being gilded and opulent, while others remain barren and hopeless.

Austerity is a *class* policy—it is not politically, economically, or socially neutral. It does not serve the broader community of American interests, as claimed by its proponents. It serves the interests of capital in crisis. It is not the only solution, not the neutral, "technical" solution to the debtor government. Like all social policy, it develops and emerges as a consequence and a part of the ongoing struggles that characterize the organization of a society.

Newspaper publishers and journalists, as well as academicians, scholars, writers, and activists, of both the right and the left, have all become budget conscious. Class, race, gender, and peace/war politics are all being shaped by the politics of the budget. Even the *Wall Street Journal* now fears the economic fallout from the politics of the debtor government. A prominent article emphasized the "Ever increasing burden of the federal budget" and the "dismal array of possible consequences: reignition of inflation, a return to soaring interest rates, a crowding-out of private borrowers from the credit markets and another plunge into recession." For the *Journal,* the increasing public debt and its burden of interest payments indicate that "When some people complain that we are mortgaging our futures, they are stating simple-and-ominous-fact" (*Wall Street Journal,* 14 March 1983, p. 1).

It is indeed clear and indisputable that American and Western governments at all levels, as well as those in the so-called Communist bloc, have become familiar with the problems associated with debtor nations: weak local economies and therefore unstable revenue sources; mobile capital leaving or arriving without government—and certainly without democratic or popular—consent or approval; high levels of debt and interest on the debt; and the *need,* as demanded by finance capital, for strict control over budgetary expenditures. For some nations, this process has included demands by the World Bank and the International Monetary Fund for certain economic and political policies aimed at redirecting government priorities. In simple terms, the choice is austerity or bankruptcy. Here the power of finance capital is clear, as nations find their domestic policies dominated by the international agencies of finance capital. But this power could not be exerted here, in America. Or so assert mainstream ideologists and orthodox social scientists who are committed to the vacuous theory that America has a pluralistic power structure.

The process described above is not very different from that experienced by New York City in 1974 and 1975, and yet austerity in New York has not been viewed and understood in quite this way before. The power relations, dependent on a particular set of class relations, are similar. Again, what is confronted here is the dominant ideological view of fiscal crisis and, more generally, of power in America.

Fiscal crisis, resolved as austerity, has a familiar litany of "problems" associated with it. These all congeal into the notions that "there is no money" or, more to the point, that the "government lacks the money." But beneath the surface of these notions, which are ideological and not merely statements of "fact," is class-based power. As a fiscal crisis develops, governments become ever more reliant upon finance capital and on the public sector debt markets that are controlled by a "fraction" of the capitalist class. Without the necessary financing of loans, which are then used as revenue, American governments cannot meet the obligations that have been built over the decades of relative prosperity and economic growth. And given the Reagan administration's total commitment to military buildup—regardless of financial, economic, and social cost—huge expenditures and deficits will certainly continue. And so, the public debt markets are "gearing up to handle another year of heavy volume," as state and local governments "continue to undergo significant fiscal strain," according to a Chase Manhattan Bank report cited in the *Wall Street Journal* (4 April 1983, p. 31).

Responding to the increasing pressure to reduce deficits and balance budgets, austerity is growing throughout the country. As a result, "Struggling to balance their budgets, most of [the nation's governors] . . . pushed through stiff tax increases and painful spending cuts. . . . 1983 is proving to be even rougher, with more tax increases and more spending cuts" (*Wall Street Journal,* 23 March 1983, p. 25).

The fiscal crisis of the state, characterized in part by huge budgetary deficits and a need to borrow just to retire previous debt obligations, has to be termed the "crisis of the debtor government." By referring to the crisis in this way, we are able to see the "weakness" of the state vis-a-vis finance capital. In a sense, this weakness comes from finance capital's internalization—national boundaries do not apply to finance capital. Yet this weakness also emerges from the demands made upon the state from working-class, middle-class, and poor people. The state has become the arbitrator, and often the provider, of last resort. It picks up the pieces that capitalist accumulation leaves behind. The state has an overload of demands—it must provide vehicles, incentives, for the accumulation of capital and must also respond to the demands made by ordinary workers. Indeed, the state must respond to the class demands of both capital and labor, and to other demands as well. It does not respond with equal concern, in the same manner, nor does it distribute evenly the national wealth. But it does respond. The forms that these responses have taken is part of the subject matter of this book. But one fact should already be clear: the debtor state desperately needs financing, and finance capital holds the key—at this time—to that assistance. The power of finance capital is structurally embedded in the social relations of a debtor state. This is especially true for nations whose economy is weak and dependent (such as Poland, Brazil, and Zaire), as well as for local governments in the United States.

The crisis of the debtor government has reached dramatic proportions during the last decade. In 1974, the crisis materialized for New York City. As *Business Week* stated in its July 23, 1984, cover story on the emergence of the city to world financial supremacy:

Just a decade ago, New York seemed to be dying—debt-heavy, cash-poor, held hostage by unions and other special interests, a victim of borrow-now, pay-later government policies, an object of ridicule throughout the nation. Yet it had the brains and the will to turn itself around. Once the city understood the shambles these policies made of its finances, attitudes changed and everyone chipped in. New York drew on the financial community to identify and help rectify its problems. "Now," says Major Edward I. Koch, "everyone goes to bed wearing a green eyeshade"—aware, that is, of the economic costs of any out-of-control budget.[7]

Increasingly, the "out-of-control budget" characterization of New York City now holds true for the federal government; especially with the costs of the Reagan administration's militarization. Moreover, it holds true for the international financial system as a whole. Fear of default by debtor nations sends chills through the executive offices of major Western banks. As the *Wall Street Journal* makes clear in its July 6, 1984, story, "U.S. Banks Prepare for Possibility of Third-World Debt Repudiation,"[8] financial collapse is not impossible; financial collision is very likely. There is now an international debt crisis—and this crisis hits home.

In light of this reality, both (neo) conservative and (neo) liberal politicians, in both the Republican and the Democratic parties, seem content to propose austerity as the only means of "solving" the fiscal crisis of the debtor state. It is true that there remains at this late date a variety of priorities within the broad consensus behind austerity: both conservatives and cold-war corporate liberals have fixed their programs to an austerity policy in domestic spending, which is accompanied by a historically huge increase in military expenditures. And these increases can be expected to exacerbate the fiscal crisis, thereby necessitating further austerity. Reaganomics has come to mean austerity with militarization. Together with this militarization, austerity has become a solution legitimized by the crisis of the debtor state itself.

In practical terms, austerity redirects the state and alters the structural relationships between state and economy, class and power. It functions to alter the politics of class that developed within and into the welfare state. If crisis refers to a process of "discontinuous change . . . where institutional arrangements are transformed or destroyed and new ones created,"[9] then we are now seeing such a transformation. The fiscal crisis of the state, the debtor state, and austerity all involve such a transformation from the class politic of postwar America and the welfare state. In the course of this transformation, the postwar arrangements between capital and labor, which exchanged relative labor peace for an increasing standard of living, are being overturned—not by a socialist-inspired labor movement, but rather by a capitalist class, riding the waves of change that are made possible by the fear of unemployment. The capitalist class is using the crisis of capitalism both in the workplace and in the organization of production—where high technology increasingly replaces human labor power—and at the level of the state effecting political policy. As Major Koch reminds us "the job of government is to provide a climate for jobs and business. If the economy's going up, our job is to get out of the way."[10] Conversely, we are told that if the economy is going down, government must get out of the way, deregulate, and encourage business through fiscal and monetary policy. Furthermore, government joins capital in weakening labor as a counterforce to capital's power. Whether these changes are brought by ideologically-motivated politicians, like Ronald Reagan, or practically-motivated politicians, like some of the liberal Democrats, the overall effect is similar.

Political policy becomes a captive of the needs of capital, for fear that business will pick up and leave for a more friendly political environment. Using the crisis of capitalism, capital is able to create a fiscal crisis of the state. Capital pits one government against the other; one state against the other; one city against others. A bidding war develops, as local governments trip over one another in their efforts to appease the capitalist class. In order to keep capital, in the words of Mayor Koch, "You need business to feel that they are not the enemy."[11] Clearly, the power of capital is asserting itself. Knowing no geographic boundary or national loyalty, capital is able to turn crisis into class power. Business leaves, capital is reinvested elsewhere, in a more friendly political climate, and unions are seriously weakened in the process. That is the foundation of the new class politic, and government responds with capital's policy: austerity. It is, after all, a matter of class power.

Yet, this process leaves the state mired in a fiscal crisis, while not resolving the broader crisis of capitalism. This would seem to be one of the most curious contradictions of the present crisis. As critical and Marxist-inspired social theory has indicated, most notably in the work of Claus Offe, Nicos Poulantzas, James O'Connor, and Alan Wolfe, the state in "late capitalism" is itself crisis ridden. The crisis tendencies of capitalist production spill over to the state. In its many functions, the state apparatus must mediate both the accumulation of capital and the class struggles that are its result. These state functions must be performed in addition to reproducing loyalty by legitimizing the social relations of production. As Suzanne de Brunhoff writes:

> The first major field of state economic intervention . . . concerns the regulation and management of the particular commodity labour-power. This managerial function corresponds to a *requirement of capital which capital cannot itself meet.* Several marxist authors have indicated how the reproduction of waged labour-power involves means and institutions external to capitalist enterprises. [Emphasis added.][12]

This point is crucial to understanding the relationship between a crisis within the state (i.e., a fiscal crisis) and crises external to the state (i.e., a crisis of accumulation). One task of this book is to establish the foundation for understanding such a relationship.

Here we are confronting one of the major issues of contemporary social theory—the relations of state and civil society. My own conceptualization of civil society is based on the writings of Antonio Gramsci. For Gramsci, civil society encompasses more than the sphere of private economic and material interests. It also includes the expression of organizational interests, as well as the realm in which hegemony and dominant ideologies find their cultural influence. Therefore, civil society exerts a protective presence for the state through hegemonic ideologies. Yet, for Gramsci the state and civil society are mutually interdependent spheres. They are not rigid boundaries within society. Each protects the other, as each penetrates the other. The state protects the organization of civil society, thereby maintaining the patterns of domination within capitalism. This protection is made possible, however, through the process of hegemony, which exerts its influence within civil society. For Gramsci, there is no arbitrary conceptual separation between state and civil society.

To view fiscal crisis as a process of class struggle is one approach to understanding this relationship. Both the crisis of capitalism and the fiscal crisis of the state make this view necessary. We need to gain a theoretical grasp of the process by which the state and civil society impact on, reproduce, and change one another. The state must be shown, in a historically specific and concrete analysis, to be grounded in the social relations of late capitalism; a capitalism in crisis. Equally important is the study of the state and its "relative autonomy"; a relationship which recognizes and "shows" that the capitalist state and the capital accumulation process have a relationship of mutual impact, mutual autonomy—mutual, though not necessarily equal, interdependence. Ralph Miliband's probing question needs to be addressed without evoking a programmatic, knee-jerk response. Miliband writes:

> If it is agreed that self-interest and a conception of the "national interest" have been and are powerful influences in shaping the policies and actions of the people in control of state power, the question which immediately arises is how this relates to the interests of the dominant class—in other words, what is the relationship of state power to class interests?[13]

Throughout this study of fiscal crisis and class struggle, this relationship will be probed. It will be shown that the state remains relatively autonomous, but that the degree of autonomy is in flux—subject to change depending on class struggle as it impacts on the state apparatus. By studying the fiscal crisis of New York City we will see how a component of the capitalist state, New York City's government, was transformed through the crisis process, along with the ideologies that legitimize particular state policies. Ultimately, we will see how the assault on the social welfare state was accomplished in a city that was highly dependent on it.

Certainly we must recognize the structural parameters that limit the options of class beings. All actors act within society and history under the "dead weight" of prior historical forms, structures, actions, and processes. Furthermore, class beings act within a set of ideological views, within a framework that further limits the notion of what can be accomplished. Yet, some ideological frameworks move class actors to alter the history of their times; to change the framework of action itself. In a sense, as this society moves to austerity, it might be that we are witnessing the transformation of America by the right and by the corporate class. The crisis process has immobilized the left, and delegitimized liberalism, while rejuvenating the right.

Social Theory and The Fiscal Crisis

In order to understand and theorize about the changing relations of class and power, economy and state, as they are altered by the structural dimensions of the debt crisis, a study and reinterpretation of the fiscal crisis of New York City seemed in order. The research focused on the most crucial phases of that crisis: the period between November 1974 and September 1975. During this period, a new class politic emerged in the city. Old and worn-out arrangements between the city and its residents, the city and its workers, the city's union leaders and the rank-and-file, and the city and its largest banks and most powerful financiers were all in the process of being transformed. The fiscal crisis of New York City, whereby the city's status as a debtor government became clear, was the milieu for these major transformations of class, power, economy, and state.

New York's fiscal crisis was the milieu for an assault by finance and corporate capital on the postwar class relations that had characterized the city and its governance. The allegedly supportive and beneficial arrangements among capital, labor, and state that were based upon economic growth had inhibited the institutionalization of the crisis mechanisms that resulted in austerity. As this book will show, the city's unions were isolated from effectively controlling or even influencing the direction of the city's response to the fiscal crisis. In the new class politics of austerity, labor was rendered powerless. Without a critical, oppositional labor movement, capital could take away labor's alleged status as a junior partner in the managing of the city and make it clear that the needs of business override any other human consideration.

During the 1974–1975 fiscal crisis, the old-growth politics, whereby everyone was alleged to benefit except the poor, was overturned and rendered obsolete. During this time, crisis mechanisms were established as part of this process of transformation. Both the Municipal Assistance Corporation (MAC) and the Emergency Financial Control Board (EFCB) constituted crisis mechanisms which effectively isolated city governance from popular control. Indeed, both the MAC and the EFCB were planned and instituted by representatives of capital *without* labor union input. This book will hammer home the reality that the new class politic of austerity represents the mobilization of capital and the demobilization of labor. Just as capital uses technology to transform the labor process, it has used its financial resources and its control over the investment markets to force the city to a choice between formal bankruptcy or austerity. This point will be stressed in the chapters on Banking Power (Chapters 5 and 6).

This discussion leads us to a significant theoretical point that is usually ignored by mainstream power structure analysts. For pluralist analysts, the political process in America produces no ruling class, nor does it create any dominant elite based on the organization of production and distribution. The American political process and its power structure reflect competition among a multitude of interest groups. There is no underlying structure which permits one class, now relegated to the status of a special interest group, to dominate society.

Yet this view ignores the basic structure of American society. It is, without contention, a capitalist society, albeit a society based upon a rather advanced form of capitalism. And this form of capitalism —perhaps even a particular stage of capitalism—has certain basic processes of production and distribution which form a system of power and a set of power relations that impact on society both outside of the state and within the state. The power of capital as it is exerted in everyday life outside the state has been ignored by mainstream power structure theorists. So much has political science moved away from examining the power of capital that we now see the political scientist specializing in policy studies that are far removed from the centers of capital's power in society. For example, the power of capital over America's communities is evident in its control over investment decisions—the very decisions that control the availability of employment and the economic health of a region.

In the case that we are examining in this book, it is clear that making the decision *not* to invest in New York City was based on a power held by certain fractions of the capitalist class. The mobility of capital—the flow of investment—is not controlled by the state or by labor unions or by the working class. Clearly, this flow of capital in and out of a city—or in and out of a nation, for that matter—can generate crises internal to the state. And once a crisis has been generated, the crisis can be used. This ability gives finance capital, and individual financiers, an enormous power, which is embedded in the structure of class relations of capitalism. Such a capital-generated state crisis is not accidental, nor is it merely the product of malevolent forces or individuals. It is already embedded *as a possibility* in the relations between capital and the state.

Here, then, we see the rationality of capitalism leading to crisis: not as an accident of history, nor as an inevitability. The flow of capital generates crisis in the capitalist state, but the form that the crisis takes, as well as the form that its resolution takes, are the products of human action. Hence, crisis is both a product and a process of struggle. Contending class actors attempt to use a crisis to generate "solutions" which will enhance class power and assert the "needs" and "interests" of their own class above others. Only capital, however, can affect the state through the control of finance capital and production. Historically it has been the case that workers, through labor movements and labor parties, have been able to redirect state resources to lessen their disadvantage. Nevertheless, in this case, Capital did not have to face a united opposition labor movement. Hence, capital was able to exert its needs over the resolution of the fiscal crisis of New York City. Capital was able to seize this crisis and, through the mobilization of important members of the corporate and financial community, it has turned back some of the social and economic successes of past working-class struggles. The crisis of capital in the form of the fiscal crisis of New York City, then, became the crisis of labor, the crisis of workers, the crisis of the poor, and the legitimation needed for the transformation of the social welfare state into the austerity state.

Austerity as Social Policy

Before we proceed to the main text, a few words about austerity seem necessary. As has already been stated, austerity is a policy which has as its basis the domination of society by capitalist rationality, by capital's needs, and by fractions of the capitalist class. These three aspects, combined with a mobilized capitalist class and an immobilized working class, provide the source of power that effectively instituted austerity as policy in New York City. This austerity is built on a set of social relations which have led to crisis in both production and finance. Furthermore, this crisis has spilled over into the public sector, into government, and, in broad terms, into the capitalist state.

We need to examine both crisis and austerity in relationship to struggle, not merely as social problems or political policies. It is im-

portant that we not fall into the trap of viewing political policy as an outcome of independent forces within government. As this study shows, the
policy of austerity did not emerge from the rational and independent
judgments of public servants and elected officials. Nor did austerity
emerge from a partnership of "special interests" representing the needs
of capital, labor, and the working-class and poor residents of the city.
Rather, austerity was the creation of a fraction of the capitalist class and
was instituted in a series of maneuvers which rendered powerless any
potential opposition. Therefore, austerity is best understood as a consequence of the formation during crisis of a new constellation of class
forces. During the fiscal crisis of New York, capital reseized the state and
superimposed undemocratic policy-making bodies within the allegedly
democratic formal processes of government.

Austerity is, therefore, the articulation of a new class politic; one
which redirects state activity, specifically its budgetary/fiscal politics, to
fulfill and enhance the accumulation of capital. Hence, the class forces
and relations that characterized the postwar growth years have now been
turned on their heads. In its course, this crisis generated militant action,
but it was action by capital, not by labor. As a consequence, Government
at all levels now plays in capital's ballpark, according to capital's rules,
guided by the notion that what serves capital/business will eventually
serve the broader community. The politics of austerity is nothing more
than the politics of "trickle-down" recession. Capital's recession trickles
down to everyone else. Government's benefits trickle up to capital. In
this topsy-turvy process, austerity has become national policy.

The class forces now stand in an altered relation to each other and to
the capitalist state. The terrain of the class struggle has shifted from the
place it occupied during the halcyon years of growth. The state could
provide for those who were left out, as well as for the needs that capital
could not itself accommodate. But given the current crisis, the language
of growth is replaced by a new mode of legitimation: the language of
scarcity and limitation. Capital's crisis shifted the terrain of discourse, as
the ideologies of affluence shifted to the ideologies of crisis. The shift
from affluence to scarcity now dominates public discourse, despite temporary recoveries. Given this shift, the workers, the poor, and the labor
unions were left without an ideological leg to stand on; in a sense, their
policies were past policies. They were illegitimate; the bastards of the
system. And ever so clearly, their lack of legitimacy reflected their lack
of power. This book focuses on this loss of power. Labor went from
junior partner to outsider; the poor went from living in hovels to finding
themselves homeless; the rich cash in on the public debt. Such is the new
class politics.

2

Crisis and Social Theory

American society is in crisis. The economy grows precariously and unevenly; it stagnates or it is in deep recession; it certainly does not sustain growth. Its industrial strength weakens; its smokestack industries decline; and its workers despair for lack of jobs and adequate income. Some cities decay, their neighborhoods decline, as housing stock for all but the wealthy disappears, while other cities, in Sun Belt regions, seem to thrive. The nation's infrastructure is in desperate need of repair, yet the funds remain uncommitted. On many levels it becomes clear that the "American empire," at home and abroad, is in decline. Even clearer is the impotence of the state in light of this decline.

We live in a time of systemic crisis. This should be evident to all who observe everyday life without being encumbered or blinded by tired theories of affluence and growth. Workers, bosses, owners, managers, union members and leaders, urbanites and suburbanites, students, the unemployed and underemployed, women, minorities, and the poor, as well as all who hope to enter the work force—all are experiencing the consequences of this crisis. The crisis is being lived; it is not merely an abstraction of social science and social theory.

And, as we live through this crisis, both social theory and social critiques have failed to understand its dimension; few dare to understand this crisis with theory that is liberated from the platitudes of the past. As deep as the crisis is in actuality, for everyday life, it is also a deep crisis of social theory. The old Keynesian formulas for resolving and understanding crises have failed in the context of this contemporary crisis. The old social science, of both acceptance and critique, that made sense

25

to a generation of scholars both those in the mainstream and those of the left has also failed to account for crisis. In the light of the major transformations that this crisis embodies and presages, it seems clear that we need to reexamine crisis theory; crisis theory needs to be disencumbered from analyses grounded in the past.

Product, Process, and Capital-Logic

This crisis needs to be understood in terms that are far more encompassing than those of its economic dimensions, however deep those may be. And it is not a crisis that will be wished away by supply-side economics, nor by monetary manipulations. Despite protests to the contrary, from Jude Waniski, Milton Friedman, or others, the conservatives have failed to resolve the crisis. America is still sliding downhill on its rear, desperately holding on to its hopes.

Here, crisis will be analyzed as both the product and the process of struggle. To do so, a body of data and a theoretical analysis are needed which show crisis to be a consequence, or product, as well as an ongoing relation, or process, of a specific set of class-based needs—needs that are mutually antagonistic and contradictory. Power, then, becomes a process whereby these needs are, to whatever extent, met, while other needs are repressed. Crisis is then both threat and opportunity, for both capital and labor. Central to this argument is the point that crisis must be understood both from the logic of class struggle and from the logic of capital accumulation. Furthermore, crisis presents a moment of social change: therefore crisis is a process of class opportunity. What changes are brought about and by what agencies of change; what new institutional arrangements will appear—for both capital and labor, as well as for the state itself as a social relation expressing needs internal and external to it—are all problematic within a theory of crisis as process. History does not just occur out of thin air; it is made. Crisis is a process in which many histories can be made. As a moment of great transformation, it is also a moment of alternative possibilities—a moment of many possible histories.

My argument begins with this notion that crisis is both the process and the product of struggle, as well as the "logic" of capital's "laws" or "tendencies." The separation of the tendencies and contradictions of capital accumulation from the struggles that shape capitalism's history seems arbitrary. While the position that crisis is a consequence of capitalism's accumulation process may be acceptable, it still does not hold true that capital's own logic must necessarily produce crisis. In simple terms, there can be no crisis without the struggle that creates it; furthermore, there can be no crisis resolution without struggle. The shape as well as the resolution of crisis is the result of human action, human decisions. It can therefore occur or be stalled at particular times, depending upon the activity of capital, labor, or the state, for instance. Without this notion it seems difficult to argue that crises can take on different forms, with different depths, and different resolutions—and therefore with different and alternative histories. Crisis itself, its specific character, is a social process which must be studied, even as it is created.

The reference here is to the debate within Marxist theory on the origin and shape of crises within capitalism. Referring back to Marx and, for some, to Lenin, there is an influential theory which argues that it is the "logic" of capitalism, specifically the logic of capital accumulation, that causes periodic and ever-deeper crises. Here, the logic of capital is self-propelling; it is a structural logic, which must, in the last analysis, produce crisis. Crisis is preordained, as is crisis resolution; or, if that fails, revolution. This theory closes off critical study. All that is left to do, once the domination of system imperatives are accepted as a matter of faith, is to study the particulars, the data, within a particular crisis. If crisis must occur, then there must also be necessary strategies of resolution. The crisis must be resolved by capital, together with the state, within the logic that has been predetermined by the "laws" of capital accumulation. There can be no notion here of crisis having alternative forms and alternative histories. Crisis ceases to be a process of struggle; rather, it becomes an entity with a static character. This theory is all too neatly packaged to demonstrate the force for change that crisis portends, especially this sort of crisis, for both capital and labor, for the state and for class society.

How this crisis is discussed, of course, is tied to the discourse built in the past. The theory of crisis, built from within Marxist theory, has much to tell us about the forces and the contradictions that are pulling capitalist production—and capitalist society—ever closer to its own barriers, to crisis. For Marx, the process of accumulation established its own barriers to the realization of surplus-value, as well as to expanded accumulation. Furthermore, circulation itself becomes a structural barrier to the realization of value. And, of course, for Marx the class struggle is an ever-present barrier to capital accumulation, and it enters into every phase of the accumulation process: into the production, circulation, and reproduction of capital.

Yet, the "capital-logic" theory misses the primacy of struggle in terms of the production of crisis. By emphasizing abstract economic "laws," the capital-logician loses the centrality of struggle to the entire process of capital accumulation. The class struggle within production, at the workplace, certainly presents a barrier to accumulation. The necessity, and the historical tendency, to replace labor power with fixed capital, with machinery, is a barrier to capital accumulation and the realization of surplus-value. And it is this tendency, born from class struggle, that, according to the capital-logic argument, results in a falling rate of profit, and therefore crisis. Indeed, the need established in competition between capitalists for advancement in technology—which is then used to reorganize the workplace to increase one's competitive position by lowering the cost of production, speeding up production, and reducing the labor embodied in the commodity—itself creates barriers to the capital accumulation process. So we see that capital's own logic creates a tendency for crisis.

Still, these instances are all conditioned by and result from class struggle. At each point of production and circulation, class struggle enters the process—at the workplace, in the use of science and technology, at the marketplace, at the level of the state as protector of capitalism and as the provider of the last instance of labor-power—at each place, then, class struggle shapes capital's own "logic" as well as its class needs and strategies. Why replace living labor (workers) with dead labor (machinery, technology)? Simply because this reduces labor costs, thereby reducing the cost of producing a commodity by reducing the labor embodied in it. But why not merely lower the wages of workers? The answer seems so simple: because of resistance from workers, because of class struggle. Furthermore, machines are not human: they do not need or demand free time, increased living standards, time to eat, drink, or play. Machines cannot resist alienated labor, exploitation, or oppression at work or in society as a whole. Indeed, machines become weapons within the class struggle; they are not entirely, nor even primarily, economic factors. So if the introduction of this dead labor increases the "organic composition of capital" (the ratio of dead to living labor in the production of value) and results in a falling rate of profit, is it not clear that this has resulted from the logic of capital and the logic of struggle? And is it not also clear that the logic of struggle is the result of the autonomous expression of the needs of labor?

Nonetheless, the capital-logic approach reduces all crises to a one-dimensional causality. As Henri LeFebvre points out:

For some Marxists, the mode of production is the answer to everything. This concept, in so far as it concerns capitalism, has been omnipresent ever since it was first formulated in epistemology and theory, and it has eliminated or subjugated all others. It is carefully toughened up, in the name of the perfect science. It is presented as *totality,* preexisting that which it encompasses, including the social relations. These social relations are defined and conceived theoretically only within and by means of the mode of production. [1]

If the mode of production determines all relations, it must also determine crises and the forms that crises take, as well as the forms that resolutions of crises take. The history of the crises, then, must take on predetermined forms, which are themselves dominated by the systemic logic of the mode of production. Thus history itself does not result from the actions of human actors within history, within society, or within, in this case, the context of crisis.

This is merely another manner of stating that the logic of capital, the dominating part of the mode of production, determines its own crises as well as its own destiny. The form the crises take, the mediation of the crises, and the economic, political, and social resolutions of the crises are all predetermined within the "logic" of the accumulation process. The social relations of production, including the relations of class and state, are subsumed under and dominated by the logic of capital.

The paradox here is that the crisis is a period of transformation, and yet the capital-logic approach allows no autonomy of human action within this process of transformation. Yet, if the mode of production is in crisis, it seems evident that the social relations that "mediate" crisis involve factors not easily reduced to the logic of capital. The issue of consciousness, including the relations of politics and culture, seems to be lost to the determining, overbearing economic forces. The transformation that occurs during and through crisis involves human action—however it is constituted. This action requires human agency, human decision-making, based upon perceptions of crisis and perceptions of necessary actions. There is no direct mechanism by which the "objective, economic" logic of capital is protected by the class actions of capital and the state. In other terms, crisis challenges arrangements as they are, while suggesting arrangements as they might become. This is so for both capital and labor, as well as for other classes and groups who might grasp the possibilities for alternatives. The crisis does not close possibility; it opens it. The crisis does not embody a set of prescriptions for its own health. It cannot close the alternative futures; it suggests possibilities. It does not do away with struggle; rather, it necessitates it.

Crisis does not emerge solely from the logic of accumulation. Yet capital-logic, as it understands crisis, reduces the class relation to a one-sided domination by the economic factors within capitalism. Crisis cannot then be both the process and the product of struggle, rather it is the product of the internal contradictions of capital. As Stanley Aronowitz writes, "the class struggle is seen as a reflex of capital's Achilles heel. . . . The class struggle is no longer understood as the confrontation of two historical actors, capital and labor, each obeying different, but mutually conditioned logics."[2] If the class struggle is seen merely as the result of capital's logic, then how could crisis be seen in any other light?

The frame of reference, the cause, and the determination are the same. Like class struggle, crisis is but a consequence of a self-determining, self-propelling logic.

Marx's Theory of Crisis

The capital-logic approach has its heritage in Marx himself; perhaps just a part of Marx, but still in Marx. If this theory is a one-sided reading of Marx's theory of crisis, it is still nevertheless grounded in analyses that Marx himself set forth. Marx often described capital's logic as a propellant toward periodic crises. In these discussions, he also described crises as the culmination of the necessary actions embedded within the accumulation process. For Marx, the capitalist mode of production must ceaselessly move toward periodic and ever-deepening crises.

References to this engine, which drives ceaselessly toward crises, seemingly apart from class struggle and human agency, abound in Marx. For instance, in his discussion of Ricardo's theory of accumulation, Marx underlines this point with his heading "The Very Nature of Capital Leads to Crises."[3] Marx explains here, as well as in sections of Volume 3 of *Capital,* his theory of crises as being the result of the independent logic, and movement, of capital; logic moving on its own terms without needing, it appears at first glance, even a push from the struggles of the working class. In a curious way, the theorist who posits the revolution and liberation of the working class denies the necessity of the working class in the production of capitalist crises.

For the other side of Marx, crisis emerges from both the logic and the contradictions of capital accumulation *and* from the process of class struggle, that is, the logic of labor. Crisis here is the consequence of the relation of capital and labor. It is not the self-propelled logic of capital accumulation; rather, the propellant is the class struggle between capital and labor. Here labor is not subsumed as an historical agency by and under capital. This is a side of Marx that has too often been lost in the left's critique of crisis.

It would seem, then, that Marxist crisis theory has been too quick to overemphasize crisis as emerging from capital-logic, from the contradictions inherent in bourgeois production itself, while reducing the class struggle, and the autonomy of workers, to an effect of this logic. The capital-logic theory, analyzes crisis as a consequence whose appearance emerges as an ironclad law of accumulation. Within the capital-logic theory, differences occur among the theorists, yet the fundamental position remains the same: that capital's own logic creates the necessary conditions for perpetual and systemic crisis.

For instance, Immanuel Wallerstein argues that capitalism is a world system which establishes patterns of worldwide growth and decline, stability and crisis, as well as relations between core, semiperipheral, and peripheral areas (nations) of capital accumulation. There should be no problem here with these notions, for surely the capitalist system is a "worldwide" process. Yet, this "single world economy of multiple states linked in an interstate system" follows its own logic, at least according to Wallerstein.[4] And here, the logic of capital accumulation, even where successful—perhaps especially where successful—results in crises. For Wallerstein, crisis is produced by the "success" of the capitalist world economy. In his view, the economic imperatives of accumulation have "built-in limitations" that have established the contemporary crisis of capitalism beginning in the period about 1914 to 1917 and "no doubt [to] continue through the twenty-first century."[5] Capital has its own limits, emerging from its own successes, and turning it toward its own destruction. Speaking of this process, Wallerstein writes:

> In short, the contradictions of the system have been constantly overcome. The economic stagnation which the world-economy has known since 1967 will almost certainly be overcome by 1990, and the world is likely to know a period of seeming prosperity. It is this very "strength" of the system, its recuperative power, its ability to resuscitate the engine of economic expansion, that has created, and is deepening, the structural crisis, so that a system which has functioned and thrived for five hundred years is disintegrating at the very moment that it is at its strongest and most efficient.[6]

Hence, from the logic of capital accumulation comes crisis, here defined by Wallerstein as "a situation in which the contradictions of a system, because of its internal development, have become accentuated to the point where it cannot continue to maintain the same basic structure."[7] So, it is transformed. It is within the transformation that Wallerstein finds class struggle, especially between the core and the peripheral areas. Within the process of creating crises, however, struggle seems absent; crisis is born from economic imperatives. Economism reigns here.

Other capital-logic theorists make similarly one-sided analyses. Some writers, like Mandel, Aglietta, and Braverman, place the labor process in its central role in the logic of capital (as opposed to Wallerstein's emphasis on accumulation). Nevertheless, these analyses still tend to reduce crisis and working-class resistance/autonomy to the logic of the accumulation process itself. "For them, the sphere of production remains the central dynamic of the entire capitalist system."[8] Though much can be learned from these studies of the accumulation process, the contemporary crisis, as well as the changing labor process, it appears that they reduce class struggle to a factor of production; thereby losing its centrality in the entire crisis of contemporary capitalism. Furthermore, the resulting analyses of the state, culture, and other "superstructures" are relegated to secondary and dependent status in their explanatory schema.

A brief discussion is now in order of the basic theoretical position that is called capital-logic theory.[9] A simplified version of this theory will be presented here, a form of political-economy—even though the political seems to be lost in these analyses, as is the social—without going into the more involved, in-depth arguments about value theory.

Capital-logic, as it interprets crisis, goes as follows: According to Marx in Volume 3 of *Capital,* a contradiction exists between the needs of capital to reproduce itself on an expanded scale and the barriers that capital accumulation itself sets to that need. Those barriers exist within the economics of the productive process itself; within production and circulation. In the circulation process, there is a barrier that is created by the necessity to exchange commodities for money (commodity capital for money capital). Without this exchange, the surplus-value embodied within the commodity cannot be realized and reinvested. Hence the circuit of capital—in which money is transformed into productive capital, into a commodity, into money once again, and then into productive capital again, and so on through the circuit over and over again—cannot be completed, allowing for the expansion of production. Thus, a barrier is inherent within the circuit of capital itself. There is always the possibility that the commodities produced cannot be sold, thereby disrupting the circuit, preventing the realization of the value embodied within the commodity, and, thereby preventing the expansion of production—of capitalism itself.

Clearly this general circuit through which capital is transformed has established the possibility of disruption. The abstract and general circuit does establish a general possibility of crisis: that is, a crisis defined by the inability to realize the surplus-value embodied within the commodity. This form of crisis would be recognized as a crisis of overproduction, in which "too many" commodities have been produced, which would then be left to acquire dust in warehouses until such time as they could be consumed again in the distribution process. Factories stop producing and remain idle as overproduction becomes an economic fact. Of course, this "economic fact" is merely the consequence of capital's logic, at least for the capital-logic theory. Until the circuit of capital is completed, over and over again, the crisis continues. There can be no expanded reproduction of capital, and, crisis therefore becomes recognized as a condition created by the abstract laws and logic of capital accumulation. Notice how the crisis is economic in both cause and form. Where are the political and social aspects of this form of "political-economy?"

Although the above theory has established the general barriers to accumulation, and thereby the general cause of crisis, we must be careful not to try to describe and explain the particular in terms of these abstract, general possibilities—an error too often encountered in capital-logic theory. To quote Marx on this matter:

> The *general possibility* of crisis is the formal *metamorphosis* of capital itself, the separation, in time and space, of purchase and sale. But this is never the *cause* of the crisis. For it is nothing but the *most general form of crisis,* i.e., the crisis itself in *its most generalized expression.* But it cannot be said that the *abstract form of crisis is the cause of crisis.* If one asks what its cause is, one wants to know why *its abstract form,* the form of its possibility, turns from possibility into *actuality.*[10]

Note how Marx suggests that the inherent contradictions in capital's logic establish the most general possibilities of crisis. It is the dependence and overemphasis of the capital-logic theory on the inherent and most general *possibilities* of crisis, together with the subjugation of the actual process producing specific crises, that are partially at fault. Such contradictions lead these theorists to relegate struggle to the position of being a consequence of the crisis process; hence, struggle, in relation to crisis, is viewed as a mediating effect. By emphasizing the domination of the "laws" of capital accumulation, the autonomy of class struggle is lost, and crisis is viewed in terms of the barriers to capital and the economic rationality of the "laws" of capital. Crisis becomes a process internal to the laws of motion of capitalist production.

Next, the capital-logic theorists add a discussion of the inherent "tendency" of the rate of profit to fall as the key to crisis. This tendency, which Marx refers to at various times as both a "law" and a "tendency," emerges out of the *social conditions* of capitalist production. It is the social relations of production that create this tendency, as we shall see, yet the capital-logicians fail to see it this way. Within capitalist production, there is a necessity, conditioned both by class struggle with the producing/working classes and by intraclass competition within the capitalist class, for the organic composition of capital to rise. By this we mean that machinery, technology, and automation are used to replace workers at the workplace. Here, workers (living labor) are displaced by machinery (dead labor, labor of the past embodied in machinery); in value theory terms—variable capital is replaced by constant capital.

Note that this process is characterized as a consequence of interclass and intraclass struggle: as a result of struggle against workers and among capitalists—i.e., against both labor and competing units of capital. Furthermore, as strategy to enhance one's competitive position vis-a-vis labor and capital, this process is a part of class struggle, as well as its consequence.

We will return to this point. For now, let us turn to Marx, to demonstrate that capital-logic theory is grounded in a specific reading of Marx—that it is, indeed, one side of Marx. Speaking of the falling rate of profit, Marx writes:

> This mode of production produces a progressive relative decrease of the variable capital as compared to the constant capital. The immediate result of this is that the rate of surplus-value, at the same, or even a rising, degree of labour exploitation, is represented by a continually falling general rate of profit . . . (this fall does not manifest itself in an absolute form, but rather as a tendency toward a progressive fall). The progressive tendency of the general rate of profit to fall is, therefore, just an *expression peculiar to the capitalist mode of production* of the progressive development of the social productivity of labour. [11]

Here Marx parenthetically states that the "law as such" is a tendency conditional upon factors which, in later chapters, appear to be factors of class struggle. For instance, Marx later cites such counteracting factors as the "increasing intensity of exploitation"; the "depression of wages below the value of labour-power"; the "cheapening of elements of constant capital," which itself may be due to struggle at the workplace over wages, over the labor embodied in the constant capital, or in capitalist competition; the "relative overpopulation," which suppresses wage levels; "foreign trade," which may be seen as encompassing elements of international capitalist competition and may involve the relations of colonialism and colonial relations of exploitation; and, lastly, the "increase of stock capital," which Marx does not analyze in any great detail. In this last factor, investment dividends are seen yielding a theoretical effect on the rate of profit. Certainly, investors make decisions which are influenced by the intensity of class struggle.

As Marx continued his discussion of the contradictory tendencies of the accumulation process, he again and again demonstrated the crisis tendencies of the system itself. Yet we must always be aware of the class struggle that *in actuality* creates the actual experience of capitalism. Still, the capital-logic theory ignores this struggle and sees only the inherent tendencies to crisis, and the falling rate of profit, in capital itself. Lost is the *relation that creates capital,* the relation of labor to capital at the workplace and in the property relations of production. Capital-logic theorists can read their theory many times in Marx. In Chapter 15, Volume *3,* of *Capital,* the theme unfolds of capital's own logic, inherent in accumulation, leading to crisis. It is here that we can read the capital-logic determinism in Marx himself.

We saw how capital replaces labor-power in the production process, resulting in the progressive development of technology and an increase in productive capability, at least in the absolute. We see here how the rate of profit falls, even as labor becomes more productive. In Wallerstein's terms, the success of the system itself causes its own crisis. As the rate of profit falls, capital, through competition and crisis, becomes more concentrated and centralized. Small, inefficient, and technologically backward companies can no longer compete with their more advanced competitors, and they are increasingly bankrupted and gobbled up by larger and larger units of capital. Small, noncompetitive, obsolete businesses (and even industries) are "expropriated" by ever-larger units. [12]

As this process takes place, along with a falling rate of profit, Marx asserts that it constitutes a barrier to "the formation of new independent capitals and thus appears as a threat to the development of the capitalist production process. It breeds overproduction, speculation, crises, and surplus-capital alongside surplus-population." [13]

Marx is showing here how the accumulation process itself creates a tendency toward crisis. We can argue, however, with the view of crisis that separates it from the actions of both capital and labor, in the workplace and in the community at large. In order to broaden our understanding of crisis, it is necessary to return the theory of crisis to an understanding of the struggles waged against both capital and the state. To do so requires an emphasis on the concrete actions of real beings, not on the inherent "logic" of a self-propelled, capitalist accumulation process.

It is therefore important to point out that class struggle enters into the process at each point. Though Marx seems not to emphasize this, it seems necessary to do so to retain the autonomy of the working class and its struggle in the analysis of crisis. Class struggle shapes and is shaped by production, and it certainly enters the picture as a struggle over surplus-value, over the length, the social conditions and the organization of the workday. Struggle enters into the process in direct conflict with the rising organic composition of capital, as a struggle against displacement by technology. And certainly, struggle enters into the picture at the points of circulation and distribution. Furthermore, the struggles of everyday life within the community attack the rationale of capitalism, even though at times, perhaps too often, these struggles are shaped to reflect the needs of capital. The ideological hegemony of capital finds its way into theories of crisis. By emphasizing crisis as the product and the process of class struggles, this ideological hegemony is challenged. Hence, even at the levels of community, consciousness, and ideology, struggle must enter the picture. To separate these factors and reduce their importance in the creation of crisis would be to miss the struggles that are characteristic of everyday life in capitalist society. Struggle enters, then, at the points of production, circulation, and distribution, both within the state and its relation to economy and the broader "civil society" and in the relations of class culture. To restrict one's analysis to the inherent tendencies embodied within the "laws" of accumulation, as capital-logic does, is to miss the multifaceted struggles that are the products and producers of crises.

In Marx's own analysis, there is a tendency to "prove" that crises inhere in both the production and the circulation processes. And this argument is made by Marx as if class struggle *did not* enter into the causality; as if the crisis process were independent from struggle. Marx points to the barriers presented by circulation, alluded to earlier in this discussion, which might inhibit the realization of value. Marx reminds his readers that the production of commodities is but the first act as the rate of profit falls and "the mass of surplus-value thus produced swells to immense dimensions. Now comes the second act of the process. The entire mass of commodities . . . must be sold."[14] That presents no small problem for the capitalist class. The distribution process itself becomes problematic and a barrier to accumulation. When capital changes form, as discussed earlier, the conditions for crisis are made possible. For Marx, "the general *possibility* of crisis is given in the process of *metamorphosis of capital* itself."[15] Though the worker remains exploited, the surplus-value must be realized through the sale of the commodity and the circulation of money-capital back to the capitalist class. Here there is a necessary and fundamental time and space separation that enters into the process. Furthermore, consumption itself may be limited:

> by the proportional relation of the various branches of production and the consumer power of society. But this last-named is not determined either by the absolute consumer power, but by the consumer power based on antagonistic conditions of distribution, which reduce the consumption of the bulk of society to a minimum varying within more or less narrow limits.[16]

And is not this, the "consumer power," an object of class struggle? Marx does make mention of struggle at this point of his discussion. But, tellingly, it is that competitive struggle waged within the capitalist class, between competing units of capital, to which he refers. The "consumer power" within society then seems to be the product of the *internal laws of capitalist competition*. Again, the working class is absent, even at this most crucial point; even in the struggle over distribution—the "consumer power" of different segments of society.

While we can read the entirety of Marx's argument as broader than capital-logic theory, it seems fair to trace the one-sidedness of capital-logic theory to a part of Marx. This last passage, and the one to follow, both seem clearly in the capital-logic mold. Marx seems eager to show that crisis must result from capital's own internal logic, regardless of the concrete actions taken by class beings. Here he is making his "best-case" analysis: even if capital were able to solve its "labor problem" and contain class struggle, it would still find itself facing crisis. For Marx, there can be only one conclusion: crisis is inevitable.

Marx continues in this direction by asserting that: consumer power is

furthermore restricted by the tendency to accumulate, the drive to expand capital and produce surplus-value on an extended scale. This is law for capitalist production, imposed by incessant revolutions in the methods of production themselves, by the depreciation of existing capital always bound up with them, by the general competitive struggle and the need to improve production and expand its scale merely as a means of self-preservation and under penalty of ruin. The market must, therefore, be continually extended, so that its interrelations and the conditions regulating them assume more and more of a *natural law* working independently of the producer, and become ever more uncontrollable. This internal contradiction seeks to resolve itself through expansion of the outlying field of production. But the more productiveness develops, the more it finds itself at variance with the narrow basis on which the conditions of consumption rest. [Emphasis added.][17]

For Marx then, capital's logic seems bound by its own *internal natural law,* which then appears distinct from class struggle. Crisis thus erupts from the barriers that capital itself creates. The absence of class struggle in this form of theorizing becomes all the more important when Marx makes his case that capitalism both self-destructs and self-produces in ever-more-concentrated and centralized form. Crisis becomes both a consequence of this self-perpetuation/self-destruction/self-reproduction process and an opportunity—i.e., the method of this process. But here Marx sees crisis as opportunity to restore functional relations within capital accumulation; again, within the logic of capital itself. Again I turn to Marx to make this case:

From time to time the conflict of antagonistic agencies finds vent in crises. The crises are always but momentary and forcible solutions of the existing contradictions. They are violent eruptions which for a time restore the disturbed *equilibrium.*

The contradiction . . . consists in that the capitalist mode of production involves a tendency towards absolute development of the productive forces, regardless of the value and surplus-value it contains, and regardless of the social conditions under which capitalist production takes place. [Emphasis added.][18]

Marx sees crises as a process of reproduction, as a cleansing process in which new, competitively viable capital replaces the old and the obsolete. Then he asserts in his strongest voice that "The *real barrier* of capitalist production is *capital itself.* It is that capital and its self-expansion appear as the starting and the closing point, the motive and the purpose of production."[19] Here we have the clearest statements of Marx as capital-logician. The real barrier is capital, not the struggles of the working class. Crisis is caused by capital; not by class struggle. The barrier to capitalist production and the cause of crisis are one and the same: capital.

These passages could be read so as to give predominance to capital in Marx himself; to give dominance to economism. The capital-logic approach reads Marx, and capitalist crises, in just that way. And, as has been shown, there is this side, this narrowness, in Marx. It originates in his attempt and desire to claim "scientific" status for his study of capitalism. Marx at times lost sight of the capital-labor relation, that which makes capital a social process, not a thing. His discussions of crises make it appear to be a thing—the result of preordained economic "laws." For Marx,

> . . . the whole process of accumulation in the first place resolves itself into *production on an expanded scale,* which, on the one hand corresponds to the natural growth of the population, and on the other hand, forms an inherent basis for the phenomena which appear during *crises.* The criterion of this expansion of production is capital itself, the existing level of the conditions of production and the unlimited desire of the capitalists to enrich themselves and to enlarge their capital, but by no means *consumption,* which from the outset is inhibited, since the majority of the population, the working people, can only expand their consumption within very narrow limits, whereas the demand for labour, although it grows *absolutely,* decreases *relatively,* to the same extent as capitalism develops. Moreover, all equalisations are *accidental* and although the proportion of capital employed in individual spheres is equalised by a continuous process, the continuity of this process itself equally presupposes the constant disproportion which it has continuously, often violently, to even out.[20]

And for Marx, the crisis tendency exists even given the real, concrete historical conditions which enter into any serious consideration of the social relations of capitalism: the tendency exists as "fact." Yet, another Marx begins to see through this capital-logic as he notes that "even going further into the actual relations which all constitute prerequisites for the real process of production," crises must erupt.[21] Capital inherently produces crises; yet, the "actual relations" constitute "prerequisites" for crisis. Could these prerequisites be found in class struggle?

On the one hand, Marx's assumption is that crisis *must* occur; on the other, the real and the concrete alter the very process itself. This dialectical argument in Marx is basic to the argument here: that crisis is itself both *real* (as the culmination of "barriers" to the realization of value, as well as economic crisis) and *produced* (as a class struggle in both the political and the economic contexts). In this sense, crisis is a result of both capital accumulation (the logic of capital) and class struggle (the struggle as resistance to capital). Crisis is a process of opportunity for classes to impact upon the transformations that shape their history. We shall return to this argument.

Let us digress a bit with a discussion of some contemporary forms of capital-logic analyses. The capital-logic theory falls back upon assertions that a mode of production constitutes a system of objective structures brought to bear, from the outside, on everyday human activity. There is no human subject; consequently there can be no class subject. Classes, and human beings, are *bearers* of systems logic. Since we are here concerned with Marxist theory, of a particular sort, the bearers are dominated by capital's logic.

An influential and intellectually forceful model of this theorizing is Althusserian structuralism. For Althusser, where state and crisis are concerned, there is no human subject as an autonomous agent of social change. Autonomy of action is not possible, given the deterministic logic of structurally overbearing processes. As Hirsch writes, for Althusser, "Human beings are simply the bearers of social structure, not free agents."[22] Classes, and the actions of class beings, act out structurally predetermined logics; the patterns of actions are preset by over-determining structures. The overdetermination in the last instance is, of course, the logic of capital itself.

Within this theoretical universe, capital is the cause, the subject moving society and creating history. It is, in this last instance, the determining force of society and history. Classes are here seen as consequences, and class struggle is an effect of capital. Notice how class struggle is here reduced to conforming within the logic of capital, within the necessary actions and necessary histories that capital itself presents. This is, after all, a deterministic theory of history; the determining force is capital and the laws of capital accumulation.

For Althusser, the state and the ideological apparatus function as a repressive mechanism whose major purpose is to reproduce the conditions for capital accumulation. In his essay, "Ideology and Ideological State Apparatuses" Althusser posits a state which is dominated by capital's needs. Here, capital's main need involved its own reproduction. The state, like other elements of the superstructure, acts out, albeit in sometimes contradictory fashion, the overdetermining needs of capital accumulation.

The question for this book, however, is really quite simple: if the relationships of state to economy, of politics to crisis, are contradictory, how is it, then, that human subjects engaged in class struggle, as well as other struggles, simply act out as bearers, a predetermined logic? How is it that the "bearer" knows its class needs and the predetermined logic that capital demands? Is there no place for human subjectivity? Is not class struggle *created* by those who struggle? And then, is not history changed by those struggles?

The very notion of contradiction seems to challenge the capital-logic approach. Yet, in this view, contradictions refer first and foremost to predetermined barriers within capital accumulation. Human agency cannot enter into the process—at least not as a creating force. And herein lies the problem. If capital-logic is taken as correct, how can we account for the many different historical forms that class struggle has taken? Why is there a strong state here, a weak one there? A parliamentary system here, a right-wing, authoritarian dictatorship there? And why do crises take on different forms, in different moments, in different capitalist societies, with different solutions and different consequences? While it might be comforting to fall back upon the predeterminations of capitalism as it appears in capital-logic theory, it is not quite so easy to account for the actions of living history. Capitalism as a social process of production is contradictory; so is class struggle. The logic of capital and the logic of labor are embedded within one another—even as they take on separate and conflicting logics. To reduce one, or subordinate one, to the other is to miss the unity and autonomy that coexist.

Understanding the Autonomy of Class Struggle

The main reason for this discussion is to return a theory and analysis of crisis to a theory of class struggle. The problem with capital-logic theory is its denial that class struggles have an independence, a logic, of their own. Class struggle is accorded no autonomy; therefore workers have no autonomy, and therefore no community. Capital-logic is blind to the power of classes to act and create their own histories (albeit not as they wish, nor under the conditions that they themselves would choose) and, by consequence, to alter the histories of their society. Historical development, crises, crises politics, crises resolution, the actions of classes and class fractions, the actions of the state, and classes themselves, all seem, in capital-logic theory, to adhere to and result from one logic—and that is of capital's own logic. Here capital accumulation is its own locomotive, with its own force; all else is consequence.

This theory is problematic, in that the actions of classes, as well as the state, seem not to form that logic, nor to exert their own logic on capital accumulation; indeed, they are not even accorded a logic of their own. All of which seems to take for granted something that must be explained. For this theory, the system seems to move on without and despite human action. The human subject—class or otherwise composed—is dismissed. Hence, the possibility of altering the logic of capital, and therefore history itself, seems hopelessly negated by the power and logic of capital. Only capital can create; only capital can destroy.

Certainly it is one of the dilemmas and ironies of Marxist theory that these agents of change, the members of the working class, dependent on visions of alternatives to the present, are often theorized as having a predetermined history, reducible to the logic of accumulation. When one does away with the human subject, one also precludes the possibility of alternative histories, save those provided by accumulation, or by technology and science, or by some other deterministic theory of change. If capital, as asserted, has its own logic, and this logic dominates the enfolding of history, even within capitalist society, then the logic itself must lead to self-destruction for the possibility of social change to exist. There is little room here for autonomous maneuvering within everyday life. Workers, capitalists, oppressed and oppressor all bear out the rationality of the system. Is this so far from Weber's iron cage? Here, crisis occurs because it must; struggle is engaged from within the internal core of capital; workers may revolt, but they cannot create. Human autonomy in action cannot exist on any level. The structures of accumulation act through the human (functioning as bearers), but the human loses its humanity.

Curiously, this theory elevates alienation of the human essence to its most extreme ontological expression, even as alienation as a theory, by Althusser and his followers, was relegated to the Hegelianism of the "immature" Marx. What could be more central to alienation than human actors, whose actions are both structurally predetermined and impotent? Of history, which is premade? Of crises and social change, which must inevitably come, not as a result of the struggles of liberating subjects, but as a consequence of the internal contradictions of capital accumulation? And what of a theory of crisis that cannot view crisis itself as a process involving struggles and transformation, breakdowns and resolutions at many levels? If crisis is viewed only as capital's logic, then crisis as transformation can be viewed only within the context of the needs of capital's logic. There is, after all, a set of structural imperatives within capital accumulation, which are seen to "guide" the transformation to allow for renewed accumulation on a grander scale. And how is this theory, then, anything else but a guide to inaction, class compromise, and, in its most extreme form, subordination to the historically "inevitable," whatever that might be?

But what of the impact of other classes, experiencing other logics, other needs, and demanding alternatives? Are these forces not significant in the production of crisis, as well as the process of struggling over transformations that occur in and through crisis? The jump from accumulation, to crisis, to resolution and accumulation on a larger scale seems too deterministic and, indeed, too simplistic in its economism. Lost is the notion, available in a side of Marx ignored by capital-logic theory, of crisis as both consequence and opportunity. Lost are the dialectics of crisis. It is this theme that we shall next consider.

It is important to understand that capital-logic theory is limited by its notion of crisis as inevitable. Embedded in the theory is an assertion of historical necessity and, therefore, a denial of historical specificity and human agency. As Manuel Castells argues:

> One of the dangers we must watch out for in understanding the problem of the "crisis" is the return to a certain social naturalism which, clothed in Marxist language, refers to the immutable essence of capitalism and to the necessary nature of its crisis, which in one way or another is always the same. Now, if the capitalist mode of production develops in a contradictory manner through crisis, then the nature of these crises is a historical process that must be analyzed as such and recognized in its specificity. [23]

Briefly, let us point to a few examples of the "social naturalism" to which Castells refers. We can then differentiate between these theories and alternative ones, as the first step toward reconstructing a theory of crisis which draws upon class struggle and the contradictions of capital. But first let us consider very briefly some examples of capital-logic theory.

Surely there are few Marxist economists with more insight into crisis than Paul Sweezy. For years, he and his colleagues at the Monthly Review Press have presented much-needed information about the shape and process of contemporary capitalism. They have filled, and they continue to fill, a real need for radical critique. Yet, *Monthly Review,* and specifically Sweezy, falls to capital-logic theory. For instance, in his discussion of "The Economic Crisis in the United States," Sweezy writes that stagnation:

> . . . is a consequence of the specific form of overaccumulation of capital which characterizes capitalism in its monopoly phase. . . . For present purposes what is important is to recognize that stagnation has now—as distinct from an earlier stage of capitalist development—to

be regarded as the norm to which the system is always tending. Stagnation may be held at bay for shorter or longer periods by counteracting forces such as major technological innovations, waves of geographical expansion, or wars and their aftermaths. But sooner or later any given set of counteracting forces will exhaust its strength, and the economy will enter a phase of little or no growth and chronic mass unemployment.[24]

Sooner or later, regardless of human agency, without a push from workers, the unemployed, or some other agency of social change and resistance, there will be stagnation and, in time, crisis. Even if one uncritically accepts Sweezy's argument that stagnation is now capital's norm, a significant question still remains: Where is the working class, or any other classes, for that matter, in this analysis? Where is the resistance to work and alienated labor in this analysis? Where is the struggle over the social wage, a struggle which is shown to be significant as a factor in the contemporary crisis that is the subject of this book? Where, then, is the proletariat and the other exploited and oppressed groups? Does the proletariat disappear as an agency of change? It is one position that it does, but it is not Sweezy's. Yet, the understanding of crisis as put forth here does not lend itself to the sort of analysis that sees crisis as a process produced by struggle—that is, the logic of capital and the logic of labor. Clearly, in Sweezy's view, the logic of capital is dominant. Class struggle exists, but as a part of the logic of capital—within capital. It exists, but it is not autonomous. Without an understanding of that autonomy, an autonomy built in a relation to the autonomy of the logic of capital, there can be no analysis of crisis grounded in class struggle. Change then becomes the fulfilling of the logic of capital's own internal crisis.

Erik Olin Wright makes a similar error in his book, *Class, Crisis and the State.* For Wright, the accumulation process sets the absolute ''limits'' of struggle and, consequently, of crisis. These limits set the parameters, or boundaries, for the social relations of capitalist society. In an otherwise fine essay on the Marxist theories of economic crisis, Wright ''links [these theories] through an analysis of the historical transformations of the accumulation process.''[25] Ostensibly, Wright's argument falls back upon the capital-logic fetishization of the capital accumulation process. ''In different periods of capitalist development, the capital accumulation process faced qualitatively different impediments. In each period the structural solution to a given impediment became the basis for new contradictions and new impediments in subsequent periods.''[26] Here, once again we can see the determinism of the capital accumulation process. History proceeds from the systemic logic, albeit a contradictory one, of capital itself.

Wright is not interested in merely reiterating a crisis theory based on dogmatic assertions. It is to his credit that he searches for a more empirically grounded theory of crisis. Yet, this leads Wright to a "test" of the major Marxist theories of crisis. Wright then searches for the empirical, quantitative evidence to support a theory of crisis. So while Wright plays with the notion that crises are the consequence of the contradictions of capitalism, including class struggle and capitalist competition, he falls back upon "proving" the "scientific validity" of capital-logic theory. And with this attempt, Wright subsumes class struggle under the logic of capital. Struggle becomes another factor to account for in the production of value.

In the search for a scientifically valid model of crisis, as caused by capital accumulation, Wright looks at three models—underconsumption, falling rate of profit, and profit squeeze. For the underconsumption model, crisis is caused by the inability or lack of capacity of the masses to consume; in other words, aggregate consumption is too low and impedes the realization of surplus-value. Remember, the accumulation process cannot be expanded until the circuit of capital is completed, commodities are exchanged for money, and money-capital is once again in the hands of the capitalist. Wright concludes his discussion of the underconsumption theory of crisis by stating that it is inadequate because the theory has not yet "elaborated an adequate theory of investment and the rate of accumulation," from which the logic of capital could produce crisis. [27]

Wright also looks at the theory of the falling rate of profit and concludes that the empirical evidence does not "prove" the historical validity of the theory. Citing long-term trends in the organic composition of capital, Wright concludes that the jury is still out on the validity of this theory. On the one hand:

> No one has argued that the organic composition of capital has fallen to any great extent in the past several decades, and thus one can say that it still acts as an impediment to accumulation, even though it may not be the great dynamic source of crisis that its defenders claim. [28]

Yet, Wright goes on to argue that:

> Sometimes during the first quarter of the 20th century, according to this hypothesis, a relatively stable, fairly high level of organic composition of capital was reached. Since that time, the organic composition of capital has dropped considerably during periods of crisis, and then risen back to the stable level during periods of prosperity as post-crisis un-devaluated constant capital replaced the cheap, devaluated capital acquired during the crisis. A fall in the organic composition of capital can be a solution of crisis without a rise in the organic composition being the fundamental cause of crisis. [29]

Perhaps I can now pinpoint a fundamental problem in both Wright's argument and the capital-logic arguments. Wright, like the capital-logicians, is concerned with finding the absolute *cause,* or *causes,* of crisis. Because of that concern, they enter into debates about cause and effect analyses pertaining to essentially social relations. Here positivism creeps into Marxist analyses; the dialectics of Marx are lost in an attempt to quantify the relations of capital accumulation. It then becomes necessary for these theorists to rely upon economistic data, abstracted from the social relations that give them meaning. Additionally, analysis, as well as the data gathered, are restricted to economic categories—that which is limited to production itself or to the circuit of capital. Lost is the social and the political; political-economy becomes modern, positivist economics with Marxist interpretations and leftist ideologies superimposed on a body of data that seems "objective" and "neutral." Here we see scientism in the analyses of crisis made by the left. This is nowhere more evident than in Wright's discussions of crisis, the last of which being his analysis of profit squeeze theory.

The profit squeeze theory emphasizes class struggle and its impact on rates of profit as the cause of crisis. Because of class struggle over the distribution of national income, the rate of profit tends to decline, relative to the strength of the working class vis-a-vis the capitalist class. Crises emerge from the ability of the labor movement to extract higher wages from capital and thereby reduce profit rates. These rates increase when capital effectively weakens the labor movement through disciplining measures such as unemployment. A large pool of unemployed workers functions to depress wage demands.

The broad outlines of this theory offer a great deal of potential, even though the theory could be weakened by a rigid operationalization of class struggle. If, for instance, the notion of class struggle is restricted to the battle between capital and "productive" labor, then lost is the struggle of "unproductive" labor (those who do not directly produce value), as well as community-based struggles that threaten the indirect, though socially necessary, conditions of capital accumulation. For example, as presented by Wright, this theory emphasizes the existence of a reserve army of labor as a depressant on wages. Of course, Wright and the profit squeeze theorists recognize that the social welfare state mediates this relation. However, missing is the fundamental notion that the existence of this state is itself a product and a process of class struggle. The forces limiting or expanding profits are therefore far more extensive than *class struggle at the point of production.* Again, even in profit squeeze theory based upon a notion of struggle, the struggle is seen as being *from within and internal to* the logic of capital.

Wright dismisses this theory, though citing its strength in its inclusion of class struggle, on the basis of inadequate empirical evidence. Here,

Wright's conclusion is again restricted by the determination to find the "cause" of crisis within capital's own logic. So he reviews these three theories, cites the inconclusiveness of data, and, on that basis, continues his search for an empirically quantifiable theory of crisis.

Still, he looks for data that will demonstrate how capital-logic produces crisis, what factors within the capital accumulation process cause crisis, and how the crisis is then attenuated by the "needs" of the accumulation process. Class struggle, then, is pasted on to his theory; accumulation is the prime mover and creator.

Having rejected for the time being—until more conclusive evidence is found—three major Marxist theories of crisis, Wright then matches the "impediments" of accumulation with the stages of capitalist development that they grow out of and hinder. These impediments then create the general conditions of crisis. In his analyses of the transitions from phase to phase of capitalism, Wright makes it clear that class struggle is the result of capital accumulation. Here we see the error of reducing the capital-labor relation into a one-sided entity—capital. Labor, class struggle, the social relations of production are all reduced here to an *effect* of capital itself. While as an effect they might become incompatible with the accumulation process, we then see that an adjustment is made, restoring favorable conditions—a functional equilibrium—to the accumulation process.

It is here that Wright begins to posit the relationship between class struggle and accumulation. But his discussion of struggle remains within capital-logic theory. To the extent that the "forces/relations of production" are incompatible with the existing organization of accumulation, there is crisis. Class struggle and capitalist competition have the capacity to "transform" the forces and relations of production, thereby creating this incompatibility. There then develops a problem of the reproduction of capital—hence crisis. Yet, given the organization of Wright's argument, class struggle still seems de-emphasized. It is accorded enough strength to transform relations of production, but still the problem of the political-economy of accumulation remains. Wright moves in a provocative direction, yet cuts short the necessary discussion. Is class struggle to be conceptualized as within the accumulation process or does it become relatively autonomous in relation to class needs, consciousness, culture, and everyday life? Does it take on a logic of its own—the logic of labor?

For Wright and others who write within the capital-logic approach, the productive forces of society have become reduced to capital and its internal process. It is the productive forces that are seen to create crisis and, by inference, to move history onward toward the ultimate crisis, and crash, of capital accumulation. The relation of capital to labor and each side's autonomy from the other are reduced to the determinism of capital needs and contradictions. The working class and its struggle for autonomy, community—its resistance—are dominated by the needs of productive forces embedded in capital. Hence, labor cannot take the lead and "create" alternative histories. How ironic that this logic betrays the very task to which these theorists have posed for both the working classes and social critique itself!

Crisis: The Terrain for Class Struggle

This book poses an alternative to capital-logic theory. This alternative is developed by way of studying crisis as a process in the making. Crisis presents opportunities for class struggle—though never "equal" opportunities—for members of classes, perhaps strategic representative organizations, whose needs are brought into confrontation by crisis itself. By analyzing a specific historical crisis as it developed and as it was "mediated"—the fiscal crisis of New York City—we can present an analysis of class forces in their relation to government. This analysis suggests that classes are not merely a "given" component of capital. They become a reality through struggle: social, political, economic. These political, cultural, ideological relations of class are central to class action and, therefore, to the expression and realization of a given set of class needs. These needs are not merely brought to bear on crisis from the outside; indeed, they constitute the very process of producing and mediating crisis. It is struggle that creates crisis, and, indeed, the "impediments" of capital accumulation do not become crisis without these struggles. Can we understand the crisis of late capitalism without comprehending the power of the struggle against work—a struggle which takes cultural, economic, and political form? For this work, the political form is especially crucial. Here we see the struggle against work manifesting itself in the struggle for a social wage—income from the state without productive labor attached to it as its precondition, on the one hand, and an increased wage for those who work within the public sector, on the other.

It can therefore be argued that we cannot understand crisis, whether it is the crisis of accumulation or the fiscal crisis of the state, without exploring the manner in which it is created by struggle. Here we can demonstrate the connection between struggle and crisis in both economic and political forms—within the accumulation process and within the state. Having argued that point, we will demonstrate class struggle at the point of crisis—within the crisis process itself—over the "resolution" of the crisis. Here, of course, the argument demonstrates that crisis spills over into the state—in the form of fiscal crisis—as does class struggle.

The process by which class needs—class imperatives—are instituted as public policy through class struggle will be shown in very specific detail. (Here I refer to the institutionalization of austerity as *demanded and organized* by representative interests of the capitalist class, specifically finance capital.)

It is absolutely fundamental to this argument that crisis be understood as a social process that is made by human agency—through struggle. Crisis is not inevitable, it must be made; nor does it take on a predetermined form. It is the mistakes of both the economism and the historicism of capital-logic, the "social naturalism" to which Castells referred, that we will try to critique and avoid. The production of crisis is subject to the *actions* embedded in the *social relations* of exploitation: relations which cannot be reduced to the economic process of capital accumulation. The relationship of class and state will be exposed through an analysis of crisis. In this way, the pitfalls of "social naturalism" can be avoided, and the power of an analysis that does not fall prey to the comfort of capital logic determinism can be demonstrated.

In the sense that this book does not deal directly with building a theory of economic crisis, there is no need to collect data that consume the capital-logic people. Yet it is important to understand that economic crises are forms and processes of the social relations of class struggle—they are social in form, not economic. Lost in the capital-logic theory is that very notion. For this theory—and even perhaps for the other side of Marx—class is a social category, which creates crisis through struggle. Marx, it has been pointed out, is ambivalent and contradictory on this point. One side of his analysis seems to be devoted to capital-logic; the other side more clearly approaches crisis as a process of struggle. Here Marx sees crisis as class opportunity—as both the result of, and the process of, class struggle.

Castells seems to capture this side of Marx, and the critical tradition within Marx, in the following statement:

> A structural economic crisis is not explained by the economy but by society, because the economy is not a "mechanism" but a social process continuously shaped and recast by the changing relationships of humankind to the productive forces and by the class struggle defining humankind in a historically specific manner.[30]

Castells is making a crucial point. This book analyzes a particular manifestation of crisis, within the state, in order to establish a greater understanding of the process through which crisis is produced by struggle; of how it comes to be understood as crisis; explained and understood in a particular "ideological" way; mediated through state structures; resolved through specific mechanisms, and instituted as a process of class struggle.

3

Causing Fiscal Crisis

Fiscal Crisis as the Product of Class Struggle

In the previous two chapters it was argued that crisis is both the product and the process of class struggle, within historically specific structural conditions. The assertion was made that crisis becomes a terrain of struggle, an arena of conflict over the realization of both class needs and socially-produced human needs. As crisis has been presented here, it is seen as a moment of rapid and, perhaps, profound social, economic, and political transformation. During the crisis resolution process, the institutional arrangements in which human beings live, interact, produce, and govern are open to change.

Of course, a given crisis opens only specific institutional arrangements to social change—progressive, reactionary, or otherwise. The crisis of our time involves both economic and political institutional arrangements; arrangements which organize the articulation of the class forces of our society. In that sense, the specific topic of this book—the fiscal crisis of New York City—is viewed here as a specific instance of a more general crisis: the crisis of capital and the fiscal crisis of the state.

This analysis of the fiscal crisis of New York City begins with this assertion: to understand the "causes," as well as the manner of the resolution of a crisis, we must understand it as a process of struggle within advanced capitalism. The struggle referred to here involves the relationship between government and economy; managers and workers; the union leaders and the rank and file; corporate and finance capital and government. Indeed, what this book explores is the very structure of city government, and of class relations, in contemporary America. Understanding the fiscal crisis of New York necessitates an analysis of the political foundations of the Keynesian welfare state. Furthermore, by understanding the fiscal crisis, we are able to view the transformation of America from a society wherein growth—in both the public and the private sectors—was assumed and depended upon to one where scarcity in the public sector dominates both the direction of social expenditures and the underlying ideologies of our time.

The Ideology of Causation

Such theorizing about crisis suggests that a crisis could be viewed as a terrain of ideological, as well as class, struggle. The struggle over how a crisis will be resolved includes a struggle over how that crisis will be viewed and defined; that is, the very manner in which a crisis is perceived is itself part of the struggle over contesting class interests. Will a crisis be defined as having been caused by workers, ever greedy and unproductive? Or will it be seen as having been caused by capitalists or the social relations of capitalism? Will particular public and private officials be blamed in a manner which suggests that if only one corrupt or incompetent individual had been replaced by an incorrupt and competent one there would have been no crisis? Will bureaucracy be blamed? Will blame be assigned to a particular group, leaving untouched an understanding of the total system in which individuals and groups, class beings and classes, operate and interact?

Even to talk about a crisis is to assign a particular set of ideological beliefs to it. The manner in which a crisis is understood is, therefore, not the consequence of rational and objective knowledge brought to bear on the crisis. Rather, our conception of crisis is itself the result of the conflicts within society and within the crisis itself.

Some analyses are viewed as objectively truthful and, in a politically instrumental way, correct, however. They may even be used as legitimations for a particular set of policy decisions. These views are themselves the consequence of the relationship of class and power within that crisis. They become viewed as "correct" as part of the struggle within the crisis. Hence, they are only "correct" insofar as a given class is able to exert its influence over the ideological process of defining a given reality. In simple terms, ideology is one form of class power, and the definition of a crisis—its causes, what is necessary to resolve it—is a concrete manifestation in ideas and consciousness of the power relations between classes.

The following example will be used to illustrate this point. During the fiscal crisis of New York City, an ideology of scarcity developed, which accepted without question the notion that the city had to cut expenditures drastically in order to avoid a formal declaration of bankruptcy. Underlying this ideology was a set of assumptions about causation, as well as a set of assumptions about the inevitability of drastic budget cuts. Furthermore, not only were the cuts viewed as inevitable but also there was a public sense that an organizational structure had to be superimposed on the city in order to effect a policy of austerity. And finally, it was assumed that the austerity policy necessitated scarcity for the workers and service cutbacks for the residents of the city. All the while, it was argued, the city must promote business interests by slashing taxes on corporate and banking income, while promoting business through incentives. In other words, an ideology developed which reflected union/labor weakness and corporate strength.

As this corporate ideology of scarcity seized the public consciousness, an interview was arranged with Edward Handman, the Director of Public Relations for District Council 37 of the American Federation of State, County, and Municipal Employees (AFSME), the city's largest union. His frustration showed as he detailed the inability of the union to confront the power of this corporate ideology:

HANDMAN: The *New York Times* and all the papers were calling on the mayor [Beame] for firings. You got to lay off civil servants, everybody's getting too much money and so on. And the first time he announced the layoffs the *Times* reacted and said he was a fearmonger. It was grotesque. . . . The substance of the issue still eludes most of them. They are still just bullshitting with the slogans.

In any event, when I say most people I mean the practitioners of the sport that's involved [Note: he is referring to the New York banks and the newspapers]. . . .

We would go around telling the papers, we were in the papers and TV everyday, whatever the crisis, and . . . we would tell the press that the banks were making this exorbitant money [from the crisis], just making a lot of money and calling on everybody else to sacrifice and them not sacrificing anything. Well, for months the press, the media couldn't get the banks [to question them]. They just wouldn't answer the phone. They were very wise in what they were doing. They were staying out of it. And it was very infuriating. You would go on a TV show and they would be attacking union pensions, the payroll, and whatever and we would say "What about the interests the banks are making off the city? What about all the money the banks are making off of the fiscal crisis? What about all of this?" And they would say, "Well, we called the banks and they don't answer." Literally, I'm not kidding you. We would say "Do you tell your listeners that the banks do not want to come on the show? That the banks do not want to be interviewed?" . . .

You see, we have a media that is ecstatic about this kind of thing, about any kind of sensationalism. This is the most sensational story, the most salable item that you have in New York City. It's a scandal, it's anti-civil-service, anticity, antipoor. To suggest that the city is misrun like the bankers did is tremendous copy. To suggest that civil servants are overpaid is tremendous copy; not just to suggest but to say it as if it's fact is tremendous copy. Politicians could get hearings any day in the week if they wanted to, just by saying we got to lay off civil servants, we're paying them too much, or saying that the bus driver retires with more money than he ever made. And you then tell them that 12,000 workers retired last year and that only forty of them were bus drivers, and what about the other 11,960: the others who went out with $4,000 a year, or $3,000, or whatever? They don't want to talk about it. They don't listen to you. And that kind of attitude presents a problem, there's no question about it. . . . They were so fucking hostile to hear this information from us. . . . And that's part of the whole general attitude [personal interview, December 6, 1978].

Ed Handman is highlighting here the powerlessness of the unions in relation to the media—the disseminators of information. Without access to the media-made consciousness of the fiscal crisis, the union's version of the "causes" of the crisis was largely ignored and dismissed. An ideological "wisdom" or "truth" about the fiscal crisis was publicly accepted, to the detriment of the city's workers, its unions, and its poor. This "truth" was representative of the corporate ideology that permeates American culture. It is antilabor and antipoor both in its most extreme forms and in the particular form it takes during crises periods. The ideology of scarcity that formed the consciousness of austerity was certainly no exception. We will return to this argument in Chapter 7; now, however, let us turn to a more concrete discussion of the various theories of fiscal crisis.

Theories of Fiscal Crisis

Given the analysis just presented, one must also be aware of the class interests of the theories of causation that will be presented in the following pages. Even though it might be suggested that theories are *interested*—that is, grounded in the struggle of opposing interests and forces themselves—that does not mean that *all* theories are equally invalid and biased. Theories differ in depth, insight, and their abilities to explain the social process leading to, culminating in, and resolving a crisis. Furthermore, given the struggle that the crisis manifests, the different theories present different sides of a whole—each understands a crisis from a particular angle or vantage point. For the reader, an awareness of these differences allows for a more total understanding of the phenomenon of crisis as struggle.

The following theories are not equally valid, however. Some illuminate, others cloud our understanding of crisis. Some theories protect the wealthy and powerful; others critically examine the social basis for their power and greed. Some theories serve the interests of the powerful by obscuring their class-based power. Competing theories cannot be equally valid since they emerge from people with different positions in relation to crisis. It is with this inequality in mind that the literature discussing the causes of the fiscal crisis of New York City is now presented.

For the most part, the theories of causation have been limited to a "scapegoat" analysis, which isolates one or more of the city's classes or class representatives as having caused the fiscal crisis. For some analysts, it was the unions that caused the crisis; for others, it was the banks. In either case, though, the class group is isolated and seen from outside its social relations.

Powerful Unions

The first "scapegoat" theory viewed powerful unions as the cause of the fiscal crisis. According to this theory, the fiscal crisis was created by the power of the municipal labor unions. These unions created the social conditions for the development of the fiscal crisis by forcing destructive and fiscally unsound wage and benefit settlements from past city administrations in return for labor peace. Labor peace was extorted by greedy, self-serving union leaders from weak and misguided mayors. Edward Banfield provided an early version of this analysis, when he wrote:

I don't see what's to stop the unions from shaking the city down for whatever money it can accumulate. The laws have prohibited striking all along. If the people of New York will tolerate strikes by public employees, against the law, and not tolerate politicians who crack down on strikes, then I can't see that it will be possible to get New York to live within its budget. It would require a fundamental change by the unions.[1]

Empirical support for this thesis was provided by the Temporary Commission on City Finances (TCCF), a government-appointed research commission whose function was to study the city's budget and analyze its expenditures and revenues. According to the TCCF, labor costs constituted the largest single item of expenditure in the city's budget in the years immediately preceding the fiscal crisis. For example, in fiscal year 1975, according to the TCCF, labor costs accounted for almost one-half of the total budgetary expenditures.[2] After the publication of the findings of the Temporary Commission, an interview was scheduled with its research director—Professor Raymond Horton, then of Columbia University. Professor Horton reasserted the Commission's position that the labor costs to the city were too high, given the resources available to the city. These labor costs included both wages and fringe benefits; the Commission was especially critical of pension costs.

> HORTON: From my point of view, the $22,000 a Sanitation worker earns isn't too much money to live on in New York City. You probably got to have $40,000 to live in New York City. So it's never enough from a person's point of view, whether you're talking about a comparative basis or sort of a micro basis. My whole sort of framework here is what are the costs of paying that and what are the consequences for other people of that person getting X amount of money? That's where the tradeoff between employment and compensation comes into hold here. Because what the city has done over the last few years, seven or eight years [i.e., during the early 1970s] is to basically choose between paying city employees X + 1 and financing that + 1 by reducing the number of city employees. Thereby reducing the amount of services provided to the city absent productivity gains, which have not occurred. . . . And finally, getting us into a sort of a bind where in a very sort of macro sense we become less competitive because our costs are higher and our quality of life that we're supposedly buying for that is reduced. So no, $22,000 isn't too much money in the abstract, but whether or not somebody is paid too much money or too little is something that's never possible or capable of being caught from a perspective of that personal level [personal interview, March 27, 1979].

A more direct attack on the perceived power of municipal labor unions came from William E. Simon, Secretary of the Treasury during the early years of the fiscal crisis of New York. Secretary Simon was the architect of the Ford administration's response to the city's desperate cry for help from the federal government. It is interesting to note that Secretary Simon himself was implicated in the city's borrowing of funds, eventually called excessive by the Secretary, as a member of the Technical Debt Advisory Committee, which advised the city on its borrowing needs during the years leading to the fiscal crisis. William Simon could hardly be called a disinterested and unbiased analyst, given his history of involvement in the city's accumulation of debt. Nevertheless, he offered this view of the city's path to near-bankruptcy and fiscal crisis, led by the unions and fiscal liberals:

> But clearly the most significant factor in New York's financial collapse was the cost of maintaining its municipal work force. The Cen-

sus Bureau shows that New York employed some 49 employees per 1,000 residents. The payrolls of virtually all other major cities ranged from 30 to 32 employees per 1,000 inhabitants. More striking yet were the salaries paid to New York public employees, which were among the highest in the country and far outstripped comparable salaries in the private sector. A few illustrations tell the tale.

—A subway changemaker, who was not required to change anything higher than a $10 bill, earned $212 per week. A teller in a commercial bank earned $150 per week.

—A city porter earned $203. In private industry an X-ray technician earned $187.

—City bus drivers often worked eight-hour days but were paid for fourteen. Split-shift scheduling was rare; thus, some drivers were paid for an afternoon snooze between the rush-hour periods, and they were paid at overtime rates.

—Teachers in the secondary school system earned up to $23,750, considerably more than counterparts in the private schools, and their workload had declined. Fifteen years before, a secondary school teacher had a schedule of thirty forty-five-minute periods per week and was responsible for other work. In 1975 the teacher had a schedule of twenty-five periods per week and could be asked to do nothing else.

If public salaries were absurd, the pensions of the city's workers were appalling. Between 1960 and 1970 fifty-four pension bills were passed in New York. In 1961 the city paid $260.8 million to provide its employees with retirement and Social Security benefits. By 1972 that sum had jumped 175 percent, to $753.9 million. . . .

[According to the TCCF], New York's politicians had given the municipal unions a fringe benefit package twice as expensive as the average elsewhere.

Technically speaking, this factor alone could be construed as the straw that broke the camel's back. In 1976 wages accounted for about $4.2 billion in the city budget. When this figure is increased by 68 percent [to cover fringe benefits], total labor costs rise above $7 billion. If, on the other hand, fringe benefits in New York were at the 35 percent federal level, total costs would have been some $1.5 billion less—the difference between a billion-dollar deficit and a half-billion dollar surplus.

How did the unions run off with the New York budget? Essentially the story is this. The city's unions were given the right to bargain collectively in the 1950s during the administration of Mayor Robert Wagner, but by law they were forbidden to strike. The law was unenforceable, and the unions soon discovered they had the power, by striking to cripple the city. On entering office in 1966, Mayor John Lindsay was confronted with a strike by transit workers that brought public transportation to a virtual standstill for twelve days. Lindsay, who had presidential aspirations, was polishing up his liberal credentials, and since nothing is more liberal than "solidarity" with the "proletariat" he capitulated to the transit union. All the other city unions demanded equivalent treatment. And from then on increasingly irresponsible settlements were extracted from the city.[3]

The powerful union theory has been a popularly held one. News media followed union workers to record nonproductive behavior, thereby reinforcing antiworker sentiment. When civil servants negotiated their most recent contracts, their cries of economic need fell on deaf ears. As evidence of union powerlessness, we have only to look at the contract negotiations begun in the spring of 1984. The unions and the city could not complete negotiations by the contract's expiration on June 30. The mayor proposed binding arbitration in November 1984, claiming that an impasse had been reached. This proposal showed a breakdown in collective bargaining, usually a sign of union weakness. If the unions had extracted unreasonable contracts in years past, they certainly seemed unable and powerless to do so in 1984.

In addition to the historical inadequacies that mar the analysis presented by Secretary Simon, the analysis suffers in another respect. It does not place the growth of union influence in New York City in the years preceding the fiscal crisis in the broader context of the growth of both public sector unionism and the size of the public sector throughout the country. Public employees throughout the nation were organizing and pressuring public officials for higher wages and benefits. In that context, New York City was not different from many of the major cities in the United States.[4] Therefore, the powerful union theory, taken alone, cannot provide us with an adequate explanation of the fiscal crisis. Its focus abstracts the unions from the context of the struggle itself: the operation, size, and control of the public sector.

Powerful Banks

A second explanation focuses on the power and greed of another class—bankers and their control of finance capital. This analysis lays the blame for the fiscal crisis at the doorsteps of the city's major banks. In this interpretation of the city's fiscal crisis, the bankers withheld their support for city securities in order to raise the interest rates and to transform the structure of city government. An example of this theory is provided by Jack Newfield and Paul DuBrul, who write that:

> . . . it was the bankers that did the hoodwinking [about the security of New York City's debt obligations], lying to the thousands of hapless investors, to the press, and even to the City Hall sharpies who were left holding the bag after a fullfledged market panic had commenced.

The true story [is that] New York didn't jump: it was pushed [into fiscal crisis].[5]

According to Newfield and DuBrul, the city was "pushed" into fiscal crisis because the banks no longer needed New York City securities, wanted higher interest rates for any securities they would be left holding, desired favorable tax policies from city government, and, in the broader sense, felt only one responsibility: to the bottom line and not to the needs of the city. This view was expressed by Victor Gotbaum, President of District Council 37 of AFSCME, during an interview on WCBS-TV *Newsmakers* on March 13, 1977.

GOTBAUM: Somewhere along the line the banks and the bankers will have to join the rest of civilization and become part of the city. . . . This is the sad part. I think we've done our part. . . . The single villain in this case are the clearinghouse banks. They deserved to be condemned and damned for what they did. Think very hard. Think very hard. When the moratorium hit us . . . if these men had said we're part of the problem and will be part of the solution; if they shook hands with us and worked it out instead of raising phony control issues . . . the bond market would have been calm and we could have looked forward to the future. Instead, what did they do? Think hard about it. They talked as though they're not part of the problem; the bond market had nothing to do with us. Or maybe they're right when Citicorp sent billions of dollars into the Bahamas and doesn't give a damn about this city, maybe they're right. Now the real tragedy is I get no satisfaction out of this. I'll state it and I'll state it again, because we do need that institution. I just hope to God that somebody humanizes them.

And, in the same vein, another labor leader took this point a bit further showing the banks' social position to be one of private, rather than public, interest. As Al Viani pointed out:

VIANI: The bottom line is the motto that they [the banks] live by. That is, make money and protect your money. They don't do anything for any social reasons. I have yet to see any corporation that has done anything for this country in terms of responding to social needs. Corporations respond to only one thing—make as much money as they can. And the banks are the same way. They haven't any social responsibility, I don't believe. No social conscience. And their goal was to protect their investors and that was it. There is nothing more to it. They weren't going to be so bleeding heart that they would care about the city of New York. They were only going to care about their big bucks.[6]

And last, there is the sense that runs throughout this type of analysis that bankers will be bankers. Therefore, their actions led to the fiscal crisis simply because of the inherent greed of their institutionally guided actions. But the problem is not that bankers' rationality is generous to the needs of the community. Certainly, the bottom line dominates bankers' rationality. Rather, the problem is that the banks are analyzed as independent of broader class relations, class struggles, and, indeed, capital investment markets and the economy. Removed from the class relations of capitalist society, the bankers seem to be totally independent actors, who act on personal whims and individual desires. This analysis "personalize[s] and, in so doing, seriously obscure[s] the larger social processes at work."[7] From this type of analysis, one can be misled to conclude that what is needed is to replace nasty bankers with nice ones. The structure of financing in a capitalist world economy and the place of finance capital in the New York political economy seem to get lost in this personalization.

Newfield's analysis demonstrated the duplicitous behavior of the city's bankers and their responsibility in producing the fiscal crisis. Though Newfield develops a power elite model for the city, his analysis ultimately personalizes the fiscal crisis. Hence, his work is weak theoretically and fails to understand the social process of class struggle from which the fiscal crisis developed. Nevertheless, his work, written early in the fiscal crisis, pointed to the power structure within which both the crisis and its resolution were developed. In that sense, Newfield's work was a valuable piece of muckraking.

Another variation of the powerful banks theory can be found in William Tabb's work.[8] Tabb's analysis constitutes an empirical application of the capital-logic theory to the fiscal crisis. According to Tabb, the fiscal crisis is the consequence of the actions of bankers who act as class beings within the logic of the capital accumulation process. For Tabb, the bankers acted as they had to act; their actions were determined by an historical inevitability found within the capital accumulation process itself. By trying not to personalize, Tabb has lost the historical subjectivity of class beings. Here the actions of both capital and labor are dominated by capital-logic, and the class struggle is reduced to a one-sided analysis of the actions of finance capital and the victimization of labor. In making his argument, Tabb ignores the past victories of public sector labor unions, the poor, and community organizations, who had demanded, struggled for, and often won increased wages, benefits, services, and income without work in the form of welfare, housing, health, and food monies; in other words, a social wage. As a result, Tabb loses sight of the class struggle from which the fiscal crisis developed and of which it was a part.

Tabb is correct when he argues that the bankers acted as bankers must in capitalist society when they protected their investments above all else. He is correct when he argues that this is the rationality of banking. Tabb is also correct in arguing that the bankers seized the crisis as an opportunity to reorganize the city's financial operations. However, this argument understates the major issue. The investment community was able to marshall its forces, to mobilize and thereby reorganize city government, because the city's unions failed to counter effectively the bankers' aims and actions. Tabb seems to understate the class struggle aspect of this crisis. By stating that the crisis was "falsely blamed" on the city's unions and poor people, Tabb places himself in the position of denying the efficacy of working-class struggle, the past strength of the labor movement in the city, and the past accomplishments of the welfare rights and other community movements.

Tabb's analysis is limited by the narrowness of the capital-logic argument itself. As a consequence, he fails to analyze the crisis as class struggle; hence, his theory of crisis fails to see that there are a number of alternatives for labor and capital; for different fractions of the working class and capital; for the middle class and the poor; for the banks and the unions. Furthermore, Tabb does not emphasize that these alternatives constitute the process of class struggle within the fiscal crisis, as these class representatives struggle over the ideological conceptualization of the fiscal crisis, and therefore, of its possible solutions.

It is important to keep in mind that the issues facing capital and the state—over the transformations of international banking, the growth of the high-tech and service economies, and the internationalization of production away from the core to the periphery, is fraught with pitfalls and conflicts both within the capitalist class and between political fractions within the state. One question that looms large is how capital and the state will deal with labor unions and workers within this profound transformation. Will unions be used as system integrators, as Felix Rohatyn suggests? Or will capital and the state try to limit and bust the unions, relegating them to the scrapheap of history, as Reagan's agenda suggests?

In any case, the city did not move into austerity solely as a result of a predetermined logic embedded in capital accumulation. The city's fiscal crisis appeared as it did and was resolved as it was not merely because bankers will be bankers. Nor was the city reorganized as it was out of some inevitable character growing from capital's own, self-propelled logic. Reorganization of the city occurred as it did—and the history of the fiscal crisis unfolded as it did—because bankers struggled as a class, while labor did not. The banks and corporate capital used the fiscal crisis politically and ideologically for capital's benefit; while labor's representatives argued that the fiscal crisis was not their fault. The representatives of capital reached a degree of unity that labor did not equal. In response, labor was unable to use this crisis and the possible histories it presented. The city's workers, though not the "cause" of the fiscal crisis, were a force in the expansion of the budgetary obligations of the city, forcing it to borrow. And though the city's workers were not paid more than municipal employees in other major cities, this fact only shows that the gains of state sector workers had been obtained over a larger, national context during the past decades. Given this history of class struggle, which is discussed in the next chapter, there was more than one direction that the crisis resolution could have taken. To suggest otherwise is to assume that the history of capitalism works itself out mechanically, as a consequence of the self-directed logic of capital. To suggest otherwise is to reduce the actions of labor to the logic of capital, thereby denying the subjectivity of workers and the class struggle.

Management Crisis

A third explanation focuses on the irrationality of city management. In this analysis, the organizational structure of politically influenced city agencies allows for corruption, inefficiency, waste, duplication of agency functions, and low productivity by the city's employees. It allows for gimmickry in reporting city expenditures and revenues. The Congressional Budget Office, in its report on the fiscal crisis, pointed out that:

> . . . one cannot ignore the city's questionable accounting procedures and loose fiscal management in relation to the current fiscal crisis. These procedures masked the fact that New York officials were failing to make the difficult choices that were required if the city's expense budget was to be truly balanced as required by law. The fault does not rest with the city alone. Many of the "gimmicks" which allowed the budget to appear balanced were tolerated or even suggested by state officials and were certainly not secrets to the banking community. These gimmicks produced small deficits which were allowed to accumulate and grow, producing a problem of large and unmanageable proportions.[9]

This analysis suggests a rationality crisis in administering the processes of government. Furthermore, this analysis suggests that a contradiction exists within the state system itself. As Jurgen Habermas suggests:

> In the administrative system, contradictions are expressed in irrational decisions and in the social consequences of administrative failure, that is, in disorganization of areas of life. Bankruptcy and unemployment

mark unambiguously recognizable thresholds of risk for the non-fulfillment of functions.[10]

Accordingly, actions to rationalize management and administration are needed if government is to fulfill its task. The resolution of the fiscal crisis therefore necessitates the rationalization of city services.

The work of Claus Offe points to the tendency toward instability and irrationality in the administration of government functions in the advanced capitalist state.[11] Following James O'Connor's theoretical schema, which will be discussed in the pages that follow, Offe argues that there is a fiscal crisis inherent in the function of the capitalist state. Yet, for Offe this is a contradictory process, in that the state both protects and threatens the accumulation of capital as it expands its administrative apparatus. In simple terms, the state socializes increasing parts of the costs of production, while protecting to varying degrees the privatization of profit. So, despite the presence of tax and revenue-raising policies, the state must find its revenues falling short of its expenditures. Thus, fiscal crisis.

Offe notes, however, that administrative irrationalities exist. The state has not been able to administer away capitalist crisis. The singular aspect of the modern capitalist state, for Offe, is its failure, despite its resources, to manage the crisis process. Hence, it is unlikely that fiscal crises can be averted merely by rationalizing city services. Indeed, Offe's work points to the inadequacy of state-government policy to solve economic crises or, for that matter, its own fiscal or political crises. Offe's work, then, provides a basis for challenging the simplistic management crisis theory that fiscal and political crises are consequences of an overfunded, underrationalized state. It challenges the conservative theory of crisis so predominant today: that the overpowerful state apparatus has single-handedly caused both economic and fiscal crisis. We will return to this argument later.

The Welfare State

Of all the theories of fiscal crisis, perhaps the most politically and sociologically significant are those that challenge the efficiency, efficacy, and practicality of the modern Keynesian welfare state. Here we see both conservative and Marxist theorists challenging, from clearly conflicting moral, political, and even epistemological bases, the institutional practicality of modern welfare policy.

On the one hand, we have the position that both James O'Connor and Claus Offe have staked out. As discussed in the preceding pages, both argue that the modern Keynesian welfare state has a crisis tendency built into its very functions. And, as Claus Offe shows, while the state suffers its own fiscal crisis, it is, at the same time, unable to resolve effectively the crises that erupt in the private sector to impede the accumulation of capital. Offe critiques the welfare state by positioning himself in direct conflict with the questions posed by most political and sociological analysts. He poses the problem in the following passage:

> While there have been numerous attempts in political science to increase the reliability of strategies of political-administrative intervention through improvement of information, organizational, planning and legal techniques, there are hardly any studies which proceed from the opposite point of view. The question of why the capacity of late capitalist societies for political regulation is so slight and their capacity for "planned social change" so defective is either not asked or implicitly dismissed by conceiving the well-known limitations of state regulation as due to factors of a contingent nature which may in future be brought under control through improved administration and budgetary management.
>
> This point of view, which dominates political science, and particularly its new branch of "policy sciences," is justified neither by practical successes nor by theoretical reasons. The following contribution thus examines the interventionist, welfare state regulatory strategies of late capitalist societies not from the standpoint of how their effectiveness could be increased but rather from that of why their effectiveness is—in spite of all attempts at improvement—so *limited.* [12]

For Offe, the welfare state is infused with contradictory functions as it attempts to regulate and administer the rationalization of the privately controlled process of capital accumulation. The split between the private control, power, and appropriation of value, on the one hand, and the public administration of the "needs" of both capital and the poor, on the other, leads to an inevitable failure for the welfare state.

This analysis explains fiscal crisis partly in terms of the expansion of expenditures and the clients of the welfare state. But the question remains as to whom we mean when we speak of the clients of the welfare state? Are we speaking of the poor and the economically defenseless? Or are we speaking of the needs of capital? For Offe, we are speaking of both. Often, when analysts speak of the welfare state they make the error of limiting their vision to either the poor or, from the conservative side, the civil servant. An example of this type of truncated vision is provided by William Simon's analysis of the fiscal crisis of New York.

> And that is why New York City collapsed financially. If one analyzes New York's fiscal crisis in terms of its real, not its mythic, elements, one sees plainly that nothing has destroyed New York's finances but

the liberal political formula. Using the "poor" as a compulsive pretext, New York politicians have formed a working coalition with a portion of the middle class to run the city for their mutual benefit at the expense of the rest of the productive population. And inevitably that productive population has slowly withdrawn, gradually destroying the city's economic base. Liberal politics, endlessly glorifying its own "humanism," has, in fact, been annihilating the very conditions for human survival.[13]

According to Simon, liberal politicians, whom he perceived as antibusiness and even anticapitalist, "gave away the store" to certain nonproductive segments of the city's middle class (by which he means the city's municipal employees). As we saw in Simon's statements about the city's unions, quoted earlier, the devil in the fiscal crisis was union-oriented liberalism. However, for the next analyst, Ken Auletta, liberalism merged with socialism on the local level, causing the fiscal collapse of the city. Of course, Auletta does not distinguish in any serious way between liberalism, a particular set of policies supportive of capitalism, and socialism, an anticapitalist philosophy and politic. But one does not have to be a serious analyst to get one's views publicized and taken seriously. Auletta's views must be taken seriously, first of all because he is a journalist who possessed access to a wide audience during the fiscal crisis itself and, also, because his views on this crisis mirror the rise of neoconservative political philosophy and political analysis. In other words, Auletta and Simon represent the profound and fundamental shift in American ideology. For Auletta, the fiscal crisis developed as New York politicians:

. . . armed with that novel government philosophy, the Statue of Liberty City, home for generations of poor immigrants, commenced an ambitious, politically popular and compassionate effort to care for the less fortunate by taxing the more fortunate. *New York undertook its own partial experiment in local socialism* and income redistribution, with one clear result being the redistribution of much of its tax base and jobs to other parts of the country as middle-class taypayers and businessmen fled town.[14]

According to Auletta, redistribution through tax policy and the expansion of public payrolls is synonymous with socialism. It is certainly questionable that the city undertook a major redistribution policy, and yet Simon, Auletta, and Ray Horton all seem to argue just that. In an interview, Horton pointed in that direction. The following dialogue indicates both the degree to which this analysis has been accepted at face value and the problems that such a politic might pose to a city. The exchange was recorded in March 1979, during an interview with Professor Horton and his assistant:

> LICHTEN: But when you get away from talking about the wages of the uniformed workers, you get many workers who are poor, who make very little money; particularly the clerical workers in District Council 37. It seems hard to argue that the fiscal crisis should be taken out on them.
>
> HORTON: I'm arguing that if hospital workers are underpaid, then we ought to finance our hospital system differently. That's if hospital workers are underpaid. But what are the consequences of paying the hospital workers the desirable wage, assuming that you could ever find out what the desirable wage is, given the city's limited ability to pay? Who pays for the hospital worker? Well, for one thing, the people who need the hospital services end up paying for it, because you have fewer hospital workers by dint of the wage level that exists.
>
> HORTON'S RESEARCH ASSISTANT: As long as this redistribution takes place in one city, in one area, then the private sector has the option of moving elsewhere. . . . If it was imposed nationally, where there was no escape, then we'd have a different story. I think we would have more options.
>
> HORTON: Most people don't recognize that I'm quite close to being a Democratic Socialist. I just argue that you shouldn't play democratic socialism at the local level. It's stupid. You can't do it. And any kind of political or economic model that tries to do that, without the federal government being involved in making that possible, is ridiculous.
>
> LICHTEN: And so the Temporary Commission on City Finances argues that the costs of doing business in the city should be lowered to make the city more competitive.
>
> HORTON: Yes, for over the long run you want to move toward more, rather than less, equality of costs.
>
> LICHTEN: But does that mean you are lowering the tax base of the city?
>
> HORTON: Yes, or holding it constant; reducing it in real terms or reducing it in terms of the share of local product.
>
> LICHTEN: Isn't this a classic trickle-down theory that maintaining a constant or, more to the point, a reduced degree of taxes on business will either bring in more business or keep those that are still here?
>
> HORTON: Yes, well, not just taxes. You have got to do more than just that. It's not just taxes. It has got to do with the quality of life, which is why we spent so much time studying the management variable.

Because I don't think it's just a question of expenses, or how much you pay. It's how you manage those resources.

LICHTEN: But hasn't business been hurt by factors external to the city's control? Not just taxes. There's the national and international recessions, as well as business running away from organized labor to cheap labor forces.

HORTON: There's no doubt about that.

LICHTEN: It's almost as if you say that business has been hurt so we have to help business while workers pay the brunt of that for a future that may or may not happen.

HORTON: My own sort of resolution of that is pretty simple. I don't think it is just. I am not even sure that it is going to work. But if you believe as I do that neither New York State nor the federal government is going to do what everybody, or what most people like myself, think ought to be done for New York City, then what alternative do you have to raising revenues? Do you cut services further? Do you pay public employees even more? How long does that last? It doesn't. We saw the answer in the fiscal crisis that it doesn't last.

In that exchange we can see the political significance of this theory. Here, it is argued that the liberal programs of the welfare state, as a path to or the realization of socialism in one city, cause a fiscal crisis whose resolution demands a return to a probusiness policy. This probusiness policy may or may not work, according to Horton. Nevertheless, it is the only policy that could be considered under the circumstances of the fiscal crisis. Accompanying this policy is, by necessity, austerity for the city's workers and residents. City services will either suffer or, in Horton's preference, will be maintained by increasing the productivity of those city workers who will be paid less in real terms, for doing more. And in those terms, the austerity policy, combined with business incentives, turn back a history in which workers struggled for a higher standard of living and a reduced work day. Hence, the social contract reached during the 1960s between the poor and the government, on the one hand, and between public sector workers and their management, on the other, is here challenged and broken by *government and management.* In later chapters it will be shown that that break was accomplished as policy, as a consequence of labor's powerlessness in relation to both city management and the private sector.

The analysis of the fiscal crisis provided by Donna Demac and Philip Mattera, in the early days of the fiscal crisis, is also instructive. Their analysis points to a theory of fiscal crisis which emphasizes the dynamics of class struggle within the Keynesian welfare state of contemporary American capitalism. For these writers, the development of the fiscal crisis is explained as the result of the mobilization of the city's working class and poor. In their view, class struggle intensified as workers and the unemployed demanded higher standards of living. They argue that this increased militance—evidenced in poor people's movements, rank-and-file wildcat strikes, and worker slow-downs resulting in lower productivity—constitutes a struggle for a social wage. This social wage, they assert, is an income independent of productivity. Basic to this argument is the assertion that advanced capitalism shifts class conflict to a struggle over the connection between wages and work. Hence, the struggle of poor people for higher welfare benefits, as well as the struggle by workers for higher wages with less work, constitute nothing short of a struggle against work. For Demac and Mattera, the fiscal crisis and the policy of austerity constitute capital's counter-offensive, which is designed to reestablish the relationship between wages and productivity.

> Something had to be done, and before long, capital's counter-offensive was launched. At its center were the imposition of a climate of austerity, the creation of scarcity, and the attempt to reimpose the discipline of work.[15]

This approach attempts to establish class struggle as the basis both of the fiscal crisis and of the solution—austerity.

Rohatyn's View

Which brings us to the final two analyses, which are basic to an understanding of the fiscal crisis of New York City. The first is offered to us by Felix Rohatyn, perhaps the single most important participant in the events leading to, and effecting, the austerity policy that "rescued" the city from bankruptcy. His views are important for providing both an overview of what happened to New York and an indicator of one possible set of policy options in the face of both national and international fiscal crises. Felix Rohatyn is on a world stage, with significant influence, and for that reason his analysis must be understood. In an interview with David Susskind, Felix Rohatyn was asked why New York City was in such trouble. Rohatyn responded with a view that challenges any analysis that finds the cause of the city's fiscal crisis within the city's own peculiar politics and economics.

Rohatyn answered Susskind's question in this way:

ROHATYN: New York's population changed dramatically in the 1950s, when there was an enormous influx of poor people, black people, coming from the South as the farms were mechanized. They were looking for employment. There were lots of people coming here from

Puerto Rico. At the same time in the 1960s as all these people were coming up here, in the 1950s and 1960s the makeup of the city changed. There was a policy in effect to help people live in the suburbs. We built roads, we gave mortgages, government guaranteed mortgages so people could buy houses. So as a lot of poor people were coming up here, a lot of middle-class people fled to the suburbs, and the tax base, the revenues of the city, the number of taxpayers began to get a little shaky. Then there was a change in technology in the 1960s. The manufacturing end of our economy began to decline and New York City lost 50 percent of its manufacturing jobs between 1960 and 1970; from 1,000,000 to 500,000, turning us into a service economy.

Now, politically at the same time, municipal employees began to have great political power, because they organized. Once they were organized they became critical factors, especially in local elections. . . . As a result of their political power, not only did they get very generous settlements over the years but their number increased dramatically. So, as our manufacturing employment went down, private sector employment went down, say, 50 percent, our municipal workforce went up from 100,000 to 300,000. And as I said, with ever-increasing generosity, as the politicians were currying the labor unions' favors and that favor was always exchanged for some very practical and concrete item.

Now, at the same time, politicians usually don't want to ask people to increase their taxes. They were running deficits as a result of these large cost increases. There was the rioting of the late 1960s, people wanted to keep the cities quiet. They spent a lot of money in the ghettos, which probably was a perfectly legitimate thing to do at the time because a lot of cities were burning. Then we had the recession and in the early 1970s our economy turned down and New York City all of a sudden had borrowed $6 billion more than it could pay back. It was running huge deficits. . . . Between 1970 and 1975, roughly $6 billion. It was running a deficit of roughly $1 billion-and-a-half per year by 1975. And the world stopped. The city couldn't refinance its bonds, refinance its notes, and it couldn't balance its budget.

Given this milieu, Rohatyn became a prime actor in the organization of austerity. As chairman of the Municipal Assistance Corporation (MAC), and even in the planning that produced both the MAC and the Emergency Financial Control Board (EFCB), Rohatyn was the major planner. And as Donna Shalala, former treasurer of MAC, described Rohatyn's power: "He had the power of his prestige; tremendous power because of his prestige and visibility in this situation. He was simply trusted by a large number of people that were involved in the process and therefore, I think he had enormous power during that period. And he, in fact, shaped the financial settlements" (personal interview, October 17, 1978).

Given that power, Felix Rohatyn's perception of the causes of the crisis, as well as the necessary steps to resolve the crisis, are significant. Later, Rohatyn would describe the overall austerity policy in the following ways:

> Business/Labor/Government cooperation coupled with courageous, interventionist political leadership saved New York City. Wealth, freedom and fairness were the subjects of continued, delicate trade-offs. A wage freeze and a Financial Control Board impinged on freedoms. Taxes, reductions in services, job losses, increased tuition fees and public-transport fares—all involved tradeoffs between wealth and fairness. There were no riots and only one short strike. We succeeded by a thin margin. We proved that intervention, liberalism and a balanced budget were not mutually exclusive. I believe this can apply to the nation at a time when the current theology is just the opposite.[16]

With the generalization of both the fiscal crisis of the state and the debt crisis to national and international dimensions, Felix Rohatyn's strategies have taken on a more international significance. Rohatyn has taken a clear position in stating that austerity is not designed to give the working class a free ride. While calling for shared sacrifices, Rohatyn comforts those who are troubled by the expansion of liberalism within the welfare state. Rohatyn writes that:

> In dealing with our budget problems, however, we cannot create the illusion that fairness means that the government will simply do more for the poor, the unemployed, the retired, the minorities. All these groups stand to suffer from a fiscal breakdown that could cripple economic growth, or cause a great surge of inflation, or both. If sacrifices have to be made to avoid those consequences, fairness means that the largest sacrifices must be made by those who can best afford them; but, unfortunately, some sacrifices will also have to be made by all groups above the poverty level.
>   This was the general principle we tried to follow in resolving New York City's fiscal crisis.[17]

The message is clear. It is not only the wealthy who must sacrifice in order to restore the profitability of the private sector and insure the stability of the public sector. Here, Rohatyn moves away from the class analysis that was suggested by his earlier description of the fiscal crisis' causation. He argues that we are all in this together, thereby drawing a conclusion that there are no irreconcilable contradictions, conflicts of needs and interests, among classes.

So, on the one hand, Rohatyn's analysis presents an overview that tells us that contemporary capitalism undercuts the security of its working classes. Indeed, one might see in his analysis a theory that suggests that the contemporary welfare state is, along with corporate capitalism, unable to effect a secure future for most Americans. The solution becomes "Business/Labor/Government cooperation"—in a sense, the expansion of the planning, administrative, and accumulation functions of the welfare state. Without long-range planning, with state participation, the crises of both the state and the economy continue. For Rohatyn, the failure of the welfare state is a failure that requires more state action. His argument leads him to call for more planning, more administration and participation of the state in economic affairs. In a curious way, by critiquing the performance of America's limited welfare state, and by actually participating in the crisis resolution process in New York City, this financial wizard has come to call for a more expanded public sector role in the private economy. His conclusions, drawn from the same set of historical conditions, lead Rohatyn away from the neoconservativism of a William Simon or a Ronald Reagan. In that sense, Rohatyn's vision represents one alternative, albeit a corporatist one, to the Reagan conservatism. If only for that reason, it is important to try to understand the New York City fiscal crisis and the austerity policy that was instituted to resolve that crisis. But first let us look at one more theory, a general one, concerning the fiscal crisis of the state.

James O'Connor and the Fiscal Crisis

In this final analysis, by James O'Connor, the fiscal crisis of the state takes place on both local and national levels and operates in government units, regardless of appearances of fiscal health.[18] According to O'Connor, the fiscal crisis results from an "overload" of fiscal demands made upon the state in its attempt to fulfill the twin, but contradictory, demands of fueling capital accumulation while legitimizing the capitalist system. These demands develop as the costs of production, in particular the social costs, become an impediment to the accumulation of capital. Capital therefore requires that these costs of production be socialized, or paid by all taxpayers, while profits remain privately appropriated. At the same time, however, the state must legitimate both the economic system, which it supports with funds, and itself. In order to do this, the state must disguise its class function as it attempts to balance these contradictory needs, which translate into conflicting budgetary pressures. O'Connor argues:

> Although the state has socialized more and more capital costs, the social surplus (including profits) continues to be appropriated privately. The socialization of costs and the private appropriation of profits creates a fiscal crisis, or "structural gap," between state expenditures and state revenues. The result is a tendency for state expenditures to increase more rapidly than the means of financing them.[19]

O'Connor argues that once the structural gap of the fiscal crisis has been established, the depth of the crisis is influenced by the actions of "special interests"—his way of representing class conflict.

> We argue that the fiscal crisis is exacerbated by the private appropriation of state power for particularistic ends. A host of "special interests"—corporations, industries, regional and other business interests—make claims on the budget for various kinds of social investment. . . . [In addition] organized labor and workers generally make various claims for different kinds of social consumption, and the unemployed and poor . . . stake their claims for expanded social expenses. Few if any claims are coordinated by the market. Most are processed by the political system and are won or lost as a result of political struggle.[20]

The socialization of the costs of production, along with the demands by various sectors of the capitalist, working, and impoverished classes, create the fiscal crisis, as well as the politicization of class struggle. The intervention of the state, in turn, alters the discipline of the market and influences the connection between profits, wages, and productivity.[21]

The works by Demac and Mattera and by O'Connor attempt to establish a basis for the fiscal crisis within class struggle. Since these writers view the crisis as stemming from the class relations of capitalist society, they are able to make clear the connections among the preceding analyses. The influence of the city's workers and unions, the organized pressure from the city's poor, as well as the greed of its bankers and the city's own administrative inefficiency all make sense, once located within such a context. Fiscal crisis then becomes an inevitable feature of the history of contemporary capitalism, and the policy of austerity is understandable as part of the crisis mechanism of the capitalist state.

Let us look more closely at the implications of O'Connor's argument. O'Connor theorized that the capitalist state must legitimize both itself and the capitalist system as a whole, particularly the private appropriation of surplus value. The state's expenditure pattern is intended both to encourage the accumulation of capital and, at the same time, to provide the ideological legitimation for that accumulation. For O'Connor, therefore, the welfare state is deemed necessary for both accumulation and the ideological hegemony of bourgeois consciousness. And yet it seems that O'Connor is postulating the capitalist state as a one-dimensional object, whose objective structure and functioning are dominated by the inherent structure and logic of capital.

At first glance, O'Connor's work seems to depart from the limitations of capital-logic theory as suggested in Chapter 2 of this book. Yet, by viewing fiscal crisis as inherent, O'Connor is arguing a form of capital-logic theory. State expenditures now are seen as legitimation devices, thereby relegating years of class struggle by workers and the poor to a dependent status in the history of the social welfare state. To speak only of the social control or the legitimation functions of social expenditures is to ignore decades of class and racial struggles.

O'Connor's theorizing makes the state's budget the victim of capital's imperatives, without locating these within class struggle. To say that the state fuels the accumulation process while at the same time providing its legitimation is not adequately addressing the question of the overall process of ideological legitimation. As this book will show, state expenditures may cease to be a legitimator when economic growth stagnates. On the one hand, ideologies of scarcity replace the ideologies of affluence that are the underpinnings of the growth of social spending. On the other hand, ideological legitimacy may be shifted outside the sphere of the state to the realm of culture, for instance. Perhaps the commodity itself replaces the state as a legitimator. In that case, the state may be viewed as impeding the ability of the economy to perform well enough to enable private individuals to acquire commodities; hence, the good life. The argument of this book is that just that has become the case. The state is now viewed as an inhibitor of capital accumulation, and one can understand the history of the fiscal crisis of New York City as a process during which the affluent state was replaced by the austere state. The ideology of affluence and state expansion was replaced by the ideology of scarcity and state contraction. Hence the state's role as legitimator through social spending has now been weakened. In that sense, the ideological terrain has shifted.

O'Connor's theorizing must in any case be addressed within the framework of the contemporary fiscal crisis. If we give O'Connor his major point, that social expenditures *were* legitimators for the overall expansion of capital accumulation, we must also locate the validity of this point for a particular and, now, limited historical period. This may have been profoundly accurate for the period of long-term economic expansion following the Second World War, up until the era of decline. Where that long-term growth left poverty, the state could justify the expansion of social welfare. Yet, if we recall the history of that expansion in the United States, it did not occur without a great deal of organized and persistent pressure, along with some rioting, from the poor themselves.[22] Joining the poor in this mobilization of class interests were the public sector unions and many of the political machines of the industrial Northeast and Midwest. And, in the sense that the state was forced to respond, then these expenditures could be viewed as a legitimating device. The state provided the ideology, concretely embedded in its budget, that capitalism was an enlightened system, a system with a "Great Society," which would rid America of poverty.

Still, this analysis begs the question. In a time of growth, ideological legitimacy also shifts to growth itself.[23] Perhaps just as important is the shift to the commodity itself that this shift engenders. The commodity and the consumer society provide a most seductive and powerful mode of legitimation.[24] And this mode of legitimacy can appear to operate outside of the state.

Here we can see that bourgeois culture provides its own legitimacy, without the prerequisite of state appearance in the ideological process. However, during crises that threaten both economic growth and state resources, we have seen that the state has shifted its legitimations to the realms of nationalism, anticommunism, new-found religious fundamentalism, and reborn individualism.

Once the depth of both the general economic crisis and the fiscal crisis was revealed, state budgets were cut back, at least in their social expenditures, at all levels of government. New York's fiscal crisis was merely a forerunner of a more general fiscal crisis. And, in that sense, James O'Connor was correct. Yet, government austerity was effected without the expected levels of dissent and resistance and, indeed, without threatening the ideological legitimacy of capitalism as a whole. The following text shows the opposite; that is, that the crisis itself became the legitimator for socially regressive policies.

Still, we need to know more. We need studies of particular historical cases, through which we can understand how this historical process, changing the relations of state and economy, power and class, actually occurs. In terms of this fiscal crisis of the state, we need to know how the crisis developed and how austerity became the basis for policy. In O'Connor's terms, fiscal crisis may be inevitable, but was austerity the only possible public policy for New York City in 1975? The notion of inevitability denies the possibility of alternative histories, of human agency; therein lies the need for an alternative analysis.

In the following chapters the argument will be presented that the fiscal crisis of New York City was the consequence of class struggle within a rapidly declining economic base. It will be shown that austerity is capital's reaction where labor has achieved significant power vis-a-vis capital in the operation of the state and that the fiscal crisis of New York was both the product and the process of class struggle. To ignore crisis as the process of struggle is to reduce the resolution of crisis to an historical inevitability, thereby relegating human action to a predetermined history. To do that, is to lose a sense of the class and power relations that define our time.

4

Precrisis Class Struggle

During the latter part of 1974, the most powerful factions of the banking and financial sectors of New York City's corporate establishment became concerned with the already huge and growing debts that had been accumulated by the city to cover past and present budget deficits. By this time, these debts totaled more than $10 billion, half of which were issued in short-term notes and due to mature within a few months. Indeed, debt service for 1974 alone exceeded $1.25 billion and represented nearly 20 percent of the city's operating funds (revenues minus categorical grants and transfers from capital funds) and 12 percent of the city's total revenue. Furthermore, the budget deficit for fiscal year 1974 was a huge $1,977 billion, portending increased borrowing by the city in fiscal year 1975.[1]

An October 1974 report by Bankers Trust warned that the city would have to roll-over $1.2 billion in debt before the year's end.[2] This sum represented nearly 25 percent of the total short-term debt and would further burden the city's budget for fiscal 1975, necessitating budgetary maneuvers to secure adequate funds. Such maneuvers could only serve to decrease the marketability of the city's debt offerings. To Bankers Trust and the rest of the financial community, this situation indicated that the city's finances were in deep trouble and might cause it to cease being an attractive investment. The specter of New York City being unable to borrow operating funds from the municipal credit markets became a realistic possibility for the first time in the post-World War II era. Only in 1933 had the city found itself in similar circumstances, only to be bailed out by the city's banks, who ran the city for the next four years.[3]

This huge debt was the result of the city having borrowed funds to cover the growing gap between rapidly increasing operating expenses and inadequate revenues from sales and real estate taxes. The practice of borrowing to supplement shortages of revenues began in 1971, though the city's short-term debt began to rise steadily as early as the 1965-1966 fiscal year. The short-term debt multiplied nearly five times during the years between 1965 and 1974, climbing gradually from $1.6 billion in FY 1965-1966 to $7.3 billion in FY 1973-1974.[4]

If we adjust for inflation, $1.6 billion in 1965 is the equivalent of $4 billion ten years later. We can therefore see that there was a significant increase in the city's short-term debt. Furthermore, since 1971 most of this debt was incurred solely to cover existing debt service. In other words, the city was borrowing to pay the maturing debt of the very recent past. The city had begun to borrow from creditors to pay its creditors.

This growing gap between expenses and revenues represents the "structural gap" that O'Connor defines as fiscal crisis.[5] In the city's case, it was the result of severe economic recessions, on the one hand, and the organized strength of its workers and the demands of its poor for an adequate standard of living, on the other. To make this claim is to suggest that the fiscal crisis is the result of class struggle and that it has a material base in the actions of both capital and labor. The financial community, suffering from heavy losses in real estate speculation as well as shaky investments in the Third World, recognized that the fiscal crisis presented a rare opportunity to repress the growth and strength of the city's work force through the institutionalization of austerity. At the same time, the fiscal crisis posed a real and serious threat to the stability of the banking system, and the solution to this crisis would be framed to save those with large investments in city paper, including and especially New York's major banks.

It has already been pointed out that this fiscal crisis developed out of a prolonged transformation in the economic base of the city. This transformation has been discussed elsewhere.[6] Here I will merely summarize the data that demonstrate the underlying causes of fiscal collapse. Then perhaps we can understand the threat and the opportunity presented by the fiscal crisis to a ruling class that was desperate to reimpose its discipline over an organized and militant work force.

The Collapse of the City's Economy

From 1950 to the present, New York City has seen its manufacturing base eroded both by economic recession and by the movement of manufacturing out of the central city. Between 1950 and 1975, for instance, the city lost nearly 50 percent of its manufacturing employment.

The loss included 13,426 firms and 324,000 jobs between 1960 and 1974 alone.[7] Between 1969 and 1976, as the city began to increase its debt, more than 500,000 jobs were lost, nearly one-half of these in factory employment, leaving still more workers dependent upon public assistance for support. Indeed, in the 1970–1975 period,

> . . . the local economy experienced a severe contraction, losing 468,900 (12.5 percent) of its jobs. . . . Between 1970 and 1975 every industrial sector declined, including service and finance, insurance, and real estate, and some declined precipitously: contract construction, 29.3 percent; transportation and public utilities, 17 percent; wholesale and retail trade, 13.6 percent; and manufacturing, 31.1 percent. The losses in the services and finance, insurance, and real estate sectors were smaller than elsewhere—1.9 percent and 8.1 percent, respectively—but contrasted sharply with the rapid growth each sector experienced in the 1950s and 1960s.[8]

Nor were the city's largest corporations immune from contributing to the city's economic decline. In 1965, for instance, the city was the headquarters for 128 of the top Fortune 500 corporations. But by 1975 the figure had dropped to 62, with 38 of these corporations relocating to the less costly suburbs or other regions of the country.[9] The city was losing employment and revenue from both its manufacturing and corporate headquarter sectors. In the process, the economic base of the city's economy was transformed.

With this overall and significant decline in the city's economy came an increased unemployment rate, a transformation to a service-oriented economy, and a revenue base that could not maintain pace with expanding city expenses. The city found itself providing support and services to the unemployed and, for a lucky few, jobs to cushion the downturn in the local economy. As the city's unemployment rate climbed from 4.8 percent in 1970 to 10.6 percent in 1975 and "wage and salary employment dropped 13%, from 3,797,700 in 1969 to 3,287,800 in 1975, . . . municipal employment rose by 30,000."[10] These were indeed years in which municipal employment grew in leaps and bounds: the city increased its full-time employment by 43 percent between 1960 and 1970. This growth provided an organizing base for the city's municipal unions, as they increased their membership by 300 percent, thereby increasing their potential influence within the city's power structure. At the same time, the city could not possibly employ all those who were left jobless, with the resulting increase in the size of the welfare rolls.[11] In the decade between 1960 and 1970, the proportion of the city's population receiving public assistance increased from 324,200, or 4 percent of the population in 1960, to 1,094,700, or 14 percent in 1970.

As the city's welfare rolls increased, poor people mobilized to agitate for better housing, higher welfare rates, better medical treatment, day-care centers, job training, and direct participation in the city's public education system. The wageless poor were demanding a social wage—an adequate level of income to support a materially decent standard of living, even without direct productivity to serve capital or the capitalist state.[12] And while some of the funding to support these services came from New York State and from federal grants, often requiring matching city funds, the city itself contributed a growing proportion of its own revenues. Table 4.1 demonstrates this growing dependence upon city, state, and federal revenues to support the social wage and to pick up the pieces left by capital's recession and mobility.

Table 4.1: Expenditure Pattern by City Function[13]

Function	Total Expenditures		% increase or (decrease)
	Fiscal Year 1961	Fiscal Year 1976	
Welfare	12.3%	22.6%	10.3%
Hospitals	8.2	9.7	1.5
Higher Education	1.9	4.5	2.6
Subtotal	22.4%	36.8%	14.4%
Police	9.5	6.4	(3.1)
Fire	4.9	2.8	(2.1)
Sanitation	5.4	2.7	(2.7)
Education	25.6	18.4	(7.2)
Subtotal	45.4%	30.3%	(15.1%)

Function	Total Tax Levy Expenditures		% increase or (decrease)
	Fiscal Year 1961	Fiscal Year 1976	
Welfare	5.6%	11.6%	6.0%
Hospitals	8.8	5.4	(3.4)
Higher Education	1.2	2.1	0.9
Subtotal	15.6%	19.1%	3.5%
Police	12.0	11.1	(0.9)
Fire	5.9	4.7	(1.2)
Sanitation	6.2	3.8	(2.4)
Education	21.0	14.9	(6.1)
Subtotal	45.1%	34.5%	(10.6%)

SOURCE: Adapted from tables provided by the Temporary Commission on City Finances

As the data demonstrate, expenditures for welfare assistance increased during the 1961-1976 period. This was due to both an infusion of federal and state monies, as evidenced by the rising proportion of total expenditures that include federal and state aid, and an increase in the proportion of tax levy expenditures allocated from the city's collected tax revenues. And while this rise in itself does not adequately demonstrate a burden on the city's revenues, it nevertheless indicates a shift in the expenditure patterns, as the city's economy moved into serious decline. If we turn to Table 4.2 we can see this more clearly. While welfare expenditures constituted 12.3 percent of city revenues in fiscal year 1961, by fiscal year 1971, welfare expenditures had increased to 22.5 percent of total city resources. It is interesting to compare this figure to the proportion of revenues allocated for police, fire, and sanitation services, all of which decreased over this time. Nevertheless, a word of caution is advisable here. Much of this revenue was allocated from grants and programs mandated and funded by both the federal government and New York State. For example, the TCCF noted that:

State and Federal aid contributed significantly to the growth and reorientation of City expenditures during the 1961-1976 fiscal period. State and Federal aid increased from $565.2 million, or 23 percent of the fiscal year 1961 budget, to $5.7 billion, or 47 percent of the fiscal year 1976 budget. [14]

The Commission then cautions us that:

Welfare and Hospital costs, which include medicaid, are nearly $4.3 billion and represent the major functional expenditure problems faced by the City. Although 75 percent of welfare and medicaid benefits are paid for by State and Federal aid, combined welfare and hospital expenditures exceed combined police, fire, sanitation, and education expenditures. [15]

Nevertheless, according to the Commission's own data, the proportion of city taxes expended for welfare functions increased only 6.5 percent between fiscal years 1961 and 1971. And while much of the pressure to increase these funds came from the poor themselves, along with their allies in the welfare rights movement, much of this money went to support a growing maze of city agencies servicing the poor, and not necessarily to the poor themselves. [16]

We might still argue that the growth and redirection of the city's budget reflected the urban insurgency characteristic of the 1960s. The process of allocating city resources reflected the militance of the city's impoverished and working-class populations. There was rebellion in the

Table 4.2: Percentage of Resource Shares Allocated to Major Functions[17] of the City of New York: Fiscal Years 1961, 1966, 1971, and 1976

Function	1961	1966	1971	1976
Police:				
Expenditures	9.5%	9.1%	7.3%	6.4%
Tax Levy	12.0	11.5	12.9	11.1
Employment	12.8	12.5	12.3	12.0
Fire:				
Expenditures	4.9	4.5	3.4	2.8
Tax Levy	5.9	5.7	5.8	4.7
Employment	6.2	5.6	5.4	4.8
Sanitation:				
Expenditures	5.4	4.4	3.4	2.7
Tax Levy	6.2	5.7	5.2	3.8
Employment	6.8	5.8	5.4	4.7
Education:				
Expenditures	25.6	24.7	20.6	18.4
Tax Levy	20.9	20.7	18.9	14.9
Employment	[Education data were not comparable during this period.]			
Welfare:				
Expenditures	12.3	14.1	22.5	22.6
Tax Levy	5.6	7.5	12.1	11.6
Employment	4.3	6.2	8.9	9.2
Higher Education:				
Expenditures	1.9	2.3	4.0	4.5
Tax Levy	1.2	1.3	3.0	2.1
Employment	2.1	3.2	5.4	7.1
Hospitals:				
Expenditures	8.2	8.6	9.4	9.7
Tax Levy	8.8	9.5	6.4	5.4
Employment	19.2	15.0	14.1	15.2
Total Percentage of Expenditure	67.7	67.6	70.6	67.1
Total Percentage of Tax Levy	60.6	61.9	64.3	53.6
Total Percentage of Employment	51.4*	48.3*	51.5*	50.3*

* not including education
SOURCE: Temporary Commission on City Finances

city, and a redirected budget was the price to be paid for some semblance of order.

The city was forced to acquiesce and to expand services for child care, housing, education, and other services demanded by insurgents in the feminist, civil rights, black power and Puerto Rican power, poor people's, and student movements. Cities across the nation were burning; mayors faced community-sustained activism. The expansion of the public sector was demanded and was in turn received.

Major beneficiaries of this militant era were the city's labor unions. Throughout America's major cities, beginning with the mid-1950s, a new wave of labor organizing resulted in the unionization of more workers than in any previous period, with the exception of the Great Depression of the 1930s.[18] In fact, the workers most likely to be harshly affected by the current austerity, that is, municipal and public employees, were the most successfully organized and experienced the most rapid expansion of unionization during this preausterity expansionary period. Public employees at all government levels, federal, state, and city, were organized to such a degree that their numbers actually doubled between 1960 and 1968 alone. By 1968, union strength among public employees had grown to over two million members.[19] For example, membership in the AFSCME swelled from 150,000 in 1950 to 400,000 in 1972. In New York City alone, District Council 37 of the AFSCME grew to include more than 100,000 workers.[20] To further highlight the extent of the organizing effort among public-sector workers, we must recognize that this was a period in which the proportion of American workers belonging to unions actually decreased. Furthermore:

By 1974 government employees at all levels accounted for 13.5% of all unionized employees, up from 10.7% in 1968. During the same years, the proportion of the unionized labor force in this country declined, from 23.0% in 1968 to 21.7% in 1974; this in itself is a dramatic decrease from the high point in union organization of 35.5% of the labor force in 1945. Therefore, the influence of public employees among unionized workers is even greater than would appear at first glance, and they are one of the few areas of the labor force where unionization is increasing.[21]

In cities across the nation, public-sector workers were organizing, lobbying, and, most importantly, striking, regardless of legal barriers forbidding many public workers to strike. Hence, the significance of the public employee unions cannot be underestimated: they effectively shut down important city services, for however brief a time. In New York City, for instance, 25 percent of all union members are in the public sector. By 1969, these public unions had grown to such an extent as to have organized the public workers in 80 percent of cities with populations greater than 10,000 (up from a low figure of 33 percent in 1938). This very rapid organizing experience caused analysts to declare that "the 1960s have already earned a place in labor relations history as the decade of the public employee."[22]

Along with this organizing experience, public workers became among the most militant workers. They often confronted government with demands for higher wages, better health and retirement benefits, shorter hours with better working conditions, and an increase in the size of the public workforce. Across the nation, strikes by public workers became commonplace whether they were legal or not, with or without the sanction of the union hierarchy or the support of the public. In most cases, these strikes were illegal and were met with forceful resistance from governments that were intent on keeping labor costs as low as possible. In any case, strikes by public workers involved more workers, for longer periods of time, as public employee unionization picked up increasing numbers of members. "In 1953, there were only thirty strikes against state and local governments; in 1966 and 1967, there were 152 and 181 strikes, respectively."[23] Furthermore, 310,000 state and local government employees conducted 490 strikes in the year ending October 1975, according to the Census Bureau. This was a 72 percent increase over the number of strikes in fiscal 1974, as governments began to crack down on public workers.[24] At the very least, these workers had demonstrated their resolve to increase their wage and benefit packages. The more progressive unions, on the other hand, formed alliances with clients to unite in a common effort against local, state, and federal governments. Social workers in New York City were one example of an effort to unite workers and clients in a common struggle. Regardless of union strategy, public workers had indicated their potential power in the administration of city services.

Furthermore, money that might have been expended toward making business more profitable was now being allocated for increased wages and benefits to city workers. Local businesses often found themselves with increased taxes, while fewer local funds were being allocated to meet their production requirements and investment needs. The result was a "consistent, though varying, level of pressure from business to keep expenses in the public sector low in order to free investment monies for the private sector, or at least to channel public monies through contracts with private enterprise."[25] As city expenses increased, local business began to apply pressure for a decrease in the costs of labor; in other words, decreased wage and benefit packages to the city's workers. The Citizens Budget Commission (CBC), a private, nonprofit, research advisory organization whose trustees are prominent members of New

York's corporate sector, warned as early as 1969 about the possibility of a fiscal crisis, as expenses increased and revenues decreased. These warnings began even as the city's debt increased, yet they went unheeded. This was not because they were unfounded; rather, it was due to the politicization of the class struggle. Government administrations, dependent upon union support for reelection, could not merely dismiss worker demands. These demands by city employees could only be ignored at the expense of "public order" and essential city services. For the first time on such a large scale, public employees were showing their potential power.

It was within this context of the politicization of class struggle that public sector workers organized, mobilized, and pressured the government for increases in the value of their labor power. Profit criteria are absent in the public sector, and the value of a worker's labor power ceases to be measured by either the profitability of the business or the productivity of the labor power. As a result, wage and benefit packages seem to lose the inhibitions and limitations of the marketplace. Wages are set solely by the strength of contending classes, or rather by the conflict between, in this case, public workers and the government.

More importantly, public workers recognized this fact and expected higher wages as their right. Often they established a wage and benefit parity, with the most highly paid workers in the corporate sector. The ideology that wage levels should be tied to productivity or profitability became transparently political and soon lost its influence over increasingly militant public workers. Consequently, workers demanded and often won unprecedented settlements, thereby forcing government to redirect some revenues from capital's needs to the workers themselves. This redirection threatened both the administrative functions of government—as it tried to provide the social stability necessary to maintain the legitimacy of capitalism—and its economic function, that of encouraging and assisting the accumulation of capital. Indeed, it was the cost of performing the former function and maintaining the "loyalty" of the working class that threatened the latter function, as potentially "productive" and profitable expenditures were drawn away from the private sector.

This redirection of government funds away from capital posed a threat to the partnership between government and industry. Seen in this light, the fiscal crisis, the loss of manufacturing jobs, and the eventual withdrawal of credit and financing from the city all result from capital's response to this heightened and politicized mobilization of public sector workers, along with the "clients" of the welfare state. Capital needed to reassert its control over government policy, so that its needs, and not the needs of workers and the poor, would be met. Control over the budgetary process of New York City became the strongest and most direct method of reimposing control.

Before we discuss the methods through which control was reimposed, let us first examine the class struggle in the public sector that occurred prior to the fiscal crisis. We shall see that the militance of New York City's workers indeed constituted a threat to the disciplined administration of city government: the public sector was no longer isolated from the union movement.

Union and Community Activism

Marxist and mainstream social scientists alike have referred to the power of the newly formed public employee unions.[26] We have already taken note of the effect of the past militance of public employees and their unions on New York City's growing expenditures and deficits. Worker militancy during the 1960s weakened capital's control over the processes that shaped government operations. Social protest challenged administrative authority, thereby challenging the forms of accountability that had been established for budgetary procedures. Under the impact of worker activism, city management was forced to stray from the rationality that was presumed to characterize the corporate influence in city government: that is, "public" accountability, an accurate and nondeceptive means of calculating and disclosing revenues and expenses, clear jurisdiction over the use and deployment of city employees, the measurement and encouragement of productivity, and an overall emphasis on decreasing labor costs. Piven and Cloward, writing about the consequences of public employee activism, maintained that:

> Under the impact of these pressures, municipal governments in the older manufacturing cities were forced to make concessions in the form of enlarged payrolls, higher salaries and fringe benefits, and new services. Most of these gains were won by the better organized municipal workers, who had the power to shut down the services and facilities on which the municipalities depended. However, the minority poor also made gains: they got enlarged welfare benefits, a larger share of municipal jobs, and some new services in the ghettos.[27]

The pressure applied by organizations representing municipal employees and the poor forced an expansion of social services, thereby increasing city expenditures through a ripple effect: demands for increases in wages, benefits, and the size of the work force (resulting in decreases in measured productivity) allowed and, indeed, encouraged, the expansion of the total government social service network.[28] The consequence of this expansion extended to the whole organization of government and the establishment of governmental budgetary priorities, including a challenge to the rationalizing of city services through the reorganization of the labor process along standard capitalist corporate procedures. Managing cities became a precarious process of balancing community needs—as represented by militant city workers, the poor, minorities, and community activists—with corporate demands.

As Mayors struggled to appease the demands of a variety of insurgent urban groups with jobs, benefits, and services, municipal budgets rose precipitously. But so long as the cities were in turmoil, the political price exacted by the insurgents had to be paid in order to restore order. Accordingly, municipalities raised their tax rates despite their weakening economies, and state governments and the federal government increased grants-in-aid to municipalities. By these means, the cities stayed afloat fiscally, and they stayed afloat politically as well. Overall, the share of the American national product channeled into the public sector rose dramatically in the 1960s, and most of that rise was due to enlarging municipal and state budgets. [29]

The New York data, provided by the TCCF, support the above analysis. During the 1961–1976 fiscal period, New York's operating expenditures increased more than fivefold, from $2.4 billion to $12.8 billion. Furthermore, after allowing for inflation, this increase was still substantial, representing a threefold increase when the value of the dollar is held constant. Indeed, during the years most characterized by worker insurgency, 1966–1971, we see an "unusually rapid growth rate in [city] expenditures. . . . During this period, expenditures successively increased 24.3 percent, 18.1 percent, 13.5 percent, 11.7 percent, and 16.6 percent." [30]

The increase in expenditure was clearly influenced, though not exclusively caused, by the increased political influence due to the insurgency of the public work force. A partial enumeration of major job actions by New York City's workers during this period includes:

(1) A twelve-day job action by transit workers in 1966, resulting in a final labor settlement with a 15 percent increase in wages over two years, free uniforms, a $500-per-year pension bonus, as well as increased and more comprehensive health and welfare benefits. The panel chosen to mediate the strike settlement estimated the cost of the package to be between $60 million and $65 million. As important as the disruption in city life caused by the transit strike was the loss of business, estimated at $100 million per day during the duration of the strike.

(2) The transit strike was followed by new demands from police, firefighters, welfare workers, and Parks Department employees. The firefighters, with a renewed militancy, demanded that management drop

its productivity proposals, which included "lower manning ratios, consolidation of stations, adjustment of shifts to comport with the frequency of fires."[31] In addition, the firefighters rejected a wage and
benefit package that police officers had ratified, leading to prolonged
job actions, slowdowns, and the picketing of City Hall by the police. A
settlement was agreed upon only after the firefighters had rejected three
offers. It called for a wage increase of $900 and a benefit package
totaling $642 per worker for the first year. At the same time, sanitation
workers agreed to a contract calling for a more secure pension plan,
equaling that of the other uniformed services. This plan called for a
twenty-year retirement provision at 50 percent of pay.

(3) A strike by nurses, followed by a doctor's strike, crippled the
delivery of health care services. The nurses struck and won against a
wage scale "so low that 60 percent of the registered nurse positions in the
municipal hospitals were vacant"; while the doctors won a wage hike
almost doubling their hourly compensation, from $23.50 to $43.[32]

(4) A three-week teacher strike in 1967 followed a recommendation by
a fact-finding panel that teacher work loads be increased.

(5) An unsuccessful strike by welfare caseworkers perhaps best
illustrated the new and emerging activism. A strike was called, and strike
action ensued, despite active opposition from District Council 37 of
AFSCME representing supervisory personnel. The strike called into
question the organization of the welfare bureaucracy, its casework
procedures, workloads, and the meager allowances for welfare clients.
These demands at once established the bond between worker and client
in opposition to the city bureaucracy.

> Bart Cohen, a former leader of the caseworkers . . . admitted that the
> militant breed of workers who were being hired by the thousands,
> fresh from the campuses, reacted almost reflexively against the least
> exercise of management authority.[33]

In retrospect one writer, following this line of reasoning, commented
that

> the disruptive tactics of the union leaders were often completely
> irresponsible, and at times literally disruptive. Work in which they had
> long taken pride was condemned as evil and prurient by all sides, even
> by their superiors. The radical new workers looked hairy and un-
> kempt, seemed to take no pride in their work, and resisted discipline
> and normal supervision.[34]

This writer, perhaps, gave too much emphasis to hair style; still, one
point was well taken: workers in the welfare agencies, as well as in other

city departments, acted militantly and challenged the productivity work rules and requirements that had given management its strength. The effect of this antiauthority activism was to demonstrate a common class experience among the long-haired welfare workers and the short-cropped firefighters. It was this class experience that created the necessity for common, though not necessarily coordinated, political action in regard to work.

The years that followed saw insurgent actions similar to those described here, with much the same effect: through the organized application of pressure, workers effected some reorganization of the labor process as a whole. Consequently, productivity declined as wages and benefits increased. This was indeed an intensive struggle against work itself, as

real compensation for most City employees increased more rapidly in the 1970–1975 period than in the 1965–1970 period. The political power of organized workers . . . effectively insulated the labor process from the effects of resource scarcity.[35]

Not for long, however. The scarcity produced by the fiscal crisis ultimately affected the gains made by workers during these bouts of militant action. In fact, the fiscal crisis represented for city workers the abrogation of many important wage, benefit, and work process gains that had been won during the preceding decade. The crisis was used to turn back the clock and reestablish managerial authority.

The rise of militancy among public sector workers during this period has not as yet been explained. A brief overview of the recent past reveals that, contrary to public perception, New York City's unions were not very strong prior to the job actions begun in 1965–1966. Indeed, city management during Mayor Wagner's administrations was quite dominant, despite a certain sympathy toward unionism. In an interview held in August 1978, Al Viani, Director of Research and Negotiations of District Council 37 of AFSCME, provided an explanation for the rise of public worker militancy by placing it within an historical context:

VIANI: To understand the role of unionism you got to understand what happened prior to 1965 and, I would say, after the Second World War until the end of 1964. Public employee unionism was never really strong, nor was there any formalized collective bargaining rights. Most of the salary schedules were determined by unilateral determination by management . . . even under Mayor Wagner's executive order which granted some form of negotiations to the union. [In 1954, by executive order, Mayor Wagner recognized city workers' rights to organize and discuss working conditions. In 1958, Wagner issued

Executive Order No. 49, which gave city workers collective bargaining rights.] The bargaining was so structured as to be within . . . the city's pay salary plan . . . so we couldn't ask, for example, for across the board increases. They were considered not negotiable, arbitration of grievances were not negotiable, the welfare fund benefit was not negotiable. So that the whole process of determining employee wages and how and what benefits employees got, through, I would say, the end of 1964, the power was essentially in the hands of management; almost, I think, a unilateral power.

There is a consensus concerning this relative lack of power of public employee unions at that point in New York City's history. Charles R. Morris, one-time budget director and now a vice president at Chase Manhattan Bank, described Mayor Wagner's executive orders and their effect on public sector unions in the following manner:

Unions are still a relatively new phenomenon in city government . . . [and] for the most part municipal unions did not come of age until late in Robert Wagner's tenure as Mayor. Unionism and public employment were not concepts that mixed easily. Wagner's police commissioner, Stephen Kennedy, viewed a police union as unthinkable; until well into the 1960s, many teachers considered unions incompatible with their status as professionals; and a top executive in the Department of Hospitals said in 1962 that unions had no place in any agency devoted to public service.

Associations of civil servants and uniformed employees had existed for many years and had occasionally wielded respectable amounts of political power . . . but although associations were occasionally effective pressure groups, there were no organizations with the right to represent employees against the government until Wagner established the city's labor relations machinery during his first and second terms in office. . . . By executive order in 1954, he granted employees the right to organize, established grievance procedures—in which employees could be assisted by a union representative—and created labor-management committees to discuss working conditions and to foster cooperation between management and workers. The city's Department of Labor was created to certify unions, approve representation units, and assist in resolving disputes. Employee titles were simplified and rationalized into broad classes that were roughly consistent across departments, and a Career and Salaries Appeals Board that included union members was created to hear disputes over pay and classifications. The city agreed to collect union dues through payroll deductions in 1957, putting union income on a reliable footing, and union representatives were allowed release time from their city jobs for union business. The final breakthrough came in 1958, when Wagner issued his Executive Order No. 49 . . . granting unions the right to bargain collectively for their members. Despite the sweep of Wagner's reforms, there was little immediate difference in the conduct of labor-management relations. The unions were still very weak and much more absorbed in organization and survival issues than bread-and-butter problems of pay and working conditions . . . Wagner did what he could to keep them that way.[36]

Mayor Wagner's methods for keeping these newly-formed unions powerless included establishing a certification process, which fragmented them and prevented them from amassing large numbers of members, thereby limiting their potential economic and political influence. In addition, the unions were not permitted to participate in collective bargaining sessions until they represented a majority of workers in a job category—and these categories cut across city agencies. This made the task of organizing the workers both difficult and costly. Finally,

the collective bargaining rules themselves were delayed two years before being issued, and when they were finally produced, they construed the executive order in the narrowest possible terms. The order had stipulated that unions had the right to bargain over "terms and conditions" to include only pay, fringe benefits, promotions, and time and leave rules. In fact, at first everything except salaries was effectively excluded from the table; even fringe benefits were seriously negotiated only in 1962.[37]

On balance, Mayor Wagner's labor relations strategy seems to have been designed to inhibit the development of a militant, active, politically influential and progressive union movement in New York City. Anthony Russo, a management official for the city during the last four mayoral administrations, stated that "there was no real bargaining at all . . . it was more of a joke."[38] Without an effective bargaining agent or power, the city's workers were forced to accept substandard wage and benefit packages relative to the unionized private sector. In an interview, Al Viani discussed the impact this had on the city's employees:

VIANI: And over the period of time employee wages . . . kept falling further and further behind comparable kinds of employment in the private sector to the degree that it became very very severe. And I think that is the primary reason or primary cause of the tremendous growth of public employee unionism in the city. The city had in fact been solving its budgetary problems by denying employees equitable wage increases and equitable salary scales in comparison to the private sector.

By the time the first Lindsay administration had begun, the unions had already broken away from accepting this degree of powerlessness. In

1965, for instance, District Council 37 of AFSCME won a critical representation election among the workers in the Department of Hospitals. Soon afterward, the small, formerly fragmented unions were joining D.C. 37, as "the era of balkanized unions was ending."[39] When the welfare workers struck that year, the peaceful coexistence so comfortable for and favorable to management was ended, and a period of worker militancy, with its tremendously escalated frequency of strikes, slowdowns, and sickouts, had arrived.

> The welfare strike settlement signaled an irrevocable shift in the balance of labor relations power away from City Hall. Wagner had opened the door to the expansion of union influence among municipal employees; by skillful maneuvering throughout his last term, he had kept the opening to the width of a crack; but in his last year in office, he was shoved aside, and the unions came bursting through, brimming with the discontents and frustrations that had accumulated through the long years in the darkness.[40]

During the Lindsay administrations, city management found itself confronted with unions that, according to Al Viani, "had gone through a period of development and begun to develop some muscle; political muscle as well as economic power." Workers engaged in job actions that were designed to increase their wages and benefits, while decreasing the amount of work required of them. Mayor Lindsay, more often than not, found his adversary strong and persuasive and very willing to utilize all available strategies. The resulting wage, benefit, and work rules packages increased the desirability of city employment. Al Viani explained the rationale behind these labor settlements in this way:

> VIANI: Lindsay basically responded to union arguments that said in fact that the wage scales were way, way behind the private sector and that there had to be a catch-up. Prior to the Lindsay administration the wage increases were very, very minimal. They were in the range of 3, 3½, or even 2 percent. In some instances, they were nothing. Or they were dragged out over four years where there were maybe what they called one or two steps within the salary schedule. But the wage increases were very, very small. So that under the Lindsay administration the disparity had become so great that the union argued under the new collective bargaining law that there had to be a catch-up. And under the Lindsay administration the wage increases varied—some were 9 percent, some were 10 percent, and some were 11 percent. That went on for most of the Lindsay administration. The last increase that was negotiated under the Lindsay administration was an 8 percent increase. So that there was a catch-up factor as well as an attempt to keep up with the rising cost of living, which, as you know,

under the Nixon administration was running at one point at 9, 10, and 11 percent a year. So just to keep in place one would have to get very substantial wage increases without having a cut in real wages. Under the Beame administration [just prior to the fiscal crisis] we negotiated a 14 percent increase over two years that had a cost of living adjustment on top of that. That added another 1 or 2 percent to the total package. We felt that was reasonable in light of the inflationary factors that were happening in our economy.

Yet these contracts were not the result of a climate of opinion that favored a decent wage as a "human" or "moral" right. Rather, the settlements were gained through harsh and often protracted conflict, struggles against an authority that in any case could only be moved by power. Mr. Viani highlighted this when he referred to the ideological power of capital and administration. An article in *Fortune Magazine* had pointed out that the city's expenses had vastly increased in the decade prior to the fiscal crisis, due in part to the unlimited amount of credit that had been available. This "credit card" created a situation, according to the article in *Fortune,* wherein

city politicians seldom had to bring themselves to say no to anybody—whether union leaders making extravagant demands at contract time or citizens seeking benefits for themselves or others. If the city government had been forced to match expenditures more closely with revenues, hard choices would have been unavoidable. But the borrowing power, coupled with enormous political pressures from a citizenry both accustomed to costly services and suffering from one of the highest taxes in the U.S., led city officials to ignore fiscal realities. As a result, New York got committed to do more things than it could afford.[41]

Among those commitments were "a slew of services for the indigent, the young and the aged."[42] It also included an increase in the city's overall labor costs. These increases were said not to reflect the health of the city's economy nor to give adequate consideration to the need for a balanced and accountable budget. In a statement that recognized that wages, even for public sector workers, are the result of class politics, and do not come from "free" market forces, the article in *Fortune* maintained that

political considerations have had a lot to do with inflating the city's payrolls. Municipal workers number around 300,000—no one is quite sure how many there are—and they are a significant political bloc. In the memory of budget officials, no mayor since Fiorello La Guardia, who left office in 1945, had ever laid off any civil-service workers until this year [1975]. The City's labor costs, which account for about half of the expense budget, have risen by an average of more than 9 percent annually over the last two decades. In mayoral election years, the average payroll rise had been closer to 14 percent.[43]

In Robertson's article, the magazine was calling for drastic cutbacks in labor costs, thereby necessitating a large number of layoffs and/or a reduction of wages and benefits, along with an increase in productivity; eventually this became the city's strategy to reduce expenses. Mr. Viani reacted strongly to this solution for fiscal restraint and against the suggestion that the demands of the city's unions had caused the fiscal crisis.

VIANI: FORTUNE is wrong when it says these 9 percent increases over twenty years [caused the fiscal crisis]. That is pure and simple bullshit. But that's the kind of myth that's been perpetuated by a press that is essentially dominated by corporate leaders. They are corporation presidents. All the presses—they're not owned by the workers. You know corporation presidents. And they're going to lie through their teeth about what is happening with the wage scale or the fringe benefits of public employees. They have lied consistently. The Temporary Commission on City Finances lied. Ray Horton [staff director of the Commission] admitted it; that his facts were wrong. He admitted it in a public forum. [Note: In a personal interview, Ray Horton denied making any such admission and reaffirmed his commitment to TCCF data and conclusions.] His research was shoddy and cheap and it was a cheap shot. But this is the kind of bullshit that the unions have to put up with. So that's what we deal with and fortunately public opinion has some bearings on the negotiations—but it doesn't ultimately decide or determine what happens. *What really determines what happens is power—pure, simple muscle and nothing else.* And so these guys scream and yell but when it comes down to the bargaining table it is going to be power and the relative power of the unions vis-a-vis the city and whether in our eyes justice is going to be done. This last settlement that we got [June 1978] is . . . in effect what one paper said: the unions negotiated a cut in their wages.

This statement puts the decade of labor militancy in its proper perspective. Both Mr. Viani and *Fortune Magazine,* though from different class perspectives, recognized that contracts were negotiated through the politics of class struggle. During the years preceding the fiscal crisis, the city's unions were successfully negotiating wage and benefit increases along with work rules provisions decreasing worker productivity. The city's workers were receiving more compensation for less work. This indicated the strength—the "muscle"—that the city's unions had built.

In 1978, well after the austerity institutions had been put into operation and the ideology of scarcity had taken its hold on New York City's communities, the municipal unions were accepting contracts that would reduce their wages and benefits, relative to inflation, and increase their measured productivity through changes in work rules reminiscent of the classical speed-up. Work rules were changed, wages and benefits reduced; all of these changes pointed to the drastic and dramatic loss of power that the unions had suffered.

It was the case that municipal workers in New York City were able to exact generous concessions from the city during Mayor Lindsay's administration. The political and social climate during the Lindsay years was quite the opposite of the retractive economic, political, and social policies of the middle to late 1970s. Union power was, at the same time, both real and illusory. It was real in the sense that the public employee union movement had broken away from the clubhouse labor-management politic of the Wagner years. The militant activism by the city's workers was matched and fueled by a more general popular militancy within the city. The "community" movement and the union movement seemed to feed upon each other. Through their militancy, and through federal policies that encourage spending, the city's unions gained influence. A city administration besieged by minority and community activists could ill afford sustained conflicts with its workers.

On the other hand, there was a measure of illusion to this power. Increases in city expenditures were to a large extent the result of the federal government's response to urban insurgency. The city often gained revenues from the federal government in grants-in-aid to develop its social services. This expanded social service network necessitated increased numbers of city workers; and as the total number of city employees grew, so too did the potential power of city workers and municipal unions.

Furthermore, corporate leaders were not exerting pressure to resist these expenditures. Indeed, the major commercial and investment bankers were implicated in the expansion of New York City's debt obligation, which was made necessary as expenditures exceeded revenues. So there was much to be gained by finance capital in the underwriting and purchasing of tax-free notes and bonds with relatively rewarding interest rates. Through these devices, the city's major financiers actually encouraged the very debt cycle that they later blamed for the fiscal crisis. William Scott, former deputy comptroller of New York City and assistant to Albert Shanker of the United Federation of Teachers (UFT), described in an interview in December 1978 how the city's major institutional lenders encouraged the accumulation of debt.

SCOTT: Mayor Beame [and previous Mayors] was led by a group of technical advisors mostly arising, all of them arising, from the banks and financial community who for many, many years had no objection to what the city did so long as the bonds were salable. They never asked for full disclosure [of the city's financial condition]; they never forced issues; never had prospectives. They had a bond counsel that conveniently came up with reasons why the city should be able to sell its bonds and the types of bonds that they were selling. There were political pressures to do certain things with city money—to roll them over, notes, in the anticipation that the interest rates were going down, which was a bad guess; therefore, if you're able to roll them over you are able to sell them later on at a lower interest rate. There were poor decisions made, based on poor information, but based upon the only information that was available. You always had to look with some suspicion on the advice you received, because in a city this size whom do you go to for financial advice about bonds—whether they're salable and what rates should be paid—except to the same people who are going to buy and sell them? There is an inborn conflict of interest unless you're going to go to an amateur and let him give you the advice. So you always had to look with some suspicion on what was told to you.

With the workers demanding better contracts, and community residents demanding better and more social services with the encouragement of both the federal government and the city's financiers, it is understandable why the growth of expenditures outpaced its revenues. The roles of the private sector and the federal government make it difficult to assess the actual power of the city's unions during the Lindsay period. The most powerful elements of the private sector encouraged the increase in city expenditures, because it served their class needs. New York City's economic base was changed, as manufacturing declined and services became more predominant. Increased city services stilled a potentially troublesome population, while keeping the city's workers cooperative through the dual policy of increased wage and benefit packages along with decreased productivity. Labor peace was essential to this transformation, and a smooth one was more likely while the city spent its funds and borrowed more, rather than while it was cutting back. To put it simply: the expansion of city expenses and debts assisted corporate needs in ways that a retracting budget could not.

James O'Connor argues this point and substantiates it in great detail in an analysis that has already been examined here.[44] We can now see that the accumulation and legitimation functions of public expenditures served a major transformation in the political-economic structure of New York City. An expanding budget provided ancillary services to capital, while performing the legitimation functions that capital required to mask its power. The expanding budget, with expanding deficits, signaled to both capital and labor that the city was to meet both of their class needs. At the same time, this policy provided increased benefits to the city's workers, while giving them the illusion of power that could guarantee influence even under different circumstances. The fact was that their power was only available when these policies did not threaten the city's corporate and financial elite. When the economy was jolted by a severe and sustained crisis, the corporate and financial sectors could no longer permit workers to exercise influence over government, nor could they permit government to respond to citizens' demands for increased services. A fundamental shift in the balance of power was necessary for capital to reassert its needs over city government. The moment when labor and capital could benefit from the same government policy had passed.

Capital demanded an austerity-based economy to meet its own class needs. In time, capital withdrew its financial support of New York City and withheld it until it could itself assume the reins of government. In an interview in October 1978, Donna Shalala confirmed that point:

SHALALA: Remember that was a bad period for the banks. They were going through some changes. They had taken tremendous losses in their real estate ventures. They no longer needed whatever tax breaks the municipals [notes and bonds] would give them. They essentially had gotten themselves into such financial problems that they just didn't need all those other municipal obligations and tax exempt obligations. So they didn't need all those other kinds of fancy tax breaks. Their prestige, the New York banks' prestige, was deeply affected during this period.

The conditions that had been favorable to influential public employee unionism had been altered. The federal government, under President Nixon, withdrew its support for local governments' social service efforts; finance and corporate capital no longer needed to encourage the city's expanded debt; meanwhile, community activism was suppressed and ultimately dissipated. Having already left behind the activism associated with their early organizing years, the municipal unions found their power to be more illusion than real. They were no longer able to threaten and cajole the city government into beneficial labor contracts. Faced with a contracting city budget and an economy in recession, the city's unions found themselves unable to sustain their former influence. As William Scott maintained in an interview in December 1978:

SCOTT: If you go back in the history of public unions, and they exist for many, many years in this city, they always negotiated in an upgoing economy. Maybe you didn't get what you wanted, but you got more than what you went in with. And when the economy in the Northeast, particularly New York, started downgrading, this was a new experience for unions. They were not used to bargaining in this way.

Despite the contention that "of all workers, the public employees have been among the least willing to yield their gains" during the fiscal crisis, New York City's workers were unable to organize effective opposition to austerity.[45] They did not produce an antiausterity movement of any real political consequence. In the following chapters it will be shown that in the face of a contracting private economy, a withdrawal of capital to the city by its financiers, and a city in fiscal crisis, the unions of New York adopted a strategy of cooperation with management which resulted in an austerity policy to the detriment of the city's workers.

5

Precipitating Crisis: The Banks

The previous chapter argued that the fiscal crisis was both *produced by* and *the result of* a prolonged history of class struggle. We saw the developing influence and organized militance of the city's labor unions, as well as its workers. I argued that the fiscal crisis must be understood as originating in the struggle between public sector workers and their workplace—the city bureaucracy—on the one hand, and, on the other, between the class needs of major New York corporate and banking interests and the community at large. This struggle ensued within a severe and prolonged economic recession, which was most evident in the decline of the city's manufacturing base.

In the following chapters this argument will be continued, with details of the actions taken by the city's major financial and corporate "representatives" that both *used* and *produced* the city's fiscal crisis. Of particular import here is the suggestion that this crisis was both real and produced; that it was both real in economic terms and manipulated by corporate elites. The fiscal crisis was real in the sense that banking and corporate interests had much to lose had the city been formally bankrupt. The fiscal crisis was manipulated in the sense that it presented an opportunity to achieve class aims. Indeed, the very task of this chapter is to argue that the fiscal crisis—even though it was the culmination of years of economic decline and class struggle—was used to promote corporate interest through the restructuring of city government. Therefore, the fiscal crisis represented both threat and opportunity for New York's financial and corporate elite.

Producing the Crisis

In late 1974, with the city's debts piling up, the financial community began to show its "concern" over the city's fiscal stability. In separate, independent memorandums, analysts at the Chase Manhattan Bank, Citibank, Bankers Trust, and Morgan Guaranty Trust all expressed reservations over the marketability of future city bonds and notes.[1] In internal bank memorandums, as well as in the city's mass media, discussions of the city's shaky financial condition were circulating. By October 1974, the city's precarious fiscal condition became the subject of discussions between city officials and major banking figures. As reported by the Securities and Exchange Commission (SEC), investigating the city's fiscal crisis on October 7, 1974:

> A monthly meeting was held of the Comptroller's Technical Debt Management Committee (CTDM Committee), a committee first established by Goldin's predecessor, Abraham D. Beame [once the city's Comptroller and, in 1974, its mayor], to advise the Comptroller on debt issuance, the condition of the municipal securities markets, and related matters. Present at the meeting, besides [Comptroller] Goldin, were Dr. Seymour Scher, First Deputy Comptroller; William T. Scott, Third Deputy Comptroller; Sol Lewis, Chief Accountant; and various other members of the Comptroller's staff. John Devine of Chase, Gedale D. Horowitz of Salomon Brothers, Richard R. Kezer and Paul S. Tracy, Jr., of Citibank, Zane Klein of Berlack, Israels, and Liberman, Richard B. Nye of First Security Co., Wallace O. Sellers of Merrill Lynch, Pierce, Fenner, and Smith, Frank P. Smeal of Morgan Guaranty Trust Co., and James F. Trees of Fisher, Francis, Trees, and Watts, Inc., all members of the CTDM Committee, were also present.
>
> At this meeting, the Comptroller announced various changes in the City's borrowing schedule. . . . Deep concern was expressed by CTDM Committee members about the potential saturation of the market because of the magnitude of the City's projected borrowings; that a point might be reached where the City would not be able to market its securities at any yields; and that difficulties might arise with the next scheduled bond offering on October 16th.[2]

Between this meeting and the end of the year, the city and its advisors, including its bankers, held meetings, passed memorandums, and discussed in detail the possibility of a fiscal crisis. One such memorandum, written from Weiner [Special Advisor to Comptroller Goldin] to Goldin, Scher, and Scott concerning the market from the city's short-term debt noted that major banks were finding it *"unprofitable to carry tax exempt debt for trading and holding purposes because other types of loans and leases had provided the banks with sufficient tax shelters for their purposes, thus eliminating the value of tax exempt obligations.''*[3] [Emphasis added.] Given this, New York's banks no longer had an interest in continuing their heavy investing in the city's debt obligations. Furthermore, the memorandum went on to indicate that the municipal securities market was saturated with the city's offerings, suggesting trouble in further marketing of its securities. "Commenting generally on market absorbability, the memorandum referred to . . . tables that showed that City short-term issues, as a percentage of all municipal offerings, comprised 20.56% of all 1973 issues and 27.57% of all issues in the first half of 1974. It was indicated that both percentages would soon increase substantially . . . "[4] With the city's huge borrowing needs of late 1974 through 1975, any conclusions drawn from this information could not be realistically optimistic.

With such concerns in mind, the banking community began to mobilize. Indeed, even the Clearinghouse Association, representing New York's major clearinghouse banks, which had underwritten and marketed city securities in the past, had been alerted to the potential danger of the city offering debt that was not covered within its constitutional limits and to the possible cool reception of investors to such an offering. For example, the SEC reported that a December 1974 letter from Richard L. Tauber, a vice president of Morgan, "advised" a substantial investor that the city was indeed in a financial crisis.

> The letter stated that although the author believed that the rating agencies [rating city securities] would give the city the benefit of the doubt, a downgrading was very possible if the financial deterioration of the city continued; this would narrow the market for City securities. The letter recommended that the client reduce his holdings of City securities by not renewing maturing obligations and by tax loss trading.[5]

Yet, at that very moment, the *Wall Street Journal* carried a report that substantiated the great demand for the last offering of city securities.[6] Individual investors were quite excited about purchasing part of the December 2, 1974, offering of $400 million in Revenue Anticipation Notes (RANs) and $200 million in Tax Anticipation Notes (TANs).[7] In part this demand was due to the high interest rates: 9.4 percent on the TANs and 9.5 percent for the RANs. The demand was also partly caused by the "low" $10,000 denominations.

The city had offered this "low" denomination for the first time in its history during its marketing of $600 million of short-term notes on November 22, 1984. Previously, city notes were marketed at substantially higher denominations. But fearing saturation of the municipal debt markets, the city resorted to seeking individual investors in recognition of the fact that both sophisticated, "large" investors and institutional investors might very well stay away from the city's notes. Indeed, the city was offering $2,500,000,000 of its notes to investors within a two-month period, between early September and November 12, 1984. On top of that, the city was to offer another $2.3 billion of city notes to investors between November 12, 1974, and February 20, 1975. Given this astronomical sum, the city's outside financial advisors in the CTDM Committee advised that smaller denominations be offered for the first time. As a consequence, the $10,000 denominations were marketed to the general investing public.[8]

In its report, the SEC concluded that:

A key role in the nationwide distribution of the City's securities was played by the City's principal underwriters: Chase, Citibank, Morgan, Manufacturers, Chemical, Bankers [Trust] and Merrill Lynch. The underwriters, through their own investments and by selling the City's securities to the investing public, enabled the City to raise billions of dollars in short-term debt issues through the Spring of 1975.

Approximately *four billion dollars* of City notes were underwritten during the period October 1974 through March 1975, a time when the City's fiscal condition was critical. Faced with a marketing problem, caused by saturation of the market through previous billions of dollars of City issues and the growing doubts of the financial community as to the City's financial status, the City and the underwriters reached out for the smaller investor.

Thus, beginning in the winter of 1974, City notes began to be marketed in denominations as small as $10,000. This had the effect, at least in part, *of shifting the risk for financing the City from the City's major banks and large institutional investors to individual investors.*[9]

Small investors were now being attracted to the city's precariously backed debt instruments. Indeed, they were encouraged to buy the city's notes by high interest rates, the promise of a tax-free return on their investments, and by the security of knowing that the city's major banks and financial institutions were underwriting these notes. They did not know, of course, that these very same underwriters were warning their major clients not to invest in these very same notes. Nor did they know that these very same institutions were refusing to invest in the city by holding these notes in their accounts.

On January 4, 1979, a prominent banker was interviewed, who played a significant role in the investment community's efforts to move the city toward an austerity budget. At the time of the interview, Jac Friedgut was a vice president of Citicorp's Municipal Securities Division. I asked

Friedgut about the practices of investment bankers, their criteria for their actions, and his response to the SEC's report relating to the banks' underwriting and investment roles at this point in the fiscal crisis. He responded as follows:

FRIEDGUT: Investment bankers never, never, never hold large blocs of anything in portfolio. An investment banker is clearly acting as an intermediary. He will go to a municipality or a state and say "sure, I'll sell $100 or $500 million for you," and he'll find people to sell it to and he'll make the difference on the spread. The commercial banker has two pieces to him in this regard; actually three. First, he has a dealer department, which in this regard is identical to the investment banker. He just wants to buy and sell and get out. But then he also has an investment portfolio department, which makes investments on the bank's own behalf. . . . The third area, which I wouldn't even mention except the SEC does, is the trust accounts for customers. And we are required to have what's called a "Chinese Wall" between that and all other parts of the bank. So that we cannot go to the trust department and say "you must do this" or say "hey, you do the trust work for General Motors. How are they doing?" We can't do that. And indeed, when the SEC says we were underwriting and the same time our trust department was unloading the notes, in a sense that just demonstrates how well the Chinese Wall works. We can't talk to each other. We aren't supposed to.

When asked whether that was a legal requirement, that there be no coordination between the departments, he answered: "Well, saying we're not talking to each other is overstating the case. But the legal requirement is that each [department] has to make its own decisions and they can't have sort of joint decisions."

In its report on the fiscal crisis and the role of the underwriters, the SEC was unambiguous about this aspect of the banks' behavior. They reported that

As the City's fiscal crisis worsened, the public was subjected to a confusing and contradictory financial picture, with the result that the public, unlike the City and its underwriters, was deprived of a basic understanding of the City's finances. While the public was left largely uninformed, the City's underwriters had an increasing awareness of the range of problems underlying the City's fiscal crisis.

During 1974 and early 1975, certain of the underwriters of City securities ceased purchasing City securities for their fiduciary accounts. Despite the shift of investment policy, they continued as underwriters to market these securities to the public. The underwriters did not disclose this significant change in their investment strategy and policy. . . . The City's securities offerings were carried out without adequate disclosure. As a result, the public's principal source of information, besides the stream of confusing and contradictory statements in the press, was the representations by the City and the underwriters attesting to the safety and security of City notes.[10]

Apparently the SEC was not convinced by the "Chinese Wall" argument. Nevertheless, there is still a serious issue that must be considered here. It has to do not with what bankers do as individuals, but rather with the actions of bankers as class beings, operating within banking institutions as class institutions that direct and manage the flow of finance capital. And in that capacity, New York's banking community, the underwriters of the city's notes and bonds, clearly redirected the city's debt offerings away from their own portfolios, away from the portfolios of their largest clients, and into the portfolios of smaller investors. The problem here is not merely in the lack of honest disclosure of the city's worsening financial condition by either the bankers or the city's own officials. The problem lies deeper: it is within the relationship of finance capital to the capitalist state as it is concretely articulated in a specific situation, a specific crisis. The problem concerns the contradictions of the relations of class and state, of public funding based on private appropriation of capital, profit, and the private control of investment (finance) capital. In simple terms, the situation demands an analysis of class and power, not of misguided, or ignorant, or malicious individuals. It is striking that analyses of the actions of bankers, city officials, and investors, have, for the most part, ignored the issues and relations of class and power, capital and government. This is one weakness of the SEC report that is cited throughout this chapter. Nevertheless, the report does clearly demonstrate a particular *power* relationship between the financial community and city government. It is to this relationship that we now return.

As the city's financial weakness and its increased need for short-term borrowing grew, toward the beginning of 1975, the banks privately discussed the serious lack of fiscal security behind the city's debt obligations. Publicly, the underwriters were calm—indeed, reassuring. Privately, memorandums warning of crisis circulated among officers of the city's major banks. For instance, the SEC reported that in December 1974,

Karen Gerard, a researcher for Chase, wrote an internal memorandum entitled "The City's Fiscal Situation—The Budget Gap Is Real." It noted that a "budget crisis" was an annual event in New York City but, unlike previous ones, this crisis was real. Ms. Gerard presented a general overview and analysis of the City's budget problems. She concluded that the City's economic base had been weakening at the same time that expenditures had grown at a more rapid rate than revenues, thus compounding the City's long-standing fiscal problems.[11]

And in another memorandum, at another of the city's major banks, written to Donald Platten of Chemical Bank, Richard Adams, senior vice president for the Investment Division, stated that the "market for City securities was narrow and dependent on the New York City banks. Problems in the 1976 fiscal year loomed large, with expenses outgrowing the economic base of the City. He declared that there was a need to reorganize the City's debt structure."[12] There were also memorandums written and circulated within Citicorp, Morgan Guaranty Trust, and Bankers Trust, all indicating the city's worsening financial condition and the need for the city's financial reorganization. And on January 2, 1975,

> David Gaston, investment officer [of Citibank], reported to Paul Collins, Senior Vice President, that Citibank held $23 million par value in New York City obligations in accounts for which the bank had fiduciary responsibility. Mr. Gaston also reported that the bank was not purchasing City bonds for fiduciary accounts at the present time.[13]

As further indication that the banks were recognizing that not only the city but they themselves were in trouble Richard Adams reported to Donald Platten, as follows:

> Support of the City of New York by the New York banks and "lending institutions" has been enormous. Chemical Bank holds an amount of N.Y.C. obligations which far exceeds the amount it could or would lend to any other borrower, except the U.S. Treasury. . . . [He noted that] (1) there was still an oversupply of City securities in the market; (2) there was much negative publicity about the City in the marketplace; (3) the market was continuing to narrow, with several institutions withdrawing; (4) the real size of the City's deficit for fiscal 1975 was in doubt ("we just don't know the facts"); and (5) figures between $1 billion and $2 billion had been discussed as the deficit for fiscal 1976.[14]

Holding an amount of obligations which "far exceeds the amount it would lend to any other borrower" surely placed these banks in a most precarious position. How could they disinvest in the city and, at the same time, protect their economic and political positions? Their behavior at this time, as they began their disinvestment in the city's debt obligations, led one union leader to remark that: "They always deny that it was them—that they did that. They said they were just representing people throughout the country. But that was bullshit. They weren't caught by surprise by the fiscal crisis. They dumped their notes, so maybe they knew what was coming. They just got out." Did they have to know the exact figure for the 1975 and 1976 budget deficits to know that they were overinvested in the city? That their huge investments might not be safe? That the city was in trouble? The banks did indeed "get out" by dumping the notes that they held, at least as much as the overcrowded market would bear. But that is getting ahead of ourselves at this point. Let us now return to late 1974, to show how the banks formulated strategy to produce an austerity policy.

Throughout late 1974 and early 1975, the banks continued to circulate internal memorandums warning of potential trouble ahead. Indeed, warning of fiscal collapse and investor wariness of the city's debt offerings, the bankers began to formulate strategies to avert financial collapse and fiscal crisis. A memorandum from Amos T. Beason, vice president of Municipal Credit and Finance, Morgan Guaranty Trust, to Frank Smeal, executive vice president of Morgan Guaranty Trust, suggested that part of the problem was that:

> City officials did not appear to comprehend the seriousness of the situation. It was asserted that, in the recent past, the City's problems were solved by more borrowings, budget gimmicks and increased Federal and State aid receivables. The reported attitude among dealers and investors was that the New York City financial institutions and the State and Federal governments would not permit the demise of the City to occur. However, investors were said to need concrete signs that the City's problems were being addressed by City officials and the financial institutions.

The memorandum went on to suggest that the bank

> apply some financial discipline to the City's operation . . . [and then recommended the following course of action]
> (1) a substantial moratorium on capital expenditures
> (2) a substantial cut in the City payroll
> (3) the development of "honest three-year plans" on revenues [and expenses]
> (4) a review of the City tax structure
> (5) an analysis of the City's overall debt structure . . . by officials of the City, State and City's business community . . . [with] the results of the study [to include] suggested remedial legislation.[15]

The memorandum further suggested that the banks would agree to *fund the city by lending substantial capital in short-term loans if the city undertook a rigorous program of fiscal recovery.* In fact, the banks had already decided that austerity was necessary—even prior to the refusal of investors to buy city securities.

All the while, the mayor and the comptroller could not agree on the size of the budget deficits nor on the methods required to close the budget gap. The public bickering, along with the actions of the clearinghouse banks and the saturation of the market, pushed interest rates higher. So it was that on October 16, 1974, the city issued $478.58 million in long-term bonds, at an average interest rate of 7.3318 percent. A November 4 issue of $500 million RANs and $115 million of TANs was marketed at an average rate of 8.3359 percent by a syndicate led by Morgan Guaranty. But by December 2, the interest rates had climbed to 9.5 percent for the RANs and 9.4 percent for TANs. This indicated a marketing problem; it also indicated that the banks' perception that the city was becoming unmarketable at any price might have affected the marketing process itself.

Even so, the squabbling between Mayor Beame and Comptroller Goldin certainly could not assure investors of the city's financial stability. As the city moved to greater and greater debts, the actions of its elected officials only served to verify the deep trouble that lay ahead. As Jac Friedgut suggests:

> The major impact of the dispute was felt after a bidding syndicate had already purchased a new bond issue from the city but before the bonds were resold by the underwriters to the public. Prices on the bonds fell sharply as investors felt the need for a higher interest rate to compensate them for greater uncertainty, and the underwriters were forced to sell bonds into the market at very substantial losses. Meanwhile, the Technical Debt Advisory Committee [whose members were bankers] had warned the comptroller that the city's heavy schedule of short-term debt offerings were likely to meet market resistance, resulting in higher interest rates. [16]

So it was that interest rates continued to climb. With this climb, the city's debt service increased, thereby necessitating further borrowing. The data that follow demonstrate the increased costs of borrowing. As the data indicate, by fiscal year 1975 the city was allocating 14 percent of its budget to pay off its accumulated debt (see Table 5.1).

In November 1974, the city began to cut its expenses. Its solution then was to be the same throughout the next three years: expenses would be cut by layoffs, attrition, and austerity. November saw 1,500 layoffs of civil servants and provisional workers, followed by 3,725 the next month. The December layoffs, however, included uniformed personnel as well as teachers. In addition, up to 2,700 workers faced forced retirement. In a series of meetings with the city administration, the finan-

Table 5.1: Debt-Service Expenses (in thousands of dollars)

Fiscal Year Ending 6/30	Debt Service*	Expense Budget*	Proportion of Budget for Debt
1970	705,753	6,722,824	10.5%
1971	781,819	7,744,761	10.1
1972	847,433	8,659,194	9.8
1973	1,099,101	9,560,928	11.5
1974	1,175,973	10,287,546	11.4
1975	1,826,965	11,895,019	14.0

* Extracted from *New York City's Annual Reports of the Comptroller.*[17]

cial community continued to press for more layoffs and stricter control of city expenditures. The financiers were willing to cooperate with "saving" the city, but the price for this cooperation was the austerity program.

The city and its financial advisors, representing the financial community, continued to meet throughout December. It is instructive to look at the meeting and events of December 17 for an indication of the events to come. According to the *New York Times'* chronicle of the fiscal crisis, December 17 was a day that brought the following:

> Saying that spending economies [including the layoffs listed above] should be matched by borrowing reductions, Comptroller Goldin cuts a planned January issue of $500 million in bonds and an unspecified amount in notes to an issue of $620 million in one-year notes and the sale of $450 million in bonds to the city pension funds. With city securities reportedly making up 30 percent of the municipal debt market, the move will "give the market a breather."
>
> Some people in the financial community still advocate "massive layoffs," wage freezes, and an end to such city services as free tuition at the city university, transit subsidies, and others.[18]

The financial community, especially the underwriting banks and brokerage houses, was reeling from substantial underwriting losses from a city bond offering in October 1974. The *New York Times* on December 16 reported that these losses might be as high as $40 to $50 million. Underwriters make their money by acting as intermediaries between buyers and sellers; they do not make money by holding the debt obligations themselves. Apparently, with the market saturated, and their own institutions not investing in the city either for their clients or for themselves, it was more and more difficult to market city debt. With this as the backdrop, the CTDM Committee met with city officials and, as the SEC reports, the following occurred:

[1] The meeting of the CTDM Committee reconvened at Gracie Mansion. A memorandum by Frank Smeal indicates that Messrs. Beame, Goldin, Cavanagh, and Lechner [Director of the Budget] apparently caucused for fifteen minutes prior to the start of meeting. [2] At the reconvened meeting, Mr. Sellers of Merrill Lynch told the Mayor that the City securities market was a "total disaster" in recent weeks. [3] Therefore, he stated, it was likely that there would be no bid on the January bonds. The CTDM Committee did not question the City's ability to pay its debt, but indicated that the market could not absorb offerings of the magnitude contemplated. The basic problem was said to be the size and frequency of the borrowings. He stated that purchases by the pension systems [that had previously saved the jobs of city workers faced with layoffs] could afford only temporary relief, and borrowing to finance deficits was no longer a viable procedure.

The Mayor disagreed . . . about the effect of the purchases by the pension funds, indicating that these purchases could continue as long as the rates of interest remain high. Furthermore, he asserted that it was the timing and not the size of the borrowing that was the problem and the banks should help "sell" the City and not just tell the City to reform. In addition, *because of the ever-growing militancy of the municipal unions, Mr. Smeal indicated that there were doubts as to whether City debt really had a first lien on revenues.* Mr. Sellers stated that the losses on the October bonds totaled nearly $50 million and it was important to the City that the banks survive. . . . The CTDM Committee indicated that the institutional market was closed to City securities and that the out-of-state banks were not buying these obligations. [Emphasis added.][19]

Following this meeting, the press release detailing the changes in the city's scheduled borrowings were announced by Comptroller Goldin. Note that the bankers had connected the question of their financial needs to the militancy of the municipal labor unions. Frank Smeal was indicating that the unions were a "problem" that had to be contained. And, in the case of bankruptcy, Mr. Smeal wanted to be certain that the needs and "rights" of investors were met before those of workers. He recognized, in his statement of concern, that militant unions could alter the scenario for the resolution of the fiscal crisis that the banking community was building.

In light of the financial community's concern over the first lien on city revenues in the event of bankruptcy, both the mayor and the comptroller repeatedly assured investors that they did indeed have that right. It was not all that clear, however, that investors had a constitutional right to a first lien. An investigation by city officials indicated that such was probably not the case at all. Nevertheless, in an effort to reassure and appease investors, city officials repeatedly promised a first lien. As the SEC reported:

Both Mayor Beame and Comptroller Goldin made unqualified statements that bond and note investors had State Constitutional and legal guarantees of a first lien on all City revenues, including all City taxes and all Federal and State aid. There had been no public statement which might be said to indicate, even obliquely, that the first lien guarantee might not exist or was qualified. This was a misrepresentation with respect to the holders of anticipation notes, which comprised the major part of the City's offerings during this period . . .

At the time these unequivocal statements were released, representatives of the Bureau of the Budget, Corporation Counsel's Office, and the Office of the Comptroller knew or had been advised that serious questions existed as to whether the principal amounts of City anticipation notes were protected by a first lien on City revenues.[20]

This question of who had the first lien on city revenues if the city were to be forced into bankruptcy was a question that would continually arise, in the light of the city's decreasing fiscal stability. Time and again, the financial community asserted its need for a first lien, either to restore investor confidence and enable the underwriters to reduce market resistance to the city's debt offerings or to assure investors of the city's faithful commitment to back its bonds and notes. Given that this first lien would assert the needs of financiers over the needs of the city's residents—who were dependent on city services—its poor—who were dependent on city money and services—and its workers, dependent on the city for wages, it is little wonder that the banks constantly pushed for both verbal reassurance and, much more importantly, an organizational structure of control over city expenditures and city priorities. Eventually, they would gain this control through the Municipal Assistance Corporation (MAC), established in June 1975, and, finally, through the Emergency Financial Control Board (EFCB), established in September 1975. But the financial community first had to struggle with a defiant Mayor Beame and to defeat any potential opposition from the city's unions and its residents and clients. This would take quite a bit of maneuvering, as we shall see in the following pages.

The Financial Community Liaison Group

On 7 January 1974, the city marketed $620 million of RANs through Chase Manhattan and Citibank, which acted as underwriters. The mayor and the comptroller withheld these RANs until 3:00 P.M., hoping and trying to find another underwriting syndicate which might agree to a lower interest rate on the notes. In a public statement concerning the high interest rate, the mayor and the comptroller decried the "unfair, unwarranted, and outrageously high interest rate."[21]

In a meeting with representatives of the financial community, including David Rockefeller, William Spencer, Ellmore Patterson, Alfred Brittain, John McGillicuddy, and other major banking figures, the mayor complained that the banks were "bad mouthing" the city, thereby causing the concern in the markets that was reflected in the ever-increasing interest rates for city notes. The bankers responded that these interest rates reflected both the market's concern with the fiscal stability of the city and also its saturation. They asserted that the public bickering between the mayor and the comptroller over the size of the deficit did anything but reassure investors about the security of investing in New York City. The bankers wished to "work with the City to solve the market problems."[22] As a result of this meeting, the Financial Community Liaison Group (FCLG) was formed.

Apparently buoyed by the formation of the FCLG, the mayor issued a statement after the meeting, stating that " 'closer communications between the financial community and the City could provide the potential investors with information that would strengthen confidence in the City as a sound investment.' "[23] The mayor's assumption here was that with more information, investors would be reassured. However, the information they were likely to receive from the FCLG and the banking community would do anything but reassure them. The mayor was acting on the assumption that the financial community's class interests necessitated their continuing support of the city. This was an assumption which neglected the changing financial status of the banks themselves, as well as their position vis-a-vis both the national and the international markets. The banks no longer needed New York City's tax-free notes and bonds. Rather, they needed to get out safely, to disinvest. The mayor did not foresee this need.

So it was that on January 9, 1975, the FCLG was formed. Its membership included the major officers of the city's most important financial institutions, and it was chaired by Ellmore Patterson, chairman of Morgan Guaranty Trust. Other prominent members of the FCLG included David Rockefeller, chairman of the Board at Chase Manhattan Bank; William T. Spencer, president of Citibank; Alfred Brittain, III, chairman of the Board at Banker's Trust; Donald C. Platten, chairman of the Board at Chemical Bank; John F. McGillicuddy, president of Manufacturers Hanover; as well as the chairman of the Board of Merrill, Lynch—Donald T. Regan—and William Salomon, managing partner of Salomon Brothers. Heading the staff of the FCLG were David Grossman, senior vice president of Chase and former budget advisor to Mayor Lindsay; as well as members from other major banks and brokerage firms. The overt function of the FCLG was to establish a formal mechanism through which the financial community and the city could cooperatively work to reopen the municipal credit markets to the city.

Essentially, however, this committee sought to establish the power of finance capital over the city's fiscal affairs. At this point, that power was exerted through a mechanism, the FCLG, which had no legal authority to mandate the city's actions and policies. Although the FCLG was able to exert a powerful influence over both the municipal credit markets and the city, its power was informal and depended upon an atmosphere of "cooperation" and "responsibility." In this regard,

> the underwriters and the City were brought together in a series of meetings at which the fundamental concerns about the clash between the City's budget gap and its constant need for new debt were aired in great detail. Among the principal problems discussed were the inability of the City to continue on the path of ever-increasing budget gaps and short-term note issuances, the use of budget gimmicks to disguise the true state of the City's deficit, and the need for immediate City action to remedy the situation. A recurrent theme during these meetings was a recognition of the scope of the problems, the need for immediate action, the consequences of the failure to take such action, and the difficulty, given political realities, of taking effective action.[24]

On January 10, one day after the formation of the FCLG, David M. Breen, a municipal bond analyst for Weeden and Company, spoke before the City Club of New York and outlined the city's problems as he saw them. They included a deteriorating infrastructure, an economy in decline since 1969-1970, a high rate of real estate tax delinquency which was exacerbating the city's already declining tax base, and a city deficit "substantially larger" than the figure estimated by Mayor Beame. He then suggested three alternative remedies, all of which involved austerity. These were:

(1) mass firings of City workers;
(2) a procedure whereby the financial institutions would manage the City's fiscal affairs, similar to what occurred in the 1930s; and
(3) reorganization pursuant to Chapter IX of the Bankruptcy Act.[25]

This would not be the last time that the financial community sought to monitor and manage the city's fiscal affairs. Such an objective became the major demand that the bankers kept pressing; a control board that would institutionalize their banking rationality over the city's finances, budget, and expenditures. In a very real sense, they sought to isolate the city's budget from influence by the city's unions, its workers, its poor, its minority communities; that is, by all who might oppose their first lien on city revenues.

On January 15, Mayor Beame announced the third phase of his

budget-cutting program, which was designed to alleviate the fears of the financial community by demonstrating that the city was getting its house in order. He outlined a policy which would result in the layoffs of 4,050 policemen, firemen, teachers, and other civil servants. The expected savings from these layoffs would be a measly $15 million; hardly a dent in the city's projected deficits. The policy was intended to be largely symbolic. It may be remembered that the bankers had drawn a connection between their need to invest safely and the wages and benefits of the city's workers. The question of who had the first lien on city revenues was part of a larger question: Where would the city's resources be committed? To paying off its debt and reducing its budget deficit? Or to its workers and to those who were dependent on it for services and support? As reported by the *New York Times,* in the face of these layoffs "union leaders loudly and bitterly begin to talk of job actions and strikes."[26] Union concessions and funds, however, were able to save many of these jobs, at least for a short while. According to Seymour Mann and Edward Handman, of D.C. 37, AFSCME, the unions faced these layoffs and the fiscal crisis as:

the same dilemma as all other elements in this unprecedented situation. The actual dimensions of the budget deficit seemed to elude everyone. . . . The only constant was the clamor from all sides [except the unions] for the mayor to lay off civil servants and cut benefits and pensions.

The *New York Times* and the *Daily News* assailed the mayor for his "softness" and inability or unwillingness to cut the city payroll deeply enough. From the beginning of 1975 and for the next 18 months, editorialists adopted the line that New York was a profligate city with excessive services and a bloated, overpaid, underworked civil service. The understanding that New York reflected the problems of other older American cities was not to seep into the editorial consciousness for many months.

The cry to cut payrolls and services unnerved the city's work force but, at the same time, began to stir the consciousness of the rank and file that their unions represented their single hope to emerge intact and employed.[27]

It is important to note that the unions' version of the events of early January 1975 leading to the layoffs and the high interest rates is quite different from the banks' version. The unions' version represents the uniting of the mayor's office, the banking community, and the newspapers against a reality: the fact that the early 1975 notes sold despite warnings from the banking community of impending disaster from the "markets." In an interview, Edward Handman recalled the events of those days in this way:

HANDMAN: The mayor, the way he reacted he was like a punching bag and he was very responsive to the editorials in the paper. If they told him he had to be tougher, he was tougher that day. His office was run like a press agent's office. He was only concerned with what the *News* and the *Times* and the *Post* said and how they would look. . . . It was totally a public relations position with no substance. . . . I mean he was there with everyone attacking him and he was not responding with anything. It was all just bullshitting with the slogans. . . . In any event, January 1975 the banks were talking about they can't sell the bonds and they got to raise the interest and the credit for New York is terrible and so on. In January they put out an issue, I think it was $500 million [it was $620 million] at 9¼ or 9½ percent [it was 9.4 percent] interest—the highest they ever put out. And the issue broke on a Monday, and on Friday I get a call from a friend of mine, and he says "You know, there's something going on you ought to know. I went to buy one of those notes. You can't get them. They're now at a premium price." Which meant that they're paying less interest because of the demand being so high. And this is when in every day's headlines the banks were saying that they couldn't sell the bonds. So they drove up the interest.

These notes did indeed sell quickly. They had a very high interest rate; they were tax free, and, for city residents, they were triple tax free—free from federal, state, and New York City taxes. They also had an "A" rating. So they were desirable notes, even with the distress from the banking community about the city's worsening fiscal situation. This discrepancy between the reception of those notes and the banking community's publicly expressed concerns and warnings, led Handman to state:

HANDMAN: So that put us, the union, onto the banks and we then started to rally. We started to attack the banks, saying they were making money out of all of this. Which they were. And we were really the first, I think, to put some focus on them. That these guys are not just holding a mortgage, and that the whole city has to turn upside down to satisfy the mortgage. These guys were part of the problem, you know, a big part of the problem and they got to take some responsibility. But they . . . had marketed [notes] in July 1974, and October, November to January, and they made lots of money. . . . I think there was one issue that slowed down [in fact, that was in October] that took them a while to sell. But the fact is that the key was in January 1975—they sold out in a week. There was a cash-flow problem. The City had a cash-flow problem. . . . But there wasn't the necessity for the kind of panic and hysteria that we had. . . . The fact that attacking the City and attacking the public servants was such a handy thing for everybody, that it just kept escalating and skyrocketing.

At the meetings between the FCLG and the city, the FCLG stressed the fact that effective and significant expenditure-cutting actions must be taken if investors were to be impressed and, reassured that the city was not a risky investment. On February 11, 1975, the staff of the FCLG denied that its major activity should be to concentrate on analyzing the "City's budget problems . . . [to develop] a long-range plan for the City's financial management."[28] The staff would concern itself with the methods by which the city financed itself. In order to reassure investors, the FCLG would insist that "reforms" be made in these financing methods and in the city's budgetary processes.

Throughout January, February, and March of 1974, as the fiscal crisis materialized and the city grew closer to the moment when its debt instruments would be closed to the municipal debt markets, the FCLG met often with city officials. As the crisis deepened, the mayor's Council of Business and Economic Advisors, itself a committee of prominent banking and corporate figures, met with the mayor eight times during 1974 alone. These actions and meetings indicate the banking community's concern and, in fact, its mobilization for action on the crisis. This fact becomes important regarding the bankers' claim that they did not foresee the coming of the fiscal crisis. After the crisis hit the city, and, especially after the SEC investigated the actions of all who were involved in the fiscal crisis, the bankers let out a united cry: "We didn't have adequate information. We didn't know what the problems were." Or, as Ellmore Patterson was to say: "We feel we didn't have any information the public didn't know."[29]

It is interesting to note how many prominent and important figures in the city's fiscal crisis later claimed that they had no prior knowledge of its depth and seriousness. For example, the bankers argued that their knowledge of the city's fiscal problems did not predate the actual fiscal crisis. One banker, Jac Friedgut of Citibank, argued that the fiscal crisis crept up on both the public and the banks. This was, he asserted, due to the inadequacy of credit analyses of the city. In an interview in January 1979 Friedgut maintained that:

FRIEDGUT: On the surface, through 1974 or so, it was not manifestly clear to anyone other than a very astute observer, like the Citizen's Budget Commission, that there was a huge accumulated imbalance which, if anything, was getting worse. Maybe it should have been clear and maybe the banks should have had people spending an awful lot of time on this, say in 1973 and 1974 . . . but . . . I don't know that any bank had anyone that had in-depth knowledge and understanding [of the problems]. Now, you'll find memos which are reported in the SEC [report] by people from Citibank, Chemical Bank, Chase analyzing the city's figures, but right from 1974 there were no really in-depth studies that got at some of the real raw problems and growing problems.

Now, I came on the scene in late February 1975, and my job was to brief our own people [at Citibank] as to what is the real situation in city finances. Now I should add that I'm not a credit analyst. The credit analyst looks at ratios that in 99 out of 100 cases will tell the story. In New York's case it didn't and that's why we all missed it. The reason we did is, for example, if you take a look at total debts and related it to almost anything that credit analysts relate it to and take a look at the growth of this over the years, for New York City it doesn't look so bad. What had happened was the amount of total debt which in effect was used to fund deficits was growing at the expense of indebtedness for true brick and mortar capital purposes. And unless and until you made that differentiation, you wouldn't discover where the real problem was. So that New York City was underborrowing for capital purposes for over a decade and grossly overborrowing to, in effect, fund deficits for that same time. I was put onto this line of inquiry by the Citizens Budget Commission. . . . When I looked at the total increase in short-term debt, plus the capital borrowing for operating budget purposes, and added these two things together—it just increased astronomically.

Raymond Horton joined many others in indicating that it was indeed likely that the banks did not have adequate information. Horton was asked how the banks fit into the fiscal crisis. He responded:

HORTON: Well, I tend to see them as rather guilty partners in this whole thing. I'm not sure, I don't think I know for sure in my own mind if it was acts of omission or of commission. But I think the banks made an awful . . . Well, they had a good business going. Let's put it that way. As the city increased more and more debt, I mean they were involved in that business. And I think that they were rather ignorant in terms of following the city's finances. They were like a lot of people in organizations. When things are going well you don't really examine them. Then, as you pointed out, the banks got caught with the REITs [Real Estate Investment Trusts], and all of a sudden they had a lot of liquidity problems and they began to get out, and structure a situation to protect themselves, because it became clear they couldn't get out all the way. And that to me is what the Emergency Financial Control Board is all about.

According to Horton's analysis, the banks may very well have been caught by surprise in 1974, with their investment portfolios down and exposed, so to speak, when their investment needs changed. One aspect of this change was their unsuccessful speculation in real estate. The Real Estate Investment Trusts lost quite a bit of money when the real estate boom collapsed in 1974, leaving the euphoria of the early 1970s real estate markets well behind. This bust left the banks with less need for New York City's tax-free securities. So was it ignorance, or was it a changing investment picture, that led the banks to reevaluate New York City's debt obligations? It very well may be that Horton was correct when he argued that the banks "had a good business going." Why shake up a good business? Only because the business had changed.

Still, other analysts argued that the bankers did not fully understand the fiscal crisis and city finances. Donna Shalala, an "expert" on public financing in New York State, maintained that the banks were indeed weak in collecting information regarding municipal finance. In an interview with Shalala, conducted after she had finished serving as treasurer of the MAC, the following exchange took place:

LICHTEN: Did the banks have adequate information?
SHALALA: No. I thought that was the most interesting thing about the banks—that they really did not know what was going on half the time and that they did not have good information. They had relatively weak staffs in this area. They were dependent upon the rating firms. They themselves knew little about municipal finance. I don't think there were many people who cared very much about municipal finance, and the bankers had their weakest people in their municipal finance divisions. So that my view of the banks was that we have less of a conspiracy theory and more of a view that they simply did not know for a long time what they were doing; they did not know or understand what was happening.

Even now, this interpretation is still being offered to the public. On the Susskind Show in late 1984, David Susskind asked Felix Rohatyn, the architect of the city's rescue plan and chairman of the MAC, whether Mayors Lindsay and Beame really knew how bad the city's finances were. The transcript of the interview is quoted at length, even through the discussion of the formation of the MAC jumps a bit ahead of the analysis at this point.

ROHATYN: Between 1970 and 1975 [the deficits were] roughly $6 billion. [The city was] running a deficit of roughly one-billion-and-a-half dollars per year by 1975. And the world stopped. It couldn't refinance its bonds, refinance its notes, and it couldn't balance its budget.

SUSSKIND: What did you do?

ROHATYN: Well, in 1975, the city ran out of time and it ran out of money. And the governor, Governor Carey, who was governor at the time, had to make a decision as to whether the city should go bankrupt, should file for bankruptcy. Or, whether we should try to do something about the budget deficit, the short-term borrowing, and all the things that had led it there. The governor had appointed four of us to give him a recommendation on the subject. And there was a very wonderful and eminent jurist, Simon Rifkind; there was the chairman of Macy's, Don Smiley; there was the chairman of the Metropolitan Life Insurance Company, Dick Shinn; and myself. And we had a couple of weeks to study this. Nobody had any numbers that were worth anything. The statistics we had, the data we had, was just woefully inadequate. Which turned out to be a blessing in disguise. I believe that if we had really known how bad it was, we would have advised the governor that it was hopeless. That we should have an orderly bankruptcy and forget it.

SUSSKIND: You didn't know how bad it was?

ROHATYN: We didn't know I'd say within a half a billion a year what the deficit was. We didn't know until the night we were bringing the MAC, which was the state agency which finally refinanced the city. We didn't know how much short-term debt the city had. We thought it had $3 billion of short term debt. We found out in the middle of the night and in the middle of June of 1975 that it had $5 billion of short-term debt because it was mislabeled, it was called something else. And we didn't know how many people were on the city's payroll. We didn't know how much cash the city had. It was a very interesting time.

SUSSKIND: Now, these men are very good friends of mine so I say this with friendship and tact. You mean that Mayor Lindsay and Mayor Beame . . . didn't know of this condition? Or, knew it but preferred not to face it?

ROHATYN: I think that everybody knew that the city was in a great deal of trouble. Everybody knew that at some point the music had to stop. I don't think that anybody knew just how bad that it was because everybody assumed that, even though, something in the back of their mind must have told them that it couldn't go on like this. There was a school of thought that said well, it will go on like this. It's gone on like this forever and the banks have always bought our notes and when the deficit gets bigger we will sell more notes. And it will go on. I think it was a combination of knowing something is very wrong and not knowing how bad it really is.

Yet, there was information being generated by both the city and the banking community. As stated in the preceding pages, the banking community had encouraged the city to go deeper and deeper into debt through the advice given the city by the Technical Debt Management Committee (TDMC). This committee was organized by Abraham Beame while he was the city comptroller, before he was elected mayor. This committee was made up of representatives from Chase Manhattan Bank; Salomon Brothers; Citibank; Merrill Lynch, Pierce, Fenner, and Smith; Morgan Guaranty Trust Co.; Berlack, Israels, and Liberman; First Security Co.; and Fisher, Francis Trees, and Watts, Inc. In other words, the financial community was well represented, and it advised the mayor and comptroller on appropriate fiscal matters. This committee routinely assisted the comptroller in assessing the marketability of city securities, based on its assessment of the city's financial and economic status. As William Scott, then the third deputy comptroller, who was present at the TDMC meetings with the city, stated in an interview: "You had to look with some suspicion on the advice you received, because in a city this size who do you go to for financial advice about bonds, whether they're salable, and what rates they should be paid, except to the same people that are going to buy and sell them."

One last but equally important point is that the banks in question, along with everyone else, had access to reports issued by the Citizens Budget Commission (CBC). As early as 1967, the members of the Citizens Budget Commission had warned of the possibility of a fiscal crisis.[30] Their reports, warning of its inevitability if fiscal policy was not altered, were quite detailed, with no lack of appropriate data. It is interesting to note that Jac Friedgut mentions the CBC's reports, and yet the banking community claimed ignorance. Even more interesting is the membership of the CBC. In 1973, well before the crisis, William S. Renchard was its chairman. He was also the chairman of the Executive Committee of Chemical Bank. Other members and trustees of the CBC were Norborne Berkeley, Jr., President of Chemical, William R. Cross, Jr., Senior Vice President of Morgan, John J. Larkin, Senior Vice President of Citibank, Raymond T. O'Keefe, Executive Vice President at Chase, William R. Salomon, Managing Partner of Salomon Bros., and Robert G. Wilmers, a Morgan Vice President.[31] How many more bankers and financiers did the CBC need before the financial community could read its reports?

The notion that the bankers, along with everyone else, were ignorant of the impending crisis, was challenged by the SEC's report on the city's fiscal crisis. The report maintains that:

Long before October 1974, the financial community realized that the City's fundamental problem was the insufficiency of revenues to meet expenses, resulting in a chronic and ever-increasing budget gap. The financial community had also come to understand the consequences of using short-term debt issues to close its budget gap and questionable budgetary practices to conceal the gap.

As early as March 7, 1966, Herman Charbonneau, Vice President, Municipal Department of Chemical, who was later to play a significant role on behalf of the bank during the City's crisis period, wrote an internal memorandum decrying the City's practice of making up the gap between current expenditures and revenues by selling RANs and other short-term debt instruments. In the memorandum, Charbonneau concluded that the use of such "deficit funding is an inherently unsound operation, and one which can lead to disaster."[32]

To reiterate, it seems clear that the banks had access to data that detailed the serious financial crisis toward which the city was heading. These banks had representatives serving on the Technical Debt Management Committee, as well as on the Board of Directors of the Citizen Budget Commission. Ignorance does not seem to be a well-supported argument. And how could the ignorant worry about a first lien on city revenues without first knowing the precarious state of the city's finances?

Still, the financial community pressed for more influence over the city's financial affairs and, in so doing, assisted the climate of investor insecurity that was pushing the city to fiscal collapse. In order to gain more control over the process, the financiers would find it necessary to exert control over both the city's financing arrangements and the city's expenditures. Hence, they would find it necessary to control the budgetary processes of the city. This, in turn, would require formalized, legal authority. The bankers began pushing for austerity budgets as well as a formal control mechanism to impose such budgeting.

Two such recommendations came from Citibank. In a February 20, 1975, memorandum to Walter Wriston, William G. Herbster suggested that a "Hoover Commission" be created for the city government. The scope of its responsibilities were not spelled out. Additionally, the following program of austerity was outlined:

(1) reduce the number of City workers;
(2) increase productivity;
(3) institute certain service cutbacks, such as the elimination of costly unproductive training programs;
(4) institute certain changes to bring these charges closer to the actual cost of the services, e.g., increase the subway fare; and
(5) make major reductions in capital expenditures which mandate future operating costs e.g., the CUNY building program.[33]

Another memorandum passed from Jac Friedgut, vice president of Municipal Securities at Citibank and an important member of the FCLG. In a February 25, 1975, meeting of the FCLG, Friedgut circulated a memorandum in which he suggested that the city must institute a complete and rigid program of reducing city expenditures. Included in this memorandum were suggestions that the city institute the following:

(1) review [of] . . . all City programs and . . . cutback in low priority items;
(2) freeze on jobs;
(3) joint effort [with] the business community to [secure] Federal and State funds;
(4) increase [city workers'] productivity;
(5) [reduce] debt and an immediate termination of the issuance of debt for operating expenses.[34]

These recommendations, if followed by the city, would require huge budgetary cutbacks. These cutbacks would be necessitated by the reduction of operating funds due to the absence of funds acquired through the credit markets. In effect, Friedgut was suggesting that the city operate only on its revenues, without substantial credit. New York City had not accomplished this in a decade, and such a program would seriously erode the quality of essential services.

February and March of 1975 were critical months for the city, as its securities increasingly became more difficult to market. In the last week of February, the city had to cancel a $260 million debt offering of Tax Anticipation Notes (TANs). The TANs had to be canceled after two syndicates, one led by Bankers Trust, the other by Chase Manhattan, refused to accept delivery of the notes. Although the city was willing to certify that its tax revenues were sufficient to cover the TANs, the bond counsel for the Bankers Trust syndicate refused to render a legal opinion concerning the TANs, saying that it was not quite clear from the available data whether the TANs were within the city's borrowing limits for this type of note. Without a "clean" legal opinion, the Bankers Trust syndicate withdrew, followed by the Chase syndicate. The TANs were aborted. With this cancellation, the city's ability to meet its financing needs was seriously in doubt. The city was moving closer to default and, perhaps, to bankruptcy.

During March, the city's budget gap, and its growing troubles with the banking community, pushed it closer to the brink. The city's need to borrow was growing, yet its access to funds was not. The city would offer nearly $1 billion of debt obligations during the first two weeks of March. By now, according to the banks' own estimates, taken at a meeting of the FCLG, the banks now "held over $1.2 billion in City securities, or 20 percent of their combined equity."[35] Yet, the city needed them to market notes. As would become clear later, the banks were not themselves investing in these notes. The banks feared having to keep the notes themselves. They did not intend to "take down" the notes for their own portfolios.

One such debt offering of RANs on March 13 was marketed only after bankers had secured a guarantee that a certain amount of state per-capita aid would be designated to retire the notes when they matured in three months. This offering of RANs underscored the trouble that the city was having in marketing these securities. Before they would market these notes, the financial community *demanded* that the revenues to repay them be secure and identified. Only in the event of bankruptcy could there be a question about repayment. During an interview in January 1979, Jac Friedgut emphasized the significance of the events that transpired during the negotiations and marketing of these notes. Asked when Citibank had realized that the city was in deep trouble, Jac Friedgut replied as follows:

FRIEDGUT: I started to realize it in late February. By March 14, which was a Friday, two things had come together in my own mind. First of all, this realization . . . about the growth of the debts which weren't real debts [since they were incurred to pay for expense items, and not capital spending]. Coincidentally with that, on March 13, the day before, was the sale date of a very short-term New York City note; which was a three-month note with a return to investors of about 8 percent. . . . It was a Revenue Anticipation Note with a very explicit agreement between ourselves [the underwriters] and the city that they would pay that note out of the proceeds of the State per-capita aid, which they would be getting on June 25, or whatever date it was. So even though we may not have had, you know, if there had been an intervening bankruptcy, I'm not sure that the noteholders would have been able to have an absolutely water-tight legal claim to those state aid monies. But in any event short of bankruptcy, those noteholders had better protection than New York City noteholders had ever had before. And as a matter of fact, when the state subsequently had agreed to in April, a month later, to advance aid to the city, and the state initially said "O.K., we'll give you your revenue sharing per-capita aid in April instead of June" we went to the city and state and said: "you can't do that because that has been identified as being there to repay our RANs." And the city and the state agreed. It was there that the state made this advance to the city, of welfare monies or something like that, due later in the year.

What happened was we were offering investors, and Citibank ran that particular note sale, a very short coupon—three months—a good rate, and much better security and an identifiable source of repayment, than had ever been offered before. And of course the fact is that these notes were repaid and didn't go into moratorium or anything like that. *They stayed away in droves.* So the skelter that came together in my mind on that Friday, the 14th, was that (a) the city was in really big trouble, and (b) that whether or not they knew the reasons for investors' sense that the city was indeed in trouble.

Then I put these two things together and said that, which I still think was the correct judgment, if the city recognized any of the depth of its troubles and the depth of investor suspicion of the city, and therefore did something very dramatic and real; that would be both real and dramatic to show that they intended to get control of their finances. So that was the only way the market [would accept city paper]. The market was quickly evaporating, as evidenced by that note sale. Only less than half of it was taken and the other half was just sitting with the syndicate.

Now the SEC reports the famous discussion that three top bankers had with Mayor Beame on Monday morning the 17th. And that was based essentially on input which the bankers had gotten from myself and Frank Smeal of Morgan. . . . I was not at that meeting between the bankers and Beame, but it is my understanding that he was told that the city was running out of gas and he had to do something very dramatic.

Before discussing that meeting, it is important to refer back to a memorandum that Friedgut sent to William Spencer of Citibank. This memorandum circulated on March 5, and in it Friedgut recommended that the city, in his words, "bite the bullet" and institute a strict austerity policy, by which the city would be forced to live within its means; that is, without market access. In order to do this, he recommended that a freeze be imposed on all labor costs, including wages and benefits, as well as an across-the-board reduction in city services. Still, Friedgut maintained that his recommendations were not to be conveyed to the mayor to pressure him; rather they would be communicated to him only if the mayor asked for advice and specific recommendations. His "bite-the-bullet" memorandum was intended for William Spencer, president of Citibank, and Spencer alone. In his own words, Jac Friedgut describes that memorandum and its intent.

FRIEDGUT: I recommended to Bill Spencer, who is our president, and was at that meeting with the mayor, that is the type of thing that the city had to do in order to regain the market's confidence. Spencer felt that would be presumptuous of us, or anybody in the private sector, to start making specific policy options. So I can't say that that part [mentioning biting the bullet] was necessarily transmitted to Beame either written or verbal. I think what Spencer had in mind is if Beame had said "You guys are right. I have a terrible crisis. My budget's a mess and I have lost market access. What can I do?" At that point Spencer might have said "One of our guys has put together some ideas as to a possible set of actions and you may want to take a look at this." But unfortunately, we never got to that stage because Beam never admitted he had a serious problem.

In a meeting on March 17 between the mayor and David Rockefeller, Ellmore Patterson, and William Spencer, the banks' contention that the city was at a crisis point was conveyed to the administration. As Friedgut's memorandum suggested, drastic action would be necessary to calm investors. Time was running out. These prominent bankers wanted this meeting to be kept from the public, so as to not exacerbate the fiscal crisis. Furthermore, throughout the producing of the crisis, the bankers wished to keep a low profile and conduct their business away from the public eye. The bankers feared that

> knowledge of the participants, purpose and the message of this meeting could trigger a real panic in the market for New York City securities and have a serious impact on markets, worldwide, because of the extensive ownership of the billions of dollars of New York City securities and especially because of the concentration of that ownership among the large New York City banks.[36]

At this meeting, the bankers told the mayor that the traditional market sources of funds were no longer open to New York City. At that time, only 15 percent, or $375 million of the RANs and $535 million of the BANs, had been successfully marketed to the public. The banks, as underwriters, were holding the remainder. Nor could these banks, the mayor was told, with one-quarter to one-fifth of their capital invested in city securities, afford themselves to hold additional securities. Essentially, Mayor Beame was told that the city could no longer borrow from the municipal credit markets or the clearinghouse banks: the city's lifeline of funds to cover its operating expenses and to retire its maturing debt had been closed. Before it would reopen, the bankers told the mayor, the "confidence of the banks and the underwriters must be restored."[37]

The bankers were operating with information supplied to them from Jac Friedgut of Citibank and Frank Smeal of Morgan Guaranty Trust. Jac Friedgut confirmed, during an interview, that Mayor Beame was told that "the city was running out of gas and had to do something very dramatic."

On Tuesday, March 18, Friedgut met with the New York City congressional delegation in Washington, D.C. Edward Koch, then a congressman and now the mayor of New York City, was the secretary of the delegation and had arranged the meeting. Friedgut described that meeting during the same interview, as follows:

FRIEDGUT: Now what happened, and this is how I got the notoriety I did more than anything else, was that I believe the next day, Tuesday, the 18th of March, I had a meeting with the New York congressional delegation in Washington, of which ironically Ed Koch was the secretary and the guy who set up the meeting. I was invited by them because they had heard that I had a different view of the city's finances than the official party line that the mayor had. I had a chart presentation that I showed to them. I had been told that everything would be off the record and wouldn't be given to the press, and I spoke very frankly and candidly. . . . I felt that sooner or later, and actually sooner than later, that Washington had to be dragged in and these would be the people who would have to get Washington in. And before they get Washington in, so that we don't look like a bunch of fools, they should realize not only what is Washington's role, but also what is New York City's own role. And in my charts and my presentations I pointed out some of the facts . . . and I told them that the dimension of what had to be done on an annual basis is at least $500, $600, $700, $800 million worth of budget-balancing dollars. That this would involve biting the bullet on the city front and also having to go to Washington. It would be a combination of the two. And as part of my presentation I said, and this phrase got to be notorious, because Beame kept quoting it out of context, the totality of what I said was unless the city takes drastic steps, the city's paper would be unsalable at any price. Now we were talking about the runup in the increase in the interest rates and how Beame had been very critical that the interest rates were so high. And I said that it won't even be a question of price. It will be a question of availability, and that unless something dramatic is done, city paper would be unsalable at any price. What Beame then started quoting out of context was that Friedgut of Citibank said that city securities are unsalable at any price, and that's a self-fulfilling prophesy. Now if I had said that as a flat-out statement being an officer of the major bank, I think he's right. It would be a self-fulfilling prophesy. What I did say was that unless drastic action was taken that this would happen. But since such drastic action wasn't taken—how can they say and what was the self-fulfilling prophesy? The combination of his [Beame's] inaction and the market response to that inaction.

These statements were leaked to the public, and soon the city's securities *were* unmarketable at any price. Given the importance of this statement, Friedgut was asked whether the banks were indeed the market. Would the market have closed, had the banks not acted as if the city's securities were a bad and risky investment? And was the market flooded not only by the city's latest debt offerings but also with the securities that the banks were themselves holding and unloading? He responded in the following manner:

FRIEDGUT: There are some things that all the banks and all the underwriters in the world can't do. They cannot open the market even if they all agreed. . . . Unless there is some feeling of confidence, which we can help to inspire up to a point, then the people who are actually going to buy these notes and hold them as an investment—it ain't going to be done. So in that regard you can't say that we are the market. It is true that if all of us would sign a public statement saying New York City securities are lousy, that would be sufficient to close the market even if, in point of fact, they weren't lousy. So in that regard one could say that yes, we are the market; which is very difficult to say whether it is true or not. But what is true is that if investors who buy to hold, which bank dealers' departments don't and investment houses don't; if investors who buy to hold don't like something, and this is a general prevailing perception, no combination of people like myself in the world in and of itself is going to make them buy it. And that's why . . . the timing is extraordinarily important [in the city's fiscal crisis]. It's only after I saw that the market out there, despite efforts by the banks and the investment houses to sell the underwriting—because the worst thing for underwriters is to get stuck with stuff in their hands—so it was only after we saw that, that I put that together with what I had just discovered and said in effect that. If I personally were to be criticized by anybody for fouling anybody's nest, I really should be criticized by the bank. Because I really shouldn't have spoken up if my words helped to make the market worse until after we had gotten that stuff off our hands, see? What happened was, and of course being a good soldier of the bank it was no intention of mine to go and make a public announcement "Hey, New York City securities are lousy," because then we would be stuck with the whole thing, the RANs. I'd made it on an off the record basis to the House Congressional delegation with the full belief . . . that if they had been able to say to Beame "Hey, you schmuck, you got to know what you're doing here and you got to do something dramatic." If they had been able to persuade him, I am confident that the market would not have closed; that we then would have gone through the same angst and so on . . . as we have gone through in the past couple of years and for the next few years in terms of cutbacks, budget balanced, and somehow look over the city's shoulders to make certain that it gets done. Now politically it just may have not been feasible without the governor stepping in, staring bankruptcy in the face. But economically, and in terms of the market, even though it was rapidly closing, I think that it is always easier to stop something from closing than to let it close and then to reopen it. . . . But if the mayor had announced the next day: "Look, I can see what the market is telling me. I have a problem. I'm going to have an immediate wage freeze. I am going to start full attrition, layoffs, close seven hospitals, close half the City University, including the Graduate School." Do some of these things which he ended up doing anyhow. If he had done that there would have been a remarkable recovery immediately in the market for city securities, and over time, it would have kept going in a way that would have had credibility and reality to it. But maybe that has more economic reality than political reality to it.

Banking's Divestiture of City Holdings

But there was another economic reality that affected the possibility of marketing the city's securities. Further exacerbating the erosion of confidence in the city's ability to retire its debt and market new debt was the unloading by the major New York banks of their own holdings of city debt. The very same banks that had advised the city for years about its debts; the same banks that had underwritten these debt obligations; these very same banks, with the possible exception of Chemical Bank, were flooding an already flooded market with their own holdings. At the very same time that these banks were underwriting city securities and meeting with the Beame administration "to keep the market open," these banks were divesting themselves of their own very substantial holdings of city securities. Jack Newfield reported that "the big New York City banks, as well as major banks across the nation, quietly dumped approximately $2.3 billion in New York City securities on the market between the summer of 1974 and March 1975."[38]

The banks were playing the dual role of both underwriting and divesting themselves of city securities. All the while they "advised" the city of possible measures to secure investor confidence in the stability of the city's finances. Yet, their actions could only exacerbate the glut in the municipal securities market, which was already burdened by the enormous amount of city debt. By March 31, 1975, the city had a total debt of over $14 billion, as shown in Table 5.2.

As the city relied more and more heavily on short-term debt, the proportion of its budget going to repay the debt, in debt service costs, increased. As was seen in Table 5.1 (p. 103), the proportion of the city's budget allocated for debt service increased from 10.5 percent in fiscal

Table 5.2: New York City's Outstanding Debt as of March 31, 1975

Total	Type of Debt
$7,887,733,170	(Long-Term) Funded Debt
1,102,000,000	Tax Anticipation Notes
1,767,655,000	Bond Anticipation Notes
3,185,000,000	Revenue Anticipation Notes
107,610,000	Other Short-Term Debt
$14,049,998,170	Total Debt

SOURCE: Securities and Exchange Commission, *Report on Transactions in Securities of the City of New York,* "Introduction and Summary," p. 2.

year 1970 to 11.4 percent in 1974 and 14 percent in 1975. The burdens of the higher interest that the city was forced to pay as the crisis deepened increased both the need to borrow more and the need to sacrifice other city expenditures—most notably, its labor costs and service levels. "As the City's Chief Accountant is claimed to have said in March 1975, absent the ability to borrow, the City could go bankrupt."[39]

Despite New York City's increased need to borrow, however, the banks carried out a systematic disinvestment in the city's notes and bonds. The data in Table 5.3,[40, 41] provided by the SEC, demonstrates the extent and the rapid pace of disinvestment between September 1974 and April 1975. The difference between the September '74 and April '75 columns does not convey the entire extent of bank disinvestment. As the table shows, a good deal of the holdings still retained by April '75 consisted of virtually unmarketable March '75 RANs and BANs. In a sense, these holdings (third column) were "forced," and do not indicate an ongoing confidence in the city's fiscal health. To correctly measure the banks' intent to disinvest, we must subtract the RAN/BAN holdings from their total holdings of April 1975.

There can be no doubt that, once we take the holdings of unmarketable March '75 RANs and BANs into account, there is a consistent pattern of disinvestment for all the major New York City banks

Table 5.3 Holdings of City Notes by Major New York Banks, Including Holdings of Unmarketable Notes (in Millions)

	Sept. '74	Apr. '75	RANs/BANs
Bankers Trust	$119	$ 58	$40
Investment Acct.	48	43	33
Chase	165	58	43
Investment Acct.	74	0	0
Citibank	24	30	30*
Investment Acct.	0	[totally divested by June '74]	
Manufacturers	180	163	64
Investment Acct.			
Morgan Guaranty	51**	0***	98
Investment Acct.			
Chemical Bank	232	227	
Investment Acct.	187	224	33

*Thirty million is an estimate; SEC report stated only that the "great bulk" of Citibank's April '75 holdings were RANs/BANs.
**Morgan held this $51 million as late as 30 Nov. 1974; holdings plummeted as Morgan divested.
***Morgan did not purchase City notes until March RANs/BANs.

with the exception of Chemical Bank. In its report on the fiscal crisis, the SEC wrote:

> During 1974 and early 1975, a number of the underwriters determined not to purchase City securities for their fiduciary accounts. . . . The underwriters were apparently unwilling, if they could avoid it, to take down for their own investment any significant portion of new offerings of City notes, and, in fact, followed a policy of eliminating or reducing their positions. These practices reflect a significant limitation of the market for City notes. It also reflects, as does the policy adopted with respect to fiduciary accounts, the banks' own evaluation of an investment of City notes. [42]

Indeed, had Bankers Trust been able to not "take down" $40 million BANs and RANs from March '75, its total disinvestment would have been approximately $100 million, excluding the $38 million disinvestment from the investment accounts over which it held fiduciary responsibility.

Chase Manhattan's planned disinvestment would have been $150 million in its portfolios, and it *was* $74 million in its investment account. In any case, if we look at the figures for all the banks, excluding Chemical Bank, it is clear that the banks had decided to take their investment capital elsewhere. Yet, they did so with the full knowledge that the city was in dire need of capital. In a sense, during the latter months of 1974 and the early months of 1975, the banks' actions, including their own disinvestments and their lack of full disclosure concerning the city's finances to the general public, might be viewed as a holding action. The bankers were trying to get themselves out of the city's crisis without endangering what remained of their investments. What other conclusion can there be? [43]

It is important to note that the banks' positions relative to New York City do not exist independently of the banks' positions relative to national and international financial speculation and investment. The possibility of holding bad debts from New York must be weighed against other bad debts that the banks might have held. For instance, Ernest Mandel reports that:

> When the sudden threat that the City of New York might go bankrupt loomed on the horizon in autumn 1975 it was reported that at the time the twelve largest New York banks were holding more than $4

thousand million in "bad debts" ($2 thousand million in obligations of the City of New York, $1 thousand million in loans to airline companies, $400 million in loans to W. T. Grant, and more than $500 million in loans to other municipal governments threatened by bankruptcy). And all this comes on top of the $11 thousand million in doubtful real-estate loans.

In certain cases the total of the bank's capital and its reserves with which to cover losses on defaulted loans was less than the total value of the REITs and the obligations of the nearly bankrupt City of New York. As of 1975 this was the case for at least two of the twelve largest New York banks, Chemical and Bankers Trust. [44]

Given the losses in real estate speculation, currency speculation, and the weak investments cited here, it is little wonder that the banking establishment was nervous about holding and taking down New York City securities. In an interview, Donna Shalala summed up this point in the following way:

SHALALA: Remember, that was a bad period for the banks themselves. They were going through changes. They had taken tremendous losses in their real estate ventures. They no longer needed whatever tax advantages the municipals would give them. They essentially had gotten themselves into such financial problems that they just didn't need all those other municipal obligations and tax-exempt obligations. So they didn't need all those other kinds of fancy tax breaks. Their prestige, the New York banks' prestige, was deeply affected during this period.

The crisis of capital, international in scope, came home to roost in New York City both in its economic decline and in its fiscal stability. The New York banks, so dominant and so powerful, were themselves weakened by this international crisis. Given that situation, New York City seemed expendable.

In April 1975, the city could not borrow to meet its expenses and found itself dependent upon New York State to provide the funds to escape bankruptcy. The price to be paid for this aid was a crisis budget, based on austerity, and the eventual layoff and/or attrition of approximately 67,000 jobs. The city's debt was now at $11 billion, with $4.5 billion in short-term securities due to mature. For the first time, but not the last, the city was faced with the real possibility of bankruptcy. The banks had produced the fiscal crisis, as we have seen, by flooding the credit markets, refusing to purchase additional city securities for their own portfolios, and thereby adding uncertainty to an investment climate that was already shaky.

6

Using Crisis:
The Bankers' Coup

Facing bankruptcy, the city's only alternative was to seek financial assistance, as Jac Friedgut had anticipated, from both New York State and the federal government. The city recognized that it could not rely on its major banks for substantial assistance; that had been made clear by the bankers' actions during the preceding months, as the fiscal crisis deepened. Further exacerbating the problem, President Ford announced that the city would not be "bailed out" with federal funds.

Bankruptcy did not seem to be a feasible option for the corporate sector, the banks, or the city's advisors. Nor did the city's unions favor such a possibility. For all concerned, there seemed to be too much uncertainty in a city bankruptcy. Furthermore, the banks themselves still had too much invested in the city for a bankruptcy to take place without threatening the solvency of many of the nation's banks. With that in mind, and with time running out, Governor Hugh Carey asked four prominent members of the corporate sector to look at the situation. As was stated earlier, Felix Rohatyn was one of those four. The others were Simon Rifkind, Don Smiley, and Dick Shinn. All were prominent and important members of the corporate and banking community. For them, there could be no serious thought of allowing the city to go bankrupt. As Felix Rohatyn suggested in his interview with David Susskind in late 1984:

ROHATYN: The bankruptcy of the city of New York would have affected a number of constituencies in a number of ways. We start off with the people who live here. The city couldn't have borrowed money. The city has to spend by federal law a certain amount of money on welfare, on medicaid. That spending would have had to continue. . . . Everything would have been in front of a federal judge in bankruptcy [court], with various constituencies disputing their claims to whatever money was available. So at the very least we thought that the bankruptcy of the city would mean immediate layoffs of tens of thousands of employees. A sharp reduction in the level of services. Dirty streets, less protection, less education. It could have resulted in social unrest, as various constituencies really disputed whatever resources were available. I mean that if you were not paying policemen, if you were only paying them half of what they felt they were entitled to, and at the same time you were paying full welfare because of federal mandates, you could see that there would be some basis for a problem there. I think that as a result of this uncertainty, unrest, and reduction of services, a lot of people who could move would have moved out of the city. I think it would have started an exodus of business and taxpayers out of the city . . . So in terms of the city as a place to live and work, I think it would have been devastating.

The state in our judgment might have gone into bankruptcy following a city bankruptcy. . . . Then there were the banks. New York City banks, the big eleven clearinghouse banks, the key to the American banking system, had a significant part of their capital in New York City paper. And if you added New York State paper as a possibility, that the state might go bankrupt, if you added up city notes, city bonds, state bonds, state agency obligations, you came to a total of $35 or $36 billion of obligations that might go into default. And at the same time, as I recall, that was 20 percent of the capital of the entire U.S. banking system. So you had a situation that might ripple out financially throughout the entire U. S. And I think it would have.

The stakes were indeed huge, as New York City's workers, unions, and residents would soon experience. So, at the behest of Governor Hugh Carey, these four corporate representatives began to study the problem in search of a solution. They decided to discuss the crisis with the mayor and his deputy mayor. As Rohatyn describes and remembered this meeting, it went something like this:

ROHATYN: I remember when the four of us . . . went to pay a courtesy call to   . . . Mayor Beame and the first deputy mayor, Jim Cavanaugh. We went down to Gracie Mansion [home of the mayor], it was late in May 1975. . . . We were met with a kind of . . . amused, barely concealed contempt that politicians have for private citizens who think that they can get involved in the process. And the deputy mayor said to me, "You know, Mr. Rohatyn. [It's going] around in the land that we have a deficit." He said we don't have a deficit. We just have these seasonal needs for money because we collect money differently than we spend it. And we're like a wonderful finance company that would have all these wonderful assets that are backing some of these debts that we have.'' Now I may not know very much about this, but it seems to me that when you look at the numbers and your debt has gone from zero to $6 billion after five years of balanced budgets, that's why people think you have a deficit. And he said, ''Well, Mr. Rohatyn, that just proves that you don't know that much about municipal finances.'' And I said, I know. I don't know much about municipal finances but I know a great deal about baloney. And I said that what you're telling me is baloney. There's no way that you can have these numbers without running huge red numbers here. So, that didn't start our relationship off on the grandest of footings. But it was partly, I think, [that] everything had always happened alright in a world in which we always seemed to have muddled through. And we were living in a different world. There was the first oil shock. There was inflation. There was recession. There was a whole different character to the economy of the country and of the city and it was over . . . The accounting systems [of the city] were really bad . . . They were really very inadequate. I don't think he [Beame] knew how bad they were. And, at the same time . . . I think Mayor Beame deserves a great deal more credit than he's been given. For the fact that the city didn't go down. The mayor had to do some really difficult things that were almost imposed upon him by the state. Cutting the work force, freezing the wages, doing all sorts of things that were really totally against his upbringing; his political advisors, who advised him to put the city into bankruptcy. And he'd have said, ''Look, it wasn't my fault. These things happened in the previous administration. And we'll just put it into Chapter 11. We'll put it into bankruptcy.'' From his point of view it might have been better politically to do that than to take the constant humiliation and blame. He refused to do that because he thought it would be terrible for the city.

Rohatyn and MAC

To avoid a bankruptcy, some of New York's most powerful corporate and banking executives began to devise a ''rescue'' plan. Felix Rohatyn, a partner in the investment banking firm of Lazard Freres, as well as a director of ITT and six other major corporations, along with Richard Shinn and Frank Smeal of Morgan Guaranty Trust, purportedly arranged the structure and functions of the MAC on May 26, 1975.[1] The MAC formalized the power of the financial and corporate class over the city's long-range fiscal planning. Governor Carey's appointments to the MAC board included eight members, out of nine, with banking and brokerage connections. They were: Felix Rohatyn; Simon Rifkind, a corporate lawyer and director of the Sterling National Bank; Robert Weaver, director of the Bowery Savings Bank and the Metropolitan Life Insurance Company; Thomas Flynn, a director of the Household Finance Corporation, as well as trustee of the American Savings Bank; William Ellinghaus, president of the New York Telephone Company, a director of Bankers Trust, and a trustee of the Dime Savings Bank; John Coleman of Adler, Coleman, and Company, a brokerage firm; Francis Barry, president of Campbell and Gardiner, a brokerage firm; and George Gould, chairman of Donaldson, Lufkin, Jenerette Securities. The only appointee without such connections was Donna Shalala, a professor at Columbia University and an expert on state financing. By her own admission, Shalala was not within the circle of decision-makers of the MAC. In an interview held in October 1978, Shalala argued that:

SHALALA: During that period it was Felix Rohatyn and only Felix Rohatyn. It was a very small group of people [making decisions]. MAC was usually represented by one person or by two at the most. Ellinghaus, when he was chairman, with Rohatyn. You didn't put all the MAC people into a room, with all the mayor's people and all the governor's people. So in a sense, while I knew what was going on, and I certainly felt consulted, I didn't feel that I was a central person in the negotiations [to refinance the city and institute an austerity plan].

It has already been shown that New York's major banks were deeply implicated in the events that led up to the fiscal crisis. We saw that through the FCLG finance capital was exerting its influence over city policy. Yet, with the MAC, the financial community began to exert more control, in a formalized, legally authorized, state board. One union leader described the power of the banks in this way: "The banks were doing business all the time. They [had been getting] 9½ percent interest . . . and they were cracking the whip." The newest "whip" was to be the Municipal Assistance Corporation. Jack Newfield, in his important book on the fiscal crisis, described the formation of the MAC and, later, the Emergency Financial Control Board (EFCB) as a bankers' coup.

The coup that looked like salvation transformed New York City's representative form of government. The theoretical repositories of the people's will—the mayor, the Board of Estimate, the elected legislators—lost much of their authority, which shifted decisively away from the elected mayor and the Board of Estimate to the bankers and businessmen who dominated MAC and EFCB. Decision-making shifted from the semi-public forum of the Board of Estimate to an endless round of private meetings in boardrooms, summer homes, and law offices.[2]

The bankers did not necessarily view the MAC in that light, however. Even though the MAC was the creation of an investment banker, Rohatyn, along with Rifkind, who was also a director of the Sterling National Bank, and Smeal, another banker with Morgan Guaranty Trust, there was a general denial that this financing corporation was a vehicle for the financial community to assert its interests. Indeed, what is most interesting about this denial is that the city's interests were presented as being identical with banking interests. About the drafting of the legislation creating MAC, Jac Friedgut judged the banks' influence in the following way:

FRIEDGUT: First, the effect as to how much input we had over the creation of MAC—I would say that it was, on a scale of one to ten with ten being the highest and one being the lowest, it would be about a three. We spoke to various city people and told them some of our ideas that maybe we need some sort of state agency to do the financing for the city and to, in effect, fund out long term the huge amount of short-term debt. Which is essentially the guts of what MAC was all about. But in terms of drafting the legislation and the various changes in legislation and so on, I would say we had zero influence. Not that I know of. Maybe some other people did but I think if we had, I would have known it. And I can't say for sure that some banker didn't meet at midnight sometime with someone from the state and say "How about this and this?" But in terms of meeting with officials, just a little bit of the conceptualization of how to structure the organization in terms of a state-sponsored financing vehicle on behalf of the city.

But did a banker have to meet with state officials in the middle of the night to get across the needs of the banks relative to the refinancing of the city's notes? Of course not. Built into the very organizational purpose and structure of such a financing organization are the needs of finance capital. Furthermore, those who did create the MAC were representatives of the banking and corporate community. Their notions of the crisis were grounded in their own particular class being. Why weren't the unions consulted during the planning process? Why weren't representatives of the city's poor consulted? Why weren't representatives, elected or otherwise, of the city's minority communities and of its middle class consulted? To suggest that these constituencies were consulted when the legislation was drafted and passed through the legislature and the City Council is to miss the point. By this time it appeared that there were no alternatives to the MAC. An ideology of limitations grounded in scarcity was beginning to take hold. Where was the opposition?

The staffing of the MAC quite obviously demonstrated the power that the financial and corporate factions of the capitalist class were able to exert at this point. In a very real sense, their view of the fiscal crisis became the prevailing ideology. The interests of the city were presented as parallel to capital's interests. At the same time, those interests necessitated reductions in the city's work force, as well as reduced real wages for those workers who remained. Austerity was to be introduced even as the MAC was to renegotiate the city's short-term debt into long-term, state-guaranteed MAC bonds. In the process, the city was to be saved from bankruptcy.

Shalala revealed the governor's concerns and the financial community's power when she described how staffing decisions were made:

SHALALA: It was seen as a financing problem and the governor's first inclination was to find people who were politically acceptable but knew the substance [of the problem]. Remember, the problem was credibility with the financial community, and therefore he was urged to make a series of appointments that would be looked at by the financial community, as well as by the unions and other people, as respectable people; people who, even though they had some connections with the banking community, didn't have a particular axe to grind or weren't antiunion particularly.

Regardless, the unions did not exert veto power over appointees. More importantly, they were not consulted about the legislation creating the MAC until *after* it had been drafted. Edward Handman described the union's influence—or lack thereof—over the legislation in an interview in December 1978:

HANDMAN: The same thing was happening all the time: when a crisis came they had to run to the unions . . . so that we could solve the problem. And then anytime something new was happening they would do it themselves without asking the unions [for assistance]. So the legislation [creating MAC] they drafted that themselves. And one morning we were having a Municipal Labor Coalition meeting and we suddenly learned that they got the legislation ready to go and they hadn't even shown it to us. So we had a press conference and everybody was here waiting for it and the word got to the governor that we were angry—so they held it up. And we went . . . over the legislation. But basically it was the same and an example of a unilateral document. We made some minor changes at the moment. We were in a frustrating position. They would draft something without us.

It was quite clear that the unions lacked real power in the context of this crisis. Instead, power seems to have centered on the financial community that had helped deny the city its much-needed operating funds. Jac Friedgut of Citibank and the FCLG made that point clear in an interview held on January 4, 1979. Friedgut was asked if it were true, as Jack Newfield maintained, that the bankers took control of the city after September 1975. Friedgut first distinguished between commercial and investment banking and then stated that:

> FRIEDGUT: It is true that the investment bankers, particularly Felix Rohatyn, George Gould, and Edward Kresky, probably had more say in the financial restructuring of the city on a continuous basis since the second half of 1975 than any other group. *So, in a sense, the bankers did take over the city.* [Emphasis added.]

Jac Friedgut went on to maintain that it was not the commercial, but rather the investment bankers who gained so much power. In part this may have been his analysis as a commercial banker, for, as we have seen, the commercial banks exerted a great deal of power through the FCLG and, later, through the MAC. Still, there may have been an important point here. Investment bankers could play an important and pivotal role in redirecting the financial structure of New York City and could, Friedgut maintained, mediate between labor and the commercial banks. Continuing his analysis, Friedgut argued in an interview in January 1979 that:

> FRIEDGUT: The bankers did take over the city. But these were not the commercial bankers. And you know, if you asked Jack Newfield who do you mean, he would say the Wristons of this world. Well, that's just not true. To a large extent if you said the Rohatyns of this world, it is pretty close to the mark. Now some people would say yes, but doesn't Rohatyn feel more comfortable with a Wriston than with a Jack Bigel, representing labor? And that is not true either, because Felix Rohatyn's genius is that he's been able to effect the same type of communication with Bigel as with Wriston; to somehow harmonize their positions in a way that's good for the city.

Felix Rohatyn was indeed able to effect an accommodation with the city's labor unions. Nevertheless, this accommodation was not based on an equality of power between finance capital and labor; rather, it was predicated on keeping union mobilization ineffectual or reactive to already accomplished policies. This was the case for the legislation creating the MAC and, a short time later, the EFCB.

The unions were constantly working with plans submitted by the banks. The MAC legislation was one such instance, in which members of the corporate sector drafted legislation without prior consultation with the city's labor unions. Furthermore, the function of the MAC itself served the interests of the financial community; it was intended to establish the security of investments in the city and to allow finance capital to invest elsewhere; or, in other words, to disinvest in New York. The MAC was authorized to market $3 billion of bonds. These bonds would be issued by the MAC as an agency of New York State, not New York City. The bonds would be retired upon maturity by a fund set aside and protected by law. The fund would consist of state taxes imposed on retail sales within the city, as well as a stock transfer tax. It was a financing instrument, controlled by finance capital, and, more importantly, devised by financiers.

On June 30, 1975, under pressure from both the state and federal governments, as well as the continuing pressure from the financial community, Mayor Beame unilaterally ordered a wage freeze applicable to the city's labor force. The unions, in a meeting at the Americana Hotel one month later, capitulated to these demands and signed an agreement deferring a portion of their wages. The bankers' demands for a reduction in labor costs were being met. Still, there was no rush by investors to show confidence in a city moving through the initial stages of austerity.

On July 10, the MAC began marketing its first series of long-term bonds. It was a $1 billion issue, with a high interest rate of 9.25 percent, tax free. Nevertheless, only $550 million of this was successfully marketed to the public, despite an "A" rating from the municipal bond rating agencies. The underwriting banks and brokerage houses were forced to absorb the remaining $450 million.

It was clear that investors were demanding more austerity before they could express their confidence in the city. The prominent banking and corporate appointees to the MAC were not enough to inspire confidence in the MAC issue; it had been too closely identified with New York City. Despite the security of separate funds and the status of state agency, investors refused to commit their capital to MAC bonds. The marketing of MAC bonds was not as successful as one might have thought, given the compositon of the MAC board. Jac Friedgut described the cooperation of the banks in this way:

FRIEDGUT: Now in terms of the marketing, the bank people said, "Well, we need these three billion dollars quickly, so we'll have $1 billion in July, $1 billion in August and $1 billion in September." And we said it looks like it's worth a try. And so we felt confident that we could do the billion dollars, billion dollars, and another billion dollars. And we obviously pulled all the stops to do it. Now, one of the ways we got things done for the first billion—we made sure that various banks, savings banks, insurance companies, and their brokerage institutions, for all intents and purposes on a private basis, signed up for $650 million or so worth. So essentially two-thirds of it was not done in a traditional market way. It was really done away from the market, even though it was added into the numbers. So only about one-third, $350 million, was done in the market. And it couldn't be done. What I mean by it couldn't be done is we offered it and after the offering rate, which was 8 percent or something like that, the market had no appetite for $350 million worth. And ultimately, whatever was left around, maybe $100 or $150 million worth, when the syndicate broke—that means when we said "O.K., sell it at whatever you could get for it." It broke badly and it ultimately reached the level where MAC was salable at only about 11 percent. So, you see, if we could control the market we would have sold it at 8 percent. So what that experience demonstrates is not only did we not control the market, but what is even worse and somewhat humiliating for us—we couldn't even judge the market. If we could have judged the market, we would have tried at 10% or something like that. We misjudged the market. . . . MAC was too little and too late.

By now, the MAC was too closely identified with the city. Even though the MAC was a creation and a vehicle of New York State and had its own revenues from the city, isolated from any other purpose but to pay back its bonds, MAC bonds were still identified as a shaky investment. Yet the MAC had its own source of funds to retire its debt. As Rohatyn claimed: "MAC is immune [from a city bankruptcy]. We have a revenue stream—a sales tax—that is collected by the state. It is not a city tax. It's been turned into a state tax. And we have first call on that revenue stream. That has been sanctified by the highest courts. We are satisfied, and I think that our A credit rating with Standard and Poor's was based on the fact that a city bankruptcy is not relevant to MAC. Obviously, a city bankruptcy would be a catastrophe, but in terms of 'Can we get at the revenue?' and 'Can we pay off our bond holders?' the answer is 'yes.' "[3]

With the creation of the MAC, along with its revenue source to pay back its bond holders, the financial community had what it was nervous about for so long: it had its right to first lien in case of a city bankruptcy. And even though the MAC was still tied to the city and its tax base, it would take a catastrophe of singular importance for the MAC to be threatened. As Rohatyn was quoted in the *Fiscal Observer*:

You can say the city's economic life and economic activity are relevant to MAC since we do depend on sales taxes that are collected in the city. On the other hand, we have a two-to-one coverage of our debt service, and one-and-a-half is the minimum sales tax coverage. Economic activity in the city would have to go down by a third to jeopardize the payment of principal and interest to our bondholders.

There's just no way that economic activity is going to go down by a third, because the city would be in flames.[4]

Given the assurance that the MAC bonds would be safe, even from a city bankruptcy, it was assumed that these MAC bonds would be much easier to market than they turned out to be. And as MAC was received cooly by investors, the city edged toward bankruptcy. The market had by now become much more independent of the New York banks than anyone had imagined. When Shalala was asked whether the banks had worked as hard as they later claimed in marketing MAC bonds, she responded that it was in the banks' interest to market those bonds. As she put it:

SHALALA: My view of them during that time was that they were cooperative. How cooperative is a relative question. In our first offering, at least with MAC, they broke their backs, it seemed to me, to help us sell the MAC bonds. If they were simultaneously dumping their stuff, they certainly were terribly nervous during that period. They had a lot to lose but I thought if anything they were panicky trying to figure out what to do in that situation.

The banks, citing the lack of investor confidence both in the city and in the MAC, pushed for austerity budgeting and for a stronger mechanism to monitor the city's finances. On July 17, a group of bankers led by David Rockefeller, Frank Smeal, and Walter Wriston met with the MAC board to propose the direction that the city must take. At this meeting, the bankers asserted that the MAC board must take more control over the city's finances and budget. They suggested an end to free tuition at the City University of New York, a raise in the transit fare, a wage freeze, further reductions in the size of the city's labor force, and deeper service cutbacks. In addition, the bankers questioned the ability of the mayor to take the "dramatic" steps that were needed and urged that a fiscal program be implemented and monitored by an outside agency or control board. They were suggesting that it was now necessary for a nonelected control board to administer the fiscal affairs of the city.[5] According to Jack Newfield, Mayor Beame was then advised by the MAC that further and much more drastic austerity measures were necessary.

By August, it was apparent that the MAC was not able to perform its function. The investment community was on strike—denying the city funding, even through a state agency such as the MAC. The corporate sector, and especially the city's banks, were pressing for a stronger, more powerful control board. Jac Friedgut detailed, in an interview in January 1979, the process leading to the control board.

FRIEDGUT: I think we made it clear . . . that there was no way that even MAC . . . at first we all made a joint judgment that people would differentiate between MAC and the city and therefore would buy MAC bonds, though not city bonds. That was wrong. Then we said O.K., let's try this as a judgment—that the only way that people will buy more MAC bonds will be if you make it very, very clear that the state is not only borrowing on behalf of the city but that *it's also clamping down on the city and getting the city back into line.* [Emphasis added.]

Clamping down on the city meant enforcing more drastic moves toward austerity budgeting. That would mean more layoffs, in real bodies, not just through the elimination of unfilled jobs or through attrition. Bill Tabb accurately summarizes what clamping down would mean, and why the investment community, led by the banks, was so anxious to get "the city back into line." According to Tabb,

the failure of MAC was political: the resistance of the public sector unions and of Mayor Beame to making budget cuts provoked a crisis in the financial community. It could not let wildcat strikes by sanitation workers, sickout by firemen, and blockades of City Hall by police prevent layoffs; nor could it let Beame get away with announcing layoffs while merely eliminating vacant positions, shifting lines, or quietly rehiring workers. MAC was clearly an insufficient vehicle for forcing austerity; the result was the direct assumption of power by the financial community.[6]

The next chapter includes a discussion of the role that the municipal labor unions played in this moment of the fiscal crisis. It was clear that many of the city's workers were rebelling against the aspects of the austerity plan that most affected their employment. Yet the labor unions themselves played a much less militant role, as will be shown in detail in Chapter 7. Mayor Beame, whose political career had been made in the political clubhouses of the Democratic Party, was not too anxious to force layoffs, wage freezes, service cuts, tuition at the City University, or a subway fare increase. Beame was a street-wise, clubhouse-made politician; as was his major advisor, James Cavanagh. Both men understood that making these austerity cuts was equivalent to ending their political careers. At the same time, the political ballgame had changed, making their old rules and assumptions no longer valid. In a sense, they were out of date and playing in the financiers' ballpark. It was a game that they could not win.

In the meantime, the financial community was pressing for more control, which they found in the Emergency Financial Control Board.

EFCB: The Austerity Board

In September, the "clamping down on the city" process was formally legislated, with the creation of the EFCB. This board was legislated to have the power to

> (i) review, control and supervise the financial management of the city, (ii) . . . approve . . . a plan that will provide the basis for a return of the city to sound financial condition, (iii) control . . . the disbursement of city funds, under which debt service requirements will be met as a first priority, (iv) review and audit city operations . . . to assure that sound management practices are observed or restored.[7]

It was, in all respects, a formal and legally authorized austerity board. Most important of all, its function was mandated by law, and it was able to institute austerity regardless of any potential resistance from the city's unions, workers, or residents. It had been isolated from potential popular movements against austerity.

Serving on the EFCB were Governor Carey, Mayor Beame, State Comptroller Levitt, City Comptroller Goldin, and three members of the corporate sector: Felix Rohatyn, William Ellinghaus, both members of the MAC, and David Margolis of Colt Industries.

The most powerful member of the EFCB was Felix Rohatyn. By this time, Rohatyn had become the major decision-maker in plans to introduce austerity. He devised and approved financing plans; he smoothed over any rough spots with both the banks and the unions. As Shalala stated in an interview of October 1978:

> SHALALA: He had the power of his prestige [originating from his work in the financial and corporate sectors]; tremendous power because of his prestige and visibility in this situation. He was simply trusted by a large number of people that were involved in the process and therefore I think he had enormous power during this period. And in fact he shaped the financial settlements.

This wizard of the corporate world was now setting the fiscal policy of the city, though within the constraints set by the deteriorating position of New York City in the municipal credit markets. Still, with all his prestige and power, he could not successfully market MAC bonds without the establishment of the EFCB.

The overt functions of the EFCB were to institute tight control over the city and its policies and to force austerity in the form of control over expenditures, finances, and city labor contracts. To this end, the EFCB asserted its authority over all major contracts that the city entered into

—including and especially the city's contracts with its labor unions. The EFCB usurped the mayor's authority. Consequently, the board began to force—within the context of a new three-year planned austerity program—layoffs, attrition, and a general reduction in city services. These actions, it was thought, would reassure investors that the city would reform its profligate ways. It was hoped that investors would now be reassured that the city was no longer a union town; that its unions no longer held power over the city purse. Furthermore, investors could be reassured that the mayor no longer had control over the city's government: its finances, its budget, and its labor contracts and negotiations. On September 5, 1975, the *New York Daily News* announced, in large headlines across the front page, that "ABE SURRENDERS FISCAL CONTROL." In return for $2.3 billion of aid, Mayor Beame accepted the authority of the EFCB. Although the union leaders were given assurances that their collective bargaining rights were still sacred, such assurances had little meaning in the context of the new bargaining. The unions would now bargain with the city, while the EFCB watched—with the power to nullify any agreement, any contract. Power shifted away from Mayor Beame, away from the MAC, away from the unions, and toward the EFCB. One more layer of power and authority was imposed on the city and its unions, with the fiscal crisis as both its cause and its legitimator. In the process, the city's budget was isolated from the workers and from the poor people of New York City. The crisis became the legitimator for the superseding of the power relations of the liberal state. In the process, the labor-management, city-citizen agreements of the past became null and void. The social contracts of the post-1960s era in New York City, fashioned out of conflict and class struggle, were now open to revision. And those with the power and authority to do the rewriting sat on the board, or demanded access to the board, of the EFCB. It was a turning point for both labor and capital in New York City.

The skirmishes began, first with the city's 60,000 teachers. In the preceding July, just two months before school was to begin, the city had buckled under the bankers' and the financial community's demands, and had announced major reductions in its labor force and, in effect, in its labor costs. Throughout the fiscal crisis, it was difficult, perhaps impossible, to find out exactly how many workers actually lost their jobs. As has been mentioned before, all such figures either are approximations or are figures that the city announced in attempts to calm the financial markets. In any case, by the late summer of 1975, all city workers functioned in a milieu that provoked uncertainty about their future status. As detailed by the *Times*, 8,323 layoffs of teaching and support personnel were alleged to have taken effect by the opening day of school in September.[8] In a school system in which teachers already felt overworked and harassed, this was not welcome news.

The productivity of city workers was an issue that had aroused deep suspicion concerning the responsibility of the municipal unions to the needs of the city. With layoffs occurring in each city agency, and with more layoffs to come, the issue of productivity was to emerge as a major arena of concern for both management and labor. The financial community, too, had made productivity one of its major issues. With the budget cutting that had already been accomplished, and with so much more to come, layoffs would mean significant reductions in the quality of city services, even with increased productivity by the workers who remained on their jobs.

In September 1975, the Board of Education tried to impose a new set of work rules and work conditions on the city's teachers. The United Federation of Teachers (UFT) had attempted to negotiate a new labor contract with the Beame administration, but with the new milieu defined by the fiscal crisis, this was no easy task. As stated earlier, the Beame administration's capacity to act on major contracts, expenditures, and general planning had been curtailed by the fiscal crisis, the financial community, the constraints of the market, and the imposition of superordinate layers of authority—notably the MAC and the EFCB. In such a milieu, labor negotiations could not proceed as if business were being conducted as usual. Uncertainty abounded, and the fiscal crisis tied the hands of the Beame administration. Furthermore, the union itself seemed powerless to conduct reasonable negotiations, given the pressures on the rank and file, and given the uncertain status of management. With whom were they negotiating? Were they negotiating with the city, the state, the EFCB, or the MAC?

The very first hints were beginning to appear of the new conditions that would limit the power of the labor unions. It is interesting to note that the September 10, 1975, issue of the *New York Times* had four major stories about the city's fiscal crisis on the front page. The headlines of those stories describe the constellation of forces that were altering the governance of the city itself. These headlines are as follows: "City Schools Are Crippled as Teachers' Strike Starts"; "Carey Signs $2.3 Billion Aid Plan Imposing Financial Curbs on City"; "State Will Face Record Interest: Chase Asks 7.80%"; and "8 of 10 Members of Board Oppose Tuition at City U." On the same day, the city's authority was subordinated to a control board, banks were getting record interest for assisting the city, teachers faced the imposition of more work for less pay, and the students of the City University were being told that tuition might be changed at the formerly free university. The city's working class was facing a decline in the quality of services that kept their neighborhoods from decline. Facing a desperate situation, the teachers walked out. Bill Scott, official of the UFT, explained this series of events in this way:

> SCOTT: In fact, in 1975 that was really a strike by the membership. It was not a strike that the leadership actually wanted to lead. The leadership . . . was aware of the financial crisis. The membership felt that it fell all around them, but that it never touched them. And this they couldn't accept. And when they had conditions in the contract that they didn't like, or when we couldn't get a settlement, they wanted a strike and a strike they had. That was, I think, one of the cases—strikes—one of the few strikes, in public areas where the leadership didn't lead them or encourage them. And in this case it was neither—not encouragement nor leadership. And it was a pretty costly strike. It cost the members of the strike. Of course, you may not have a background in the Taylor law, where you pay a two for one. In other words, a striking member loses pay for two days for every day they're out. Also the unions stand to be fined. . . . Eventually we did get some leniency from the courts but that was based on the feeling of the court that the leadership was not responsible for the strike and, secondly, that the leadership from the period of the strike on, had really provided leadership in assisting the city in its fiscal endeavors. . . . You know, if you go back in the history of the public unions . . . they always negotiated in an upgoing economy. . . . This was a new experience for unions. They were not used to accepting this type of bargaining. The membership felt that the leadership had failed them when in effect probably the leadership was doing the only responsible thing it could have done, which was to provide some giveups, attempt to resolve the situation so that we could continue education here in New York, and at least at some standards or some level of accomplishment.

A contract was finally negotiated with the city, but its approval and implementation would take more than a year. The problem was simple: the EFCB refused to accept and ratify the contract as punishment for the teachers' militancy. And, as William Scott correctly indicated: "That is the contract that had embodied the policy with respect to increments, and whether there was a continuation of increments, and whether certain givebacks would be enforced because of the fiscal crisis—what the limitations were and how long they were going to remain in effect." By not approving the contract, the EFCB was postponing the increments due the teachers, while prolonging any work rules changes that management was imposing on the teachers. For the other labor unions, it was a message that could not be ignored.

By now, the city's residents were paying higher subway and bus fares for a deteriorating service. By now, the austerity cutbacks were accelerating in quantity and speed. Austerity was now proceeding full speed. And the committees managing the city included the MAC and the EFCB, as well as a Management Advisory Board and a Temporary Commission on City Finances (TCCF). The management committee was assigned the task of streamlining the city's managerial systems. Furthermore, it was authorized to "install expenditure controls in city agencies, focusing first on problems such as pensions, Medicaid billings, hospitals and sanitation. Serve as consultants . . . on steps for revising budget for EFCB."[9] Serving on this board were, among others, several financiers and corporate executives, such as Richard Shinn and William Ellinghaus, and a union leader—Harry Van Arsdale. The membership of the TCCF was even more impressive, reading like a list of the power elite of the city. As Joy Cook wrote in an article about these four "panels" in the *New York Post* during September, "The city's new shadow government—associates from corporate boardrooms rather than political backrooms—is made up of four key panels that are dividing the tasks of ushering New York into a new era of austerity."[10] But the real power resided in the EFCB—as a control board with authority over the city's major expenditures and contracts—and in the members of the banking community, who could begin to move toward the back seats, now that their power was formalized through the control board. But, as we shall see, these bankers wanted still more control over the city's budget.

In May 1976, less than a year since its formal creation, the EFCB extended its control over labor policy through its authority over the city's labor contracts. On May 18, the EFCB refused to accept a contract negotiated between the city and the Transport Workers Union (TWU), saying that its settlement was too costly for the city. As reported by the *New York Times*:

> The New York State Emergency Financial Control Board successfully imposed a less costly contract on transit workers yesterday and . . . issued specific limitations for the coming round of negotiations between New York City and its municipal-employee unions.
> . . . The Control Board thus moved deeply into setting the city's labor policy. . . . The transit agreement, which the Transport Workers Union leadership accepted with a statement of reluctance, is different from the earlier pact rejected by the Control Board in that it mandates that any cost-of-living wage increase must come from increased worker productivity. It also defers part of this benefit.
> In similar fashion, the Control Board's issuance of collective-bargaining guidelines for the other major unions is based on a policy of providing labor no new city or state money, and forcing workers to realize cost-of-living raises by either increasing productivity or surrendering some fringe or pension benefits of comparable value.[11]

Traditionally, the contract negotiations and the settlement between the city and the TWU set the tone and the parameters for the forthcoming negotiations between the city and its other major unions. What the TWU got, other unions would get, with minor variations between the uniformed and nonuniformed unions. Here the EFCB was telling each and every labor leader, as well as the mayor, that these negotiations were meaningless. Policy was now being set by the EFCB and only the EFCB. Negotiations conducted in good faith were no longer relevant. Austerity was here, productivity would be here, or no new money. The EFCB was imposing its discipline both on the city's politicians and on its unions and workers. It was establishing the logic of finance capital as the dominant logic guiding the city's governance. And this logic extended to and enveloped its workplaces, its subways, its schools, its universities, its closed day care centers, its hospitals, and its streets. The city's financial community was getting nearly all it wanted.

Nevertheless, the city's banks wanted more direct control over the city and its budget and its revenues. Still a bit nervous over the first lien issue, the banks pushed for a stronger control board, along with a more politically isolated debt reserve fund. For them, the controls that were now in place were better than a policy of allowing the city's population to decide city priorities—in spending and in its revenue collecting. Now, at least, the city's budget was entrenched in the Control Board's hands, negating the influence of the city's potential opposition groups, such as its unions and its minority and citizen activist groups. But the banks wanted a still tighter control mechanism.

Despite all the controls that were in place, New York City faced repeated skirmishes with bankruptcy. For one thing, the city needed a steady source of financing. It would find this through the use of its union pension funds. Just how these funds were covered is discussed in the next chapter. But facing the financial uncertainty of the fiscal crisis, the city placed a moratorium on its short-term debt. Through the MAC, the short-term debts that had burdened the city with the possibility of default and bankruptcy were forcibly exchanged for long-term MAC bonds. In November 1975, the moratorium was placed in effect, thereby transforming $1.6 billion of short-term notes for long-term MAC obligations. The city's default was postponed. (In November 1976, the moratorium was declared illegal and a violation of investor rights.) With this financing package in place, the Ford administration accepted and approved a program of $2.3 billion in seasonal loans through June 1978. The administration had put off any assistance to New York City for months, forcing the city to institute more stringent austerity measures. When the city was properly disciplined, by both the EFCB and the financial markets, the Ford administration was ready to act. Its assistance did not cost the federal government one single dollar. President Ford and Secretary of the Treasury William Simon had whipped the liberal city—showing the rest of the country that "Peck's bad boy" would not be tolerated. Some time later, with the hindsight that history brings, Senator William Proxmire, chair of the Senate Banking, Housing, and Urban Affairs Committee, which had oversight responsibility over the $2.3 billion Seasonal Loan Program for the city, had this to say about the legislation designed to "save" the city. "Obviously, the Federal Loans have provided a convenient way for the banks to get out of New York City securities." [12]

During the city's skirmishes with bankruptcy, the battle over a first lien and, therefore, the city's priorities, was fought in the backrooms of the city's new shadow government. The city had set up a Contingency Committee on Bankruptcy, which would seek to determine the order of priorities if indeed a bankruptcy became a reality. This committee functioned whenever it seemed that the city was again on the verge of bankruptcy. It had no real power, yet its very existence provided a sense that the battles were being fought by the banks in order to establish their own priorities as the city's priorities. In the following passage from an interview with Bill Scott this committee and its interaction with its banking representatives can be seen as a microcosm of the conflict over the city's needs and the bankers' needs. As Bill Scott tells this story, it went like this:

> SCOTT: I was on the committee because the comptroller had appointed me to it. The president of the Union Dime Savings Bank was on it, as was a consultant and partner of a Wall Street firm. I think there might have been as many as ten members on it. . . . The meetings were intensive when we thought we were next door to bankruptcy. . . . The importance of this committee zigged and zagged with the financial history of the city. But what we did consider was: where we would begin; what recommendations we would make; who would take over—would it be a federal judge? would it be some other type of bankruptcy? There was a big cloud . . . over the bankruptcy of a city. Bankruptcy of a city never seems to be clear. . . . The assets of a city are a far cry from the assets of a corporation. You don't have automobiles that are on the assembly line. You don't have clothing that is in a factory. You have paved streets, subways, and you have the necessities of life which you cannot sell—you have to keep them to operate. The job is not to sell them. It's to regroup and create dollar assets. The objective of a city bankruptcy is to keep the city running under some semblance of order and some rationale. So you face a different problem of a bankruptcy. It's not what are your assets. It's what are your needs. So you have to approach it from a different view. . . . The needs of a city are multiple. There are obvious needs

. . . the police, firemen, sanitationmen, doctors and, I suppose, some sort of educational system. You can't have hundreds of thousands of kids running around the streets. . . . Schools, you got to remember, have changed. We not only fill their minds, we fill their stomachs. They have two meals a day in some areas—breakfast and lunch. So it becomes an integral part of government. But those are the obvious things. The ones that are not so obvious but they're also there are feeding prisoners, taking care of people in the hospitals, providing oxygen, providing all of the things which are bought—food, oxygen, drug problems, methadone—which is supplied. There are so many things that people don't realize that are necessary to running this city. Necessary for the health and welfare of all of us. We did discuss this. We did talk about it and we tried to line up a set of priorities. There was disagreement as to how the priorities would be and what we were talking about. For instance, the health of the city—that's a high priority. But what exactly is the health of the city? Is that methadone? Is that taking care of the hospitals or are they separate from health of the city? . . . Do you do away with water testing? These are the things we had to consider. . . . Repayment of debt was second to the continuation of the city. Now that puts it pretty high on the list. That doesn't mean that we would continue to pay the people in the Parks Department or to pay the people doing the chauffeuring of city cars. It doesn't say that the services rendered by city agencies which are deemed to be important are going to be the same as they were before. We may put one cop on a patrol, whether the police like it or not. Or we might have done away with the cars and restricted the police cars so we wouldn't be buying gasoline and put the guys out on foot. We might cut down on the manning charts of the Fire Department. Instead of having five men on a chart we might have four men or three men and do away with the remaining. They just wouldn't get paid. It said—these are service priorities that we must have. Then within that you determine how much of that priority you must have. Eventually, after you take the very, very important, the extremely essential services, and the extent to which they must be manned, and after you decided that—then the payment to the debtors came next. Everybody who buys a city bond, a government bond of any type, has to realize that there is no law that is supreme to government. You can have all the guarantees you want, but is it worthwhile to pay you and turn over the money to you and when you turn away from the cashier's window in the municipal building, some guy puts a gun in your back and takes the money from you and there's no cop to stop him? . . . Now you're going to tell me about the investor who lives in Iowa. I recognize that. But nevertheless, cities and governments have to go on.

Scott was then asked whether the bankers were trying to impose their set of priorities within this bankruptcy committee.

SCOTT: Bankers have a very narrow point of view. Their point of view is banking; that's their business. They take a point of view that if you do not pay back your lender, you will have no more lenders. When you default and refuse to pay, for whatever reasons, you realistically cut off your supply to new money for a long period of time. I would have to agree with them. We put the notes in moratorium. . . . Eventually we were forced to pay off the moratorium, which everybody knew before we even started. What we gained there was about a six months or a year delay. So we saved that money for that time. We didn't save it. . . . It was pretty well known that you can't place notes in moratorium. . . . I think we have to realize that the banks' point of view is to pay off your debts first. I think they realize that they have to maintain this point of view, because if they don't, they won't be able to sell bonds. They won't have customers. They won't have this very attractive business that they're in. On the other hand, privately they probably agree with us that payment of debt only comes after you maintain the services of the city. But they took some very hard points of view and they were very suspicious.

Their suspicion extended to the guarantees that the MAC had for the payment of MAC bonds. In early 1977, the banks made another push for a stronger control over the city's revenues and expenditures. In a memorandum from the Bankers Trust Company to Mayor Beame, dated March 4, 1977, the banks pushed for the type of control that would allow them to attain a first lien on city revenue even over the service priorities mentioned by Bill Scott. The banks proposed a Debt Service Fund, "into which all City real estate tax payments will . . . be deposited . . . Tax payments . . . will be remitted in kind . . . to a bank for deposit in a special trust account. The bank will be responsible for administration and investment of the Fund." Control over the payments of debt service will be with the bank controlling the Debt Service Fund. Furthermore, "The Debt Service Fund will be for the benefit of all outstanding debt obligations of the City."[13]

The banks also pushed for a balanced budget as demanded by law and reviewed by a new and stronger control board. According to their plan, a deficit from one fiscal year would be treated as an expenditure in the next year. Therefore, a deficit from a preceding year would result in lower service expenditures in the next. All budget modifications would require the prior approval of the new review board. In addition to the Debt Service Fund, which would serve to assure investors that short-term securities would receive payment even in the event of a city bankruptcy, the banks pushed for a similar fund for long-term debts. This "Contingency Reserve Fund" would be a separate bank account equal to 1 percent of total budgeted revenues for a given year. A reserve would be required to meet outstanding debts.

Finally, still another review board would be created "for the benefit of the City and its bondholders," to continue "for the life of new City bonds which are granted the benefits of the enabling legislation." This new review board would have the power to approve or disapprove of the city's budget, its capital budget, its "month-by-month cash flow"; and the city's three-year financial plans. Furthermore, the review board would have the power to revise the city's revenue estimates, thereby revising, if necessary, the city's expenditures. And, of course, the Review Board would review the city's major contracts, including labor contracts, in order to maintain the city's cost structure. To accomplish all this, the Review Board would have a Review Board Fund, with the understanding that "all revenues received by the City, unless exempted by the Review Board, are revenues of the Review Board Fund for the account of the Review Board." In simple terms, the Review Board was to have legal control over the City's finances, its budget, its short-term and long-term planning, its borrowing, its paying back of investors, and its labor contracts. In still simpler terms, the Review Board would control and run the city for the benefit and security of the city's investors. As Al Viani described this memorandum:

VIANI: I could show you a document that the banks proposed in terms of the city's budget that could blow your mind. It would blow your mind if you saw what they wanted. They wanted a budget that was totally—that there were no decisions to be made within it. Everything was totally automatic. If one thing happened, then something else automatically had to happen. The constraints and controls were amazing, and they wanted it for the entire state. For every locality in the state. The controls were so stringent as to make, in my estimation, the mayor meaningless. It was just pure budgetary control. It was totally geared to protecting their finances to the extent that there would be a 100% guarantee of any money that was invested in this city with absolutely no risk associated with it. It was unbelievable. They didn't get it and it was either do it my way or they weren't going to do it.

The banks seem to have lost that fight. Yet, they won a more important one. The Emergency Financial Control Board was reinstated as the Financial Control Board, and it was to control—or at least watch over—the city's finances for perhaps as long as the next twenty years. In that sense, the banks' original goals were met. They were able to divest their holdings in New York City and, at the same time, set up more rigid control over the direction of city politics. The new class politics of austerity had been established for their class needs. And all the while, the banks disinvested in the city.

Given disinvestment by the banks, the city needed a continuous flow of capital invested in either MAC or future city notes and bonds. The banks were clearly refusing to bankroll the city while it remained in such a precarious and risky financial condition. A source of funds would have to be found, and found soon, or else the city might find itself falling into bankruptcy. The source of these funds was to be the city's unions. In this way, the banks used the fiscal crisis to divest in the city, gain power for finance capital, institute austerity and probusiness policies, and restrict the influence of the city's labor unions.

The next chapter will present and analyze the strategies adopted and not adopted by the city's unions in response to the developing austerity. Through such analysis we shall be better able to understand the fiscal crisis not only as the *product* of class struggle but also itself a *moment* of class struggle.

7

The Municipal Unions and the Fiscal Crisis

Labor's Crisis Strategy

From the beginning, the unions responded to the ever-deepening fiscal crisis by cooperating with the emerging public policy, which was seemingly defined by the sacrifices of the city's workers and unions. These sacrifices became economically and politically "necessary," as the city found increasing reluctance among investors, both institutional and individual, to its note and bond offerings. In November 1974, with Comptroller Harrison Goldin admitting to a budget deficit of $650 million, interest rates on the city's debt obligations climbed to 9.5 percent, as doubt grew about the solvency of both the city and its notes.

To highlight the erosion of confidence in the city's fiscal health, one must recall that just one month earlier the city had marketed $420.4 million in Bond Anticipation Notes at a 7.79 percent interest rate. This rate was, up to that time, the highest interest rate ever paid by the city on this type of offering. The cause of still more investor anxiety was the decision by Fitch Investor's Service, Inc., to reduce its ratings of New York City bonds from an "A" to a "BBB" rating for maturities before January 1, 1980, while those maturing after that date were rated "BB." In so doing, Fitch reported that the city might soon have "difficulty in meeting all its financial obligations, debt service, as well as operating expenses."[1]

In order to attract investors, the city was obliged to offer 8.6 percent to 9.5 percent interest, and even under those conditions, the city could not attract ample investor interest. The crisis atmosphere was further com-

149

plicated and promoted by an urgent need to borrow $2.3 billion to meet operating and payroll obligations due within a few short weeks. By the end of 1974, the city had accumulated more than $13 billion in outstanding debt and was facing the real and threatening possibility of bankruptcy.

In November 1974, the controversy over the city's solvency was fueled by the actions of the city administration. Despite growing concern by the city's major financial powers and authorities, the offices of the mayor and the comptroller could not stop bickering in public over the actual size of the budget deficit. The mayor argued that the deficit was $430 million—$220 million short of the comptroller's estimate. Investors, already wary of the city's leadership, saw confirmation of their doubts in the confusion over the size of the deficit. Could the city be so poorly administered that its mayor and comptroller did not know the size of its debt?

As Mayor Beame and Comptroller Goldin argued, the major institutional investors began to pressure the city to produce a financing plan capable of closing the budget gap, whatever its actual size. In November 1974, Mayor Beame began to economize, as he announced a three-phased program designed to relieve the crisis. At first, Mayor Beame ordered $100 million in economies; then, later in the month he announced the layoff of 1,510 civil servants and provisional employees, in order to save an additional $44 million. Comptroller Goldin, however, suggested harsher economies, with additional personnel cuts. In December, Mayor Beame announced over 3,700 additional layoffs, including, for the first time, police, fire, and sanitation workers as well as teachers. In addition, 2,700 city workers were faced with forced retirement. The total savings produced by the two-phased cutback was announced by the mayor's office to have reduced the budget deficit to $135.4 million from the originally estimated $430 million: a reduction of $294.6 million in expenses.

In January 1975, with the crisis atmosphere growing, Comptroller Goldin reduced a planned bond and note offering to respond to "the market problem of oversupply." This action had been made in response to a memorandum by Frank Smeal and after a meeting with Wallace Sellers, of Merrill Lynch. Mr. Sellers had communicated the concern of the financial community with the growing crisis and informed city officials that the last note and bond offerings were a "total disaster." Therefore, he added, the January offerings would most likely not receive a bid from the financial underwriters.[2] In response to this lack of investor interest, Comptroller Goldin arrived at a plan which included issuing $650 million in notes with a one-year maturity, as well as an investment of $450 million in bonds by the city's union pension plans.

For the first time during this crisis, the union's pension funds would finance a plan requiring worker layoffs. (The implications of this strategy for the unions will be discussed later on in this chapter.) Phase Three of the mayor's plan was announced shortly thereafter and projected the laying off of 4,050 uniformed and nonuniformed personnel. These dismissals were projected to save $15 million. The total layoffs and dismissals, including forced retirements, up to this point supposedly numbered 12,700.[3] These numbers, however, were estimates at best. The confusion concerning actual totals of city workers employed, laid off, forced to retire, and/or dismissed underscored the failure of the city's administration and management to effectively rationalize city services or even the city government itself.

Clearly, this failure to effectively rationalize city government perpetuated much of the investor anxiety, as represented by the expressed concerns of finance capital (banks and investment brokers). This lack of rationality, of managerial control and predictability, was deemed fiscally unsound by those who represented investment capital. What could seem more irresponsible to capital than a managerial system that does not manage the productivity and discontent of its workers and clients? Does this not violate capitalism's operating basis?

In the face of these layoffs, the municipal unions began to talk about possible job actions and strikes. At first there was an attempt to unite the various unions through the Municipal Labor Coalition (MLC). This coalition was formed in 1967 to represent all the unions involved with the city's Office of Collective Bargaining (OCB). The MLC excluded unions in nonmayoral agencies, such as the United Federation of Teachers and the Transport Workers Union, thereby weakening its potential power. It may be theorized that one reason for these two unions' subsequent militancy was their omission from the MLC. Being left to their own independent action may have encouraged militancy. The MLC, however, was not an organization that functioned to promote militancy among union members. The function of the MLC prior to the fiscal crisis was to be the "vehicle through which the unions negotiate policy in the OCB, select their representatives in mediation and arbitration procedures, and assume the unions' share of the costs to maintain the OCB."[4] In other words, the function of the MLC was to promote the collective bargaining process and to inhibit the necessity of militant action. One might say that in that sense, the MLC functioned as a tool for the management of class conflict—for negotiation rather than confrontation. Because District Council 37 was its largest member union, its Executive Director, Victor Gotbaum, served as the chairman of the MLC.[5]

In late 1974, amidst growing calls for the mass layoff of city workers, the city's unions attempted to alter the function of the MLC. For the first time in their history, the unions in the MLC were faced with "an issue [in] which all its members could recognize as being in their self-interest" to unite.[6] Unity among these unions, however, was not easy to achieve. Edward Handman, of D. C. 37, described the problem in the following way in a December 1978 interview:

> HANDMAN: In fact, there were hostilities within the MLC—police, firefighters, sanitation all had flashpoints with each other. The uniform people were generally not too receptive to our union. There was kind of grudging participation within the MLC. However, with this first crisis, Victor Gotbaum really got the notion that the MLC had to start working as . . . the bargaining unit for all the city's employees.

The MLC, representing approximately 200,000 city workers, soon thereafter met with Mayor Beame to discuss, negotiate, and relay the unions' concern with the early layoffs. The strategy that was arrived at within the MLC was twofold, as described by Handman:

> HANDMAN: One—to prevent layoffs of civil servants, which is opposed to provisional employees. *This is really a defense posture knowing that somebody had to get laid-off.* And the second was to retain collective bargaining. Victor Gotbaum didn't want to be in a position where the city could make decisions which were uncontestable. [Emphasis added.]

With this defense-minded strategy, and with no long-term alternatives to austerity to offer, the unions met with Mayor Beame. The result seemed to portend continuing union success in avoiding massive numbers of layoffs. The announced layoffs of late 1974 were avoided, or at least temporarily postponed, by a union plan to

> substitute cash savings for jobs. Each union accounted for its share of money [saved] in its own way. District Council 37, for example, waived a $6 million payment long due its health and security fund and saved the jobs of about 650 men and women it represents.[7]

Some city workers were thus able to keep working—their pay coming from union dues and funds. Nevertheless, this was a one-time temporary, stop-gap plan, and, as it was, it never could be seen as an alternative to austerity or as a solution to the budget crisis. Some city workers kept their jobs—but for a very short time.

The December 9, 1974 minutes of the Municipal Labor Committee reveal the process by which the unions attempted to influence the city's proposed policy of worker dismissals. The sections of the minutes pertaining to the layoffs highlight the lack of concrete, long-range planning by the unions individually or by the unions collectively within the MLC. Furthermore, these minutes suggest the lack of unity that would characterize union efforts throughout the first and most significant moments of the fiscal crisis. The sections of the minutes pertaining to the mayor's actions regarding employee layoffs are quoted below.

> The Chairman then introduced discussion on the recent layoffs of civil service employees. It was agreed that the following proposal would be presented for approval to the General Membership as the MLC position on layoffs: . . . "The member unions of the Municipal Labor Committee oppose any attempt by the City of New York to effectuate budgetary savings by dismissing permanent civil service employees while, at the same time, wasting funds by contracting out services which could be performed more economically by City employees and retaining provisional, exempt, temporary and other personnel doing nonessential work."
>
> In his report, Mr. Gotbaum stated that the MLC policy on layoffs would be presented to the press and to the Mayor. He recommended that since a budgetary crisis does, in fact, exist, labor leaders should look at the situation in any attempt to solve the problem before the situation becomes more severe.[8]

Regardless of this statement's implied unity, underlying the statement was an "on your own" attitude. The member unions of the MLC were basically being told to negotiate individually with the city their own plans to avert layoffs. In other words, these negotiations and solutions were to be arrived at independently of any long-term common strategy or position. The solution arrived at, allowing the unions to buy back the jobs of some of those who had been laid off, was a temporary one at best. More significantly, the unions clearly accepted the crucial argument that the crisis necessitated layoffs and that provisional employees could be sacrificed.

In a sense, the unions had accepted what they might have very well fought and negotiated. Nowhere, in the minutes of the MLC or in any other negotiating position, was there a plan submitted by the unions by which New York City's major corporations could be taxed directly on their "surplus" profits in exchange for a continuing level of city services. Nor were there plans suggesting a renegotiation of city debt held by major institutional lenders, as these lenders had arranged for Third World debtor nations, such as Zaire, and, later, for nations throughout Latin America. The unions began their crisis strategy by accepting the one argument that would render them powerless: that the fiscal crisis necessitated their eventually sacrificing the jobs of some of their members. Already the notion of alternative solutions was being dismissed. Raymond Horton (of the TCCF), not considered a friend by the labor leaders who were besieged by this fiscal crisis, explained in an interview the unions' choices during the fiscal crisis as a choice between methods of reducing the city's labor costs. Horton explained the unions' strategy as one that had developed out of their choice to accept layoffs as opposed to any other alternative. He continued:

> HORTON: The unions claimed there were no other alternatives. Let me tell you how simple it is. New York City has lost [during the cutbacks of the fiscal crisis] by one means or another about 60,000 lines. . . . The city lost a hell of a lot of people over the last few years. Basically, and I guess that this is not Gotbaum's or Jack Bigel's fault, it is Beame's fault, but this is how it happened. Beame basically said, "Well, we got this amount of money to spend on workers. You guys [labor leaders] take your choice. You want to keep getting salary increases or do you want to hold those salaries constant or even take a pay cut and keep all your people. You choose." You see, basically the unions decided to take the salary increases, such as they were, and sacrifice the bodies. Now I happen to think that is a totally rational choice—the only one you can predict a union leader to take. He's going to get his ass in a sling if he takes anything else. The problem is that the mayor was absolutely devoid of responsibility for not asserting a different position. Because from the public's point of view, you could be a hell of a lot better off with those 60,000 people working for the city, albeit at a lower wage rate. I think that's right. But you see, my point here, is that there were options. I think the viewpoint is wrong that the unions didn't want layoffs. I think they did. The proof of the pudding is that they consistently chose layoffs or attrition rather than holding constant the wage rate. There were alternatives.

Al Viani confirmed this view, asserting that:

> VIANI: Staffing, as far as we are concerned, is strictly up to the city. The size and nature of the workforce was strictly up to the city. So that when they cut back, it wasn't in an area that we insisted we had to bargain on. They could cut back. We could negotiate what that meant in terms of the other people who were remaining. Where there were layoffs we could negotiate for things like unemployment insurance, and various other things.

I then asked Mr. Viani if they ever negotiated the numbers of layoffs. He responded "No. We never negotiated. No." Now, at first, this seems to contradict Horton's assumption that the unions chose the layoffs. Yet, if they didn't negotiate the numbers of layoffs while they negotiated salaries and fringe benefits, within a milieu of cutbacks, clearly then they were talking about sacrificing some of their members. And clearly that is what they did. As this chapter will show, the union leaders approached the crisis with a sense that worker sacrifices had to be made. Given that stance, layoffs were seen as part of the crisis resolution process. For them, there seemed to be no way around that, and, after all, laid-off members of a union cease to be members of the union. In a way, then, the union could continue and claim organizational strength, even with the layoffs.

At this early stage, there was some talk among the union leaders of job actions and strikes to halt the development of austerity budgeting. However, the crisis presented a situation heretofore not encountered by the unions; hence, a strike was deemed a radical action, with unpredictable results. The union coalition, such as it was, was characterized by disunity, leaving the union leaders suspicious of one another. The labor movement in the city was less a unified social movement than it was a group splintered into factions, each vying for the remaining city revenues. Disunity, and sometimes conflict, among the unions was therefore a consequence of the structure of labor relations in the city. In fact, it was a consequence of a complex division of labor within the public service sector itself, as well as between the public and private sector workforces. So it should not be surprising that a general strike and job actions, slow-downs, and sick-outs were talked about, as Edward Handman explained:

> HANDMAN: But nobody wanted to do it. You would hear it, but nobody really wanted to do it. For one, you always had the problem that you didn't know if everyone would go out on a general strike, particularly the uniformed people. They are adverse to striking. And nobody wanted it, because that's chaos, and much of what was going on, you have to remember, everything that was going on had never happened before. There was no experience.

While the union leaders in the MLC were ruling out any militant opposition to the mayor's layoff plan and the outcries for further austerity, their union members began to threaten resistance. Some union leaders, particularly those in the police, firefighters, and transit unions, were not in a position to accept the layoffs passively due to their lack of control over their rank-and-file membership. Hence, they were all too ready to defer, as much as possible, to the leadership of Victor Gotbaum of District Council 37. From then on, Gotbaum, as director of the union with the largest membership, would take a prominent role in formulating union strategy. In the interview mentioned above, Edward Handman explained the situation at that time in the following manner:

HANDMAN: Fortunately, and I'm the public relations person at D.C. 37, Vic [Gotbaum] was on the scene. He was the guy who clearly had the most and clearest vision of the problems that existed, of the extent of the problem and what it would take to rectify it and save it. The mayor never had it and was never conscious of it. He was conscious of a tremendous problem, and he was ready to throw in the towel. *The banks were doing business all the time. They were at that time getting 9¼ percent interest for their bonds and they were cracking the whip.* And nobody had the sense that you got to get all these pieces together or the whole city is going to go down—except for Victor Gotbaum. He was the one. He, on the other hand, had the sense that the unions had to work together, which also meant not only getting one voice in terms of understanding the problem and trying to defend our position but also getting the responsibility on the union side. It would have been easy for anybody to become a demagogic hero and call for strikes and such. And he had to keep that in mind and it was very difficult, extremely difficult, because you had dozens of union presidents and each one had his own members to perform for. It meant that they had to, on the one hand, have Victor as their spokesperson, which meant that they had to look in their own eyes perhaps like lesser figures to their own membership. Some of them were inexperienced and were reluctant to take that kind of role and lose their manhood, so to speak, to their members. Most of them were, I think, delighted that Victor was there, because they clearly were over their heads and they were delighted to leave it with him. Which is what happened. So our position was to maintain collective bargaining and to limit the firings. The first time, in November 1974, the ultimate solution was that we gave back to the city proportionately to the number of people in their respective unions fired, and we saved their jobs.

But only temporarily. Throughout the early months of 1975, investor confidence in the city severely eroded. In January, Mayor Beame announced the layoff of 4,050 city workers. However, union concessions saved the jobs of most of the workers who were threatened with the loss of their jobs. At this point, union strategy seemed to have stalled the austerity cutbacks designed to lower the cost of labor; actual dismissals totaled 1,941 after these months of public posturing, threatening, and cajoling. But during this time, the Financial Community Liaison Group (FCLG), representing the banking interests, was formed and began to exert severe pressure on the city to adopt a stringent austerity policy (see Chapters 5 and 6).

The financial pressures mounted, and Mayor Beame found the city in a "cash-flow" crisis, as the city had difficulty borrowing $260 million to pay its March bills. Speaking about the cash-flow problem, Edward Handman maintained that the fiscal crisis was being created by those who had an institutional interest in such a crisis; that is, the banking community. As Handman asserted:

HANDMAN: There was a cash-flow problem. The city had a cash-flow problem. One of the big ironies was that our deficit in 1974, fiscal year 1974, was not that large—[around] 5 percent. There were cities all over the country with budget deficits bigger than 5 percent. [I believe] the state of Massachusetts had a 14 percent deficit. So there was not a necessity for the kind of panic and hysteria that we had.

Regardless of the percentage of the deficit, clearly a problem was developing over the city's access to the financial markets. The question of whether access was being denied because of the actions of the city's major banks or because the city's own financial house was not in order seems less relevant here than the developing market resistance to New York's debt obligations. And in the context of the mobilization of the banking community to force on the city the policies that were, indeed, eventually adopted, one must wonder about the failure of the city's unions to develop a united stand. While the unions refused to act collectively, the financial community asserted its interests and its own definition of the crisis. The banking community was turning the screws, while resistance failed to materialize.

Later that month, in response to the bankers' suggestions, the mayor reduced the amount of projected borrowing for the remainder of the fiscal year from $3 billion to $1 billion. It was thought that this reduction would decrease the pressure on an otherwise glutted municipal securities market. Mayor Beame then blasted the critics who suggested that he had lost control of the city to the banks. " 'Nobody is going to tell me how to run the city,' said the mayor."[9]

This remark brings us to an important point. Throughout the early stage of the fiscal crisis, Mayor Beame maintained that it was not a long-term problem. He suggested then that only short-term remedies were required, and he therefore resisted any major realignment in the city's institutional arrangements. The only exception was his acceptance of the informal connection between the Financial Community Liaison Group and the city administration. The mayor's denial of the severity of the fiscal crisis and his conflict with the comptroller were seen by many as contributing factors to the acceleration of the crisis.[10] William Scott, then the assistant to Albert Shanker, revealed the conflicting points of view between Major Beame and Comptroller Goldin during an interview in December 1978:

SCOTT: There were long periods of time when the comptroller and the mayor did not see eye-to-eye. There was a political difference between the two men. I believe that Beame honestly did not believe that the notes and the bonds of the city were no longer salable. I think he honestly thought that this was—a conspiracy is too harsh a word—done by design by the banks and the financial institutions against the city, and even the federal government. I don't think that he really ever early on felt that there was no market for the city's securities. He felt that this was a false premise. And he was encouraged in this by his deputy mayor, Jimmy Cavanagh, who felt very strongly, in the choicest of languages, that the banks were anticity. Jay Goldin, on the other hand, felt that the banks were getting a very high rate of interest for the bonds that they happened to be buying just before the point in time when they wouldn't be buying any more. But I think that he even failed to realize that the market was drying up for city bonds.

Scott's assessment of the Beame administration's refusal to accept the depth of the fiscal crisis, and the exacerbating function this had on the crisis, was also Shalala's analysis. She conveyed this point during an interview in October 1978 in the following way:

SHALALA: There wasn't much that we [members of MAC] could do while the mayor was running around acting like there wasn't a real crisis. I remember sitting in Dallas when someone stood up and said "Hey, the mayor of your city says in the *New York Times* he doesn't know how many employees you have, or the mayor says that the crisis will be over shortly." It was very difficult, because the city wasn't acting as if there was a crisis and taking serious steps during the summer of 1975 for us to convince anyone that that was happening.

This confusion then, must be seen as critical to the remainder of the crisis. The strategies adopted here by the unions, the banks, and the city administration were to be repeated often with similar effect—the institutionalization of austerity. By this time, finance capital had mobilized and unified as a class and was demanding austerity as the solution to the fiscal crisis. Meanwhile, the city administration was floundering without direction and lacked a concrete awareness of the growing depth of the crisis. It was therefore unable to find alternative budgetary, taxing, or borrowing strategies to counter demands by capital for a planned and externally imposed austerity program. In this void, the city's unions lacked the unity and the class ideology, as well as the knowledge of the depth of the crisis and the peculiar characteristics of the city's finances, to oppose successfully the oncoming crisis resolution that was being developed, planned, and imposed by capital's representatives. It is within this context that we will analyze the functions, powers, and contradictory position of the city's public employee unions.

The Limitations of Public Sector Unions

We must be careful not to abstract these municipal labor unions from the structural and historical context within which they operated and developed their crisis strategies. Public employee unions do not control, nor do they have any direct influence over, the municipal securities markets that so powerfully affect city finances and from which the city desperately needed to borrow operating capital. The unions' only influence over these markets was an inverse one: the markets might have responded more favorably toward the city's notes and bonds had the unions voluntarily undertaken sacrifices in wages, benefits, and work-productivity regulations. However, this action would have been highly unpopular with both the union leadership and the city's rank-and-file workforce.

The paradox here is that the unions seem to have been caught between a crisis that was not yet so deep as to necessitate such stringent austerity and, on the other hand, the need to institute drastic worker sacrifices and to restore investor confidence, if the city was not to be completely shut out from market accessibility. In either case, the city's workers would have been victimized in the process. The power of finance capital seemed to lie in its control over much-needed operating capital. To counter this power, an alternative funding source had to be found. The implications of this process of power, deeply imbedded in capitalism itself, will be discussed in later sections of this work.

To develop a counterstrategy to the power of finance capital would have necessitated arousing public consciousness against the actions of New York City's financial and corporate class. The actions of the city's major banking institutions, documented in earlier chapters, provided a key to mobilizing class consciousness against capital's interests. The crisis resolution itself, that is, austerity, has been experienced by New York's working and poor classes as a real threat to the quality of everyday life. Yet the public was brought to believe that austerity was absolutely necessary in the form it took. Furthermore, public consciousness came to view the unions' actions as self-serving and against the interests of the community at large.

Labor was presented as the possessor of threatening greed, while capital was largely ignored. The news media daily published or aired stories which claimed that the city's workers were overpaid, overpensioned, and underworked. One need only recall the news stories in which television cameras followed public employees as they worked, recording how much time the work crews took for lunch. Ravaged by recession, inflation, and high taxes, the city's residents were easily convinced that the city's fiscal crisis was the direct result of profligate city

workers. *Nowhere was there a connection made between the struggles for
a better work life and a higher-quality community life.* The city's news
media seemed to be predominantly antiworker and continually ran
stories "exposing" the power and greed of city workers, which contributed to an antiworker, antiunion consciousness and played directly
into the hands of capital. Meanwhile, New York's major commercial
banks were "dumping" approximately $2.3 billion in city securities and
flooding the municipal securities market, thereby making it improbable
that the city could market any more debt obligations. News of this activity was not made available to the city's residents, however. Union
publicist Edward Handman described the situation in this way:

> HANDMAN: There was not a necessity for the kind of panic and
> hysteria that we had. The media, of course, played a tremendous role
> in that. And the fact that attacking the city and attacking the public
> servants was such a handy thing for everybody that it just kept
> escalating and skyrocketing. . . . It's a question of what they're saying
> in the *Times* about welfare reform—about the need to get federal help
> . . . We were saying that in 1974 and 1975 and they wouldn't even
> print it. The only time they would print it is they would say "Victor
> Gotbaum is raising a red herring about welfare reform," or something
> like that to take the pressure off.

Without control over the major disseminators of public information,
it was extremely difficult for the city's working class to mobilize effective
and informed mass opposition to austerity—even to recognize such a
need and such a possibility. Alternatives were not discussed or presented
as within the realm of the politically realistic. There was a *language of
limitations* that solidified and concretized the fiscal crisis and the absolute, nonnegotiable necessity for drastic action. One might say that the
language of crisis—"There is no money." "What else can we do but
make severe budget cuts?" "These city workers don't work, but they
have excessive salaries and pensions." "We can't afford teachers."
—came from the ideology of capital. The lack of alternative consciousness reflected, in part, this control over both the forum and the parameters of debate. The language of this fiscal crisis was capital's language,
reflecting capital's consciousness and needs. Bankers' logic defined the
parameters of discourse and served to restrict the possibility of development of a consciousness which viewed city government and city services
in terms of human needs.[11]

In the meantime, the now acquiescent unions left themselves institutionally isolated within the city's power structure. Perhaps they
recognized the fact that their opponents—the ideologues of the right
wing and those who maintained that the unions ran the city—had refused
to accept the fact that their power was greatly exaggerated. If anything,

the union givebacks—estimated by Victor Gotbaum to be approximately $643 million in the first three years of the fiscal crisis—indicated their lack of power. Edward Handman was asked about union power in the context of fiscal crisis. The conversation went like this:

LICHTEN: In May 1975, the Beame administration instituted a crisis budget—layoffs, attrition . . .

HANDMAN: Yes, 30,000 layoffs. That's the one.

LICHTEN: Yes, 31,000 layoffs actually. Plus there was a total loss, with attrition, of about 67,000 jobs and lines. The debt by this time reached about $11 billion, with about $4.5 billion in short-term notes. You then had the formation of the MAC. You indicated that for months before this your union was trying to get a message out and no one listened. What does that say about your union's power?

HANDMAN: Unions' power is so highly overrated, you see. The unions' power is on certain levels—it exists. The union has power. I'm trying to find a way to focus on it. There is a certain subjective power. There's a power when you have influence on politicians in the legislature, in the City Council, with people you helped get elected, if there's anyone else you might help get elected and they're responsive to you to a point. You have a certain amount of power in that people are afraid to take you on on certain things. Say there's an appointment and they say "gee, if you put this guy on, the unions are going to fight it." They don't even know what it means by the unions fighting you. There's power that comes from people who think that if they do something to hurt you, you're going to pull the whole city on strike. That's a simplification, and it's a stupid position, but there are variations on that. On the other hand, we don't really have power. You're giving the perfect example. I heard a guy this week on the radio, on a talk show. He calls up and they're talking about imports—imports of clothing. He calls up and asks why aren't the unions doing something about those imports. It is a total misperception and it is the same thing here. We don't hire the people who work for the city. We don't make policy for the city, and certainly with the media, in terms of power and getting information out, we are the last people they listen to.

The unions set their crisis strategy with the knowledge that they lacked the power to offset fully the mobilization of the banking community. And we cannot help but wonder how much of their powerlessness was a consequence of their unwillingness to use the power resources at their disposal. We are referring here to their control over the pension funds that would be used to rescue the city from bankruptcy. Their failure to use these pension funds to enhance union power, as well as to build antiausterity coalitions, stems from an ideology which has reinforced union weakness. Here is an example of an ideology eliminating a sense of strategic options and alternatives. The unions failed to develop their power resources, or even to use the resources they had, precisely because their ideological perspectives denied the validity and practicality of such action. Later in this chapter, we will discuss the pension funding of austerity. First, however, a few words are in order concerning the unions' priorities, given the fiscal crisis.

The unions' first priority was their own organizational survival. They determined that they must devise a strategy to ensure their organizational survival, along with the effectiveness of their main legitimation: collective bargaining. Mere survival was to be assured, even at the expense of many city workers. It should not come as a surprise to hear that collective bargaining, even during a crisis where wages and benefits were unilaterally reduced, was seen as the focal point of union strategy. Collective bargaining is, after all, the basis for union acceptance and legitimation within corporate capitalism. The bargaining process legitimates both capital-management and the union within the status quo of class exploitation.

Collective bargaining marks the existence of class exploitation and establishes the notion that all the worker deserves and gets is a "fair day's wage for a fair day's work." Therefore, the maintenance of the bargaining process, even if this process was more illusion than reality during the fiscal crisis, was deemed by the union leadership to be absolutely necessary.

Later, after the further institutionalization of austerity had weakened the unions and made the bargaining process an empty formality, Albert Shanker, President of the United Federation of Teachers and one of the most powerful of the union leaders, suggested the temporary suspension of collective bargaining. In a statement that angered the other major labor leaders in the city, Shanker said: "When there's nothing to be bargained for, it is a form of torture to send people in to bargain. Maintaining bargaining as usual in a period of the combination of want and bankruptcy is ridiculous." Shanker did not suggest opposition to austerity, nor mass resistance to the deterioration of the quality of city services due to the budget cutting, but rather the institutionalization of a labor-management control board similar to the War Labor Board that was operant during World War II. This type of board would establish a set of wage controls to monitor and regulate working-class wages, benefits, and productivity. William Scott, Shanker's assistant, explained this proposal made in November 1976:

SCOTT: Much to the dismay of all the other labor leaders in this city—they didn't think it was right—[Shanker made this proposal].

But he worked on a little different level. He is more international than most of the other labor leaders in this city, since he's the national president and since he represents the government and the A.F. of L. in many conventions around the world. And he had more exposure to a war board. I don't really think he meant what he said. I think what he meant was that to go in under the guise of collective bargaining and to merely bargain as to how you are going to reduce your contract is not bargaining at all. It might be better . . . to have a uniform limitation on all of labor in a particular situation, for a particular period of time, rather than to go in and let this fellow bargain away this and that . . . Basically, I guess when Shanker said "I don't want to bargain a contract down. Impose it on me," that he was really saying: "Don't give me the option of telling my members I'm going to take $10 away from them or ten days away from them. You impose it on me. Don't let me bargain for that." That's what he was saying. It was taken up generally by the press as meaning that he didn't want to collective bargain during the fiscal crisis. He didn't mean that at all. He meant that you impose your conditions during the time when you can prove you can't do anything else and when I decide that you now have come to the point when you can do something else, then I will bargain with you.

Shanker was recognizing that the basic strategy of the MLC—to maintain collective bargaining—was an empty one since there was no real collective bargaining during the fiscal crisis. Still, his suggestion—the imposition of restrictive and austere contracts through a superordinate labor-management board—also abdicated any opposition role that the unions might play. Shanker was calling for more union collaboration, not less. He was willing to cooperate with a preconceived and predefined reality that conformed to capital's best interests. This strategy accepted without question the legitimacy of austerity.

Still, the other labor leaders, however enraged by Shanker's proposal, were more in agreement with him than they would have cared to admit. After all, they adopted the diplomatic approach, which was also based on a perceived responsibility to a community larger than their membership or the city's working class. Before we continue to describe and analyze union strategy throughout the remaining early years of the fiscal crisis it is necessary to understand the origin of this type of labor strategy.

The municipal labor union leadership adopted strategies that accepted sacrifices without militant opposition. They eschewed any collective, mass resistance to austerity, as a threat to the security of the community at large. American labor unions, in the private as well as the public sectors of the economy, have similarly adopted a reformist ideology, which views the class interests of workers and capital as basically contiguous and not structurally contradictory. Collective bargaining allegedly functions to mediate conflicting class interests and to resolve potentially disruptive working-class activism; working-class activism is thereby channeled into constructing labor relations which will ensure productivity.

According to this ideology, capitalism provides room for workers' economic freedom. As a result, when workers take positive actions to gain more collective control of their labor and/or community, they are presented as a threat to the community at large and must do so without union support. Here, stability is defined as manageable class relations within a general status quo which legitimates and helps preserve capitalist social relations: equilibrium is control; fiscal health is a deteriorating wage and service network; a healthy economy is a high rate of profit and management firmly in control.

Simply put, the interests of capital are viewed as sustenance for the community at large; while the interests of workers, when expressed independently of the union hierarchy, are viewed as disruptive and chaotic. The interests of unions become identified with stability even when the consequences of this stability cause suffering for the working class. Yet this interest is not expressed in equal partnership with capital. In fact, the basis for this partnership is union acquiescence to capital's power to organize and control production in the private sector and, in the public sector, to organize and reorganize the mediating functions of local government.

As this ideology takes shape, it makes sense for the cause of the fiscal crisis not to be viewed as contained within the contradictory social relations of the labor process, but rather as being the self-serving and community-threatening activity of labor. The unions, then, must serve the community by denying workers. Yet, by doing so, the union denies the autonomy of the working class, thereby relegating the community to capital's own. Cooperation within such a "community" works against a potentially autonomous workers' "community."

The unions' reformist ideology of responsibility, so socially and politically conservative in its repercussions, finds further expression and influence when the workers labor and struggle in the public sector. Actions in opposition to management by public sector workers are seen as threatening to the public, the community. Capital seems not to enter into the conflict except as victim: the flow of labor to business may be disrupted, or the circulation of capital may be stalled. Then, capital may move out of the community to find labor peace, leading a public cry of "If only the workers were less disruptive and more cooperative and sympathetic to business needs," or "If only government paid attention to the needs of business!"

In such a labor dispute in the public sector, management is pictured as representing the public interest—after all, government is class neutral and protects the needs of the unity of the community, itself class neutral. An independent and autonomous working-class consciousness seems less critical, since it is accepted that capital's exploitation does not exist. This absence of working-class unity, as indicated by the ideological separation of public and private, isolates the public sector worker. The public employee union then finds its interests best served in collaboration with city management and corporate capital. But in this case, that of the fiscal crisis of New York City, this collaboration enabled capital to deny the city the necessary operating funds to resist budgetary cutbacks and, in the long run, austerity.

> In failing to develop an independent ideological stance of its own, organized labor in America has remained a reactive movement, always more or less captive but certainly never an equal partner of private capital.
> The same pattern holds true in the relationship between private capital and governing institutions. Again it is private capital that makes the important decisions regarding economic growth, planning, and allocation of resources and jobs. Like organized labor, local and state governments have also become captive partners, accepting the notion that what's good for business is good for the community. Moriarty of the Congressional Coalition put his finger right on the problem when he remarked that "given the nature of the capitalist system, you have to count on them all the time to carry the major load." The role of local and state governments in this partnership has always been to accommodate to the needs of private capital, and on occasion to act as a mediator between its abuses and excesses and the reactions of an angry public. [12]

In this crisis, however, there was no effective voice representing an angry public against the excesses and abuses of finance capital. Without such active opposition, capital was able to press its demands for austerity. The public employee unions meanwhile continued to act reactively and defensively, thereby abdicating the state to those who demanded worker sacrifice. In the following pages, we shall see how this union strategy, measured by its powerlessness, impacted upon the remainder of the fiscal crisis.

Pension Funding Austerity

As the fiscal crisis deepened throughout 1975, the threat of *skirmishes* with bankruptcy grew. In this milieu of fiscal and political uncertainty, the mechanisms of social control over the city's labor unions were becoming more pervasive and powerful. The key to comprehending the constraints on union activism was the adoption of the strategy to invest public employee pension funds in city and MAC bonds. This section will elaborate the process by which these pension funds were committed to save the city from bankruptcy even while the austerity policy was imposed on the city's labor unions.

In my view, the strategies adopted by the unions during this time actually contributed to the construction of an antilabor austerity. Previously, we saw the unions adopt a no-strike strategy of cooperation. Now, in this case, they used pension monies to establish a financial foundation for austerity. This action gave the city time to reorganize its finances and managerial policies and, in so doing, to restore investor confidence. The following pages will confront this issue—the connection between pension funds, bankruptcy, and austerity—since it is fundamental to our topic: class struggle and fiscal crisis.

There were not many public or private sector leaders in support of a city bankruptcy. The city's government, its unions, and its banking and corporate elite all wanted to devise an alternative to bankruptcy. The banks, we have seen, could not afford bankruptcy while they still held a large amount of city securities. As the fiscal crisis grew more serious and their investments less secure, the commercial and investment banks shifted their investments. While their investment activity focused elsewhere, the banks demanded a stringent austerity policy for the city, under the rationale that investment would not return otherwise.

It is important to note that the power of finance capital, as represented by New York City's major banks, was realized while *disinvestment* in New York was proceeding. Finance capital was leaving the city because of the city's bad investment status, while the major banks tried to reorganize the basis of power within the city in order to protect the investments they still had there. *A new class politics was emerging,* and the city's labor unions seemed ill prepared for it. This new class politics necessitated nothing short of the reorganization of city government: reestablishing managerial authority and reducing labor costs, as well as reducing the costs of services to the city's poor, working-, and middle-class communities, all of which were dependent on city services. In this new class politics, corporate and finance capital increased their power in relation to labor by withdrawing finance and productive capital. We might suggest that this withdrawal left a political vacuum for the exertion of labor's power. Where, then, was labor?

The withdrawal of credit from the city (discussed in Chapters 5 and 6) created a need for an alternative source of operating capital. One might suggest that this source had the potential to exert enormous power over the policy of city government. The source of these new-found funds turned out to be the city's labor unions. And in the context of fiscal crisis, the unions wound up funding, underwriting, and investing in their own austerity. Let us first describe how it was that the pension funds were tapped for their investment capital and, then, why it was that the union leadership was not able to halt austerity. In the context of the ebb and flow of class struggle, we shall see that this process was closely tied to the possibility of bankruptcy and the potential uncertainty that such bankruptcy would bring to the city's unions.

First let us review the previously stated position regarding the formulation of union strategy. From the beginning of the fiscal crisis, the municipal unions felt it necessary to adopt a "pragmatic" approach. This pragmatism accepted the fact that the fiscal crisis was real and severe and, therefore, that cutbacks in city expenditures were necessary, even at the expense of the city's workers.[13] As Al Viani of D.C. 37 asserted, when interviewed in August 1978, the unions were willing to make what they deemed to be necessary sacrifices:

> VIANI: . . . because those sacrifices had to be made. There was no getting away from it. The crisis was real, the billion dollar gap was there, everybody knew it and we had to deal with that. Now one could say that if the unions were strong there would have been no sacrifices and no cutbacks. But that was impossible. I mean it would either have been made up with layoffs or, if there were no sacrifices on the wages, or no deferral of wages, or anything of that sort, then it would have been made up in layoffs or dismantling of various agencies or whatever. That had to be dealt with, and from the unions' point of view in the most pragmatic kind of way. And that was to get out of what was admittedly a very severe crisis the best way we possibly could without any long-term erosion of either the basic salary structure or the basic fringe structure.

It is interesting to note that "pragmatism" had already been defined as cooperation with an antilabor austerity. As Viani and other labor leaders asserted, there was a real crisis, which inhibited labor's response. Yet it appears in their depiction of the strategy-making process that alternative strategies to cooperation with austerity—more militancy, demanding more labor input into decision-making, influence over managing services—were hastily set aside to demonstrate labor's responsibility to the "public." The separation of workers from the control of the labor process was strengthened, as management was given more control by labor without a fight. And as the crisis progressed, labor's "pragmatic," "cooperative," and "responsible" strategy was used against the city's workers to develop a formal mechanism of institutional control. We have seen that labor's responsiveness to the depths of the crisis was used against labor. In a sense, therein lies the ideological and political weakness of labor. In terms of the prevailing ideology, union militancy and demands for more workers' control might have been viewed as antipublic and anticity. Meanwhile, the banks' responsibility was to protect their investors' money. This definition allowed finance capital, as represented by the bankers and financiers now mobilized to promote austerity, to legitimize the withdrawal of credit to the city.

The fate of municipal labor was therefore tied to the city, while finance capital knew no such political or financial boundaries. Al Viani pointed to this basic social relation between labor and the community when he stated that:

> VIANI: Our considerations [like the banks] are also bottom line, but our approach is quite different. Our basic responsibility was to protect the workers to the maximum extent that we could. That is our constituency and our responsibility. But we do have a social conscience and we are concerned about the city as a city. But our primary goal was to protect the worker. And we made the judgment that it would be in the best interests of the workers ultimately if the city survived and if the city made it through the crisis. That was being truly honest in terms of what was best for the people that we represented. And so the goals of the employees and the goals of the city, in terms of survival, were just not divergent. They were the same, and once we made that decision then we decided how we would go about it—to help save the city and not clobber the employees to the extent that they have a long-term impact. And we did what we had to do. The banks, on the other hand, their constituency is quite different. The bottom line is the motto that they live by; that is, make money and protect your money. They didn't do anything for any social reasons. Corporations respond to only one thing: make as much money as they can. And the banks are exactly the same. They have no social responsibility, I don't believe, no social conscience. And their goal was to protect their investors and that was it. There is nothing more to it. They weren't going to be so bleeding heart that they would care about the city of New York. They were only going to care about their big bucks.

Within this relationship—that of labor to community and finance capital to capital gain—was the potential for and limitation of class power. The labor leaders only recognized the social-control side of this social relation. The potential for alternatives, for social change involving a labor-community coalition and unity, went unrecognized and, perhaps, feared. Viani described the uncertainty of this moment in the following way:

> VIANI: The point I have been making was that we were dealing with an entirely unknown situation, and we were feeling our way along. We didn't know . . . in retrospect one could argue with the unions' posture at various stages along the way. But it was a very delicate and

dangerous kind of situation. The city was going in over a short period of time, two or three months, for over $6 billion in financing—$6 billion that particular year, as I recall. We're at the end of fiscal year 1975 and the beginning of the new fiscal year. [Note: from June through September 1975 the city needed $3 billion. Viani is here referring to the period before June and after September.] There was some huge amount of money that was required. Actually, I thought it was $6 billion. It was a totally unknown situation—bond markets, bankers, and all that shit. The unions did not know anything about this.

This lack of knowledge led the unions to hire Jack Bigel as a financial and strategic consultant. Bigel was not tied to any rank-and-file constituency. Again, Viani:

VIANI: A few people like Jack Bigel understood it probably better than most people did, or at least had sources of information that would give him an advance warning of what the potential problems were. Basically, Bigel is a power broker. There is no other way to call such a person in this city. He has contacts in all kinds of places and in different areas and basically was the right man at this particular time. He had these lines into the financial community, as well as the city and the unions. He could serve as our focal point for a lot of the stuff that was coming on in terms of guiding the unions as to how to deal with these things. Or at least he could alert the unions to the magnitude of the problem and what the banks were saying—what the mayor was saying—and what the realities of the situation were. Everybody tried to figure a way to deal with it . . . The dumping of notes by the banks—nobody was aware of that. There were people who were arguing internally that this union, D.C. 37, should, when the threat of bankruptcy came in the late Spring and early June of 1975, say to the mayor, to the federal government and the state and the business community, fuck you—let the city go bankrupt. You don't want to open up the market, sorry, I am going to let the whole thing go down. This would have been such a horrible threat that nobody would have allowed it to happen and they would have come up with cash right away to prevent it from happening. We didn't do that; the mayor—he didn't do that, and first there was the Municipal Assistance Corporation, then the Emergency Financial Control Board *and all the power was openly taken away.* [Emphasis added.]

The unions, as has been shown, discussed more militant alternatives within a context of uncertainty about the consequences of such actions. However, regardless of actions taken against the rank and file, the union leaders returned to a strategy guided by conservative notions of pragmatism and responsibility. These notions amidst a deepening crisis led to a policy of investing pension funds in city and MAC debt obligations.

The unions were being trapped by their own ideology and by a crisis they did not control and had not, they felt, produced. All the while, layers of control were being imposed upon them. Their own trade union philosophy had been transplanted from private sector unionism. While it was often militant, it was always reformist, and that inhibited the development of concrete alternatives to cooperation with austerity. The union leaders feared a general strike and the consequences it might bring. Remarkably, they seemed to fear that more than they feared the worker layoffs and reduced wages and benefits that an austere budget would bring. As Edward Handman stated during December 1978: "There was never—let me say this point blank—a serious possibility of a general strike during those years." A general strike might produce bankruptcy and lead to judicial intervention, which might in turn cause the unions to lose the little control that they had over the situation, or so they felt. As Al Viani stated:

VIANI: What our approach essentially was from the very beginning was that we didn't want unilateralism. We recognize the severity of the problem. What is done, we want it done as a result of negotiations with the union. We don't want anything imposed upon us. We would cooperate, because that was the only way that we could get some measure of control as to what was really going to happen. Had we taken a very hard line, bankruptcy would have given control to somebody else. There might have been legislation that took control from us. So tactfully, we said we could take a hard line and maybe look good with the troops initially, in the short run. In the long run, if we don't have any say with what happens then we will really be out of the picture and they'll really just run right over us.

It was this fear of losing what little power they had that guided union strategy. They feared the loss of control and the unpredictability that a bankruptcy would entail. If labor relations is anything at all in this country, it is usually predictable, with both labor and management seeking routinization and collaboration. Bankruptcy would destroy that balance. One might suggest that the fiscal crisis had already accomplished that—to the detriment of both the city's unions and its workers. The labor leaders clinged to the hope that the labor relations of precrisis New York City would soon return. That would be impossible, they suggested, if the city went bankrupt.

William Scott expressed the unions' fear of bankruptcy and the uncertainty it would bring. Here, in this description, is revealed the underlying source of the union leaders' willingness to go along with austerity and, indeed, to fund it and the city by committing union pension funds to invest in city debt obligations. As Scott maintained, a city bankruptcy was very possible if the city's unions had refused to cooperate with austerity.

> SCOTT: [Bankruptcy] would have meant the abrogation of all contracts, including pension contracts. The people who had already retired would have had no protection. That those who were eligible for retirement would have had no protection. That the money that we had all contributed to pension funds in the city would, if not disappear, become an asset of the city and therefore be attachable by creditors. It would have been realigned by some federal judge who would reduce pensions or do whatever he felt was needed to be done because the contract and the constitutional protection would no longer be there. That was a fear. It was not necessarily a reality, but nobody wanted to test that. What would it have meant for the city? . . . It served nobody's purpose to put it into bankruptcy, because all you would do was reorganize it so that in a future time you could pay off the bondholder. If you kept it out of bankruptcy, by whatever measures you had to take, you were doing the same thing and you were leaving some sort of a reality in the city, and not a chaotic city. There were some people who saw bankruptcy as a method of doing things. Some banks thought of bankruptcy as a guaranteed payoff to their customers. . . . The *Wall Street Journal* looks for it as a way to break unions.

Yet, staring bankruptcy in the face led the unions into a position of weakness, while the banking community assumed a position of strength and power. It is instructive to look at a turning point of the crisis, in the summer of 1975, when the power of the banks to shape the crisis resolution process became overwhelming for the city and the unions. Edward Handman is quoted in depth, from the transcript of an interview with him. Handman was asked if, indeed, the whole crux of the power relations at this time was the union being forced to invest in the city. He responded:

> HANDMAN: Our power in this came from the threat of bankruptcy and the threat of chaos, and the threat that ultimately—the reason that everybody finally got to May '75 and the mayor's crisis budget-austerity announcement. . . . We were in the mayor's office, and to me this was the turning point of the whole crisis. The unions were meeting with the mayor, and the mayor said "I got to do what the banks want." He just threw up his hands, he was exhausted, he was demoralized. He was two hundred fathoms over his head . . . "They want 30,000 firings . . . or else we go into bankruptcy." Nobody knew. Nobody knows to this day, but, at that time, *certainly* nobody knew. And he stated that we are talking about bankruptcy. And all of

a sudden Victor [Gotbaum] said "Look ," and he practically got him by the throat verbally and he said: "Look, you get the fucking banks in here. You get the MAC people in here. You get the state in here. You get the business people in here. You get all the unions and we'll all sit down and start working on this fucking thing here or else we'll all go down together." That's power. What you're saying is you're not going to fire 30,000 people and expect 270,000 to stand idly by. Then you're talking about us doing something. And with that then he said: "Then all us pigs will be equal." You know, we'll all go down together.

The unions' decision to invest pension monies was not a decision made from strength, however. The unions feared bankruptcy, and because of that fear they also feared their rank and file's militancy. And so, with the city facing bankruptcy and the political uncertainty this would bring, the source of operating funds became the city's unions. Pension funds would be diverted from other investments into city and MAC bonds and notes. The unions had two choices as they saw it: to commit pension funds or to live with bankruptcy. The union leaders knew that, in Edward Handman's words,

HANDMAN: In any given crisis, we had the ability to dump it. We could sink the city. We could refuse to lend the money. We could throw a general strike, which would really kill the credit. So this was a tremendous negative power. We also had the intelligence and knowledge that we can't use it, this power. Because the most and earliest victims would be our members. Our pension system would go down the drain. Thousands of more jobs would be lost. And the city, our members live in this city, anything that happens in this city would happen to our members. So that we had this awesome power, but we really couldn't use it. So the line we were always walking was to try to use it, whatever strength we had to improve a lousy situation. You're constantly fighting a losing battle. You knew that the payroll had to be cut. You knew that the budget was in deficit. So you were just trying to minimize the suffering and to that we did some very successful things.

Of interest now is *how* the union leadership arrived at the decision to use their pension funds. There are two versions of the making of this commitment. One version—the one that makes the most sense, given the history of the crisis and the relative position of the unions at the time—was offered by William Scott in December 1978, as follows:

SCOTT: Well, let me put this into perspective. Remember now, at the time we're talking about I was on the other side, working for the comptroller. I was the seller of these bonds to the pension systems. At that time, the unions in New York City were, to say the least, not friendly toward each other. Gotbaum and Shanker didn't agree at all. In 1975, however, there was a requirement that the city had to get money out of the pension funds. And not Gotbaum, nor Shanker, nor any other union leader developed a plan of using the pension funds. The fellow who developed that plan was a fellow named Steve Clifford, who was a deputy to the city comptroller. And he worked out what you understand today to be the financing system. And he showed it to the comptroller, and I met with the comptroller in his apartment for breakfast on a Saturday morning with Felix Rohatyn and George Gould [a director of the MAC and President and Chief Executive Officer of the Madison Fund. Until 1976 he was also Vice Chairman of the Board of Directors of Donaldson, Lufkin, and Jenerette Securities Corporation, and a Director of First National Stores, and of International Controls Corporation.] And the plan was presented to them that morning. And it showed how each month's capital needs were going to be met, the expense budget, all the rest was laid out and it required that each month so much money was to be coming from the pension funds. The plan also expected that the federal government would participate, as they did later in the seasonal loans. *And that was all presented and so it was all worked out entirely without the unions.* The unions did not enter into it. The newspapers were both pro and con. There were learned newspapers that opposed the whole idea of using pension money to support city government. This business of buying the employer's securities, which is prohibited under ERISA, was the same effect as the unions buying city securities. We met with the pension funds jointly and some of them acquiesced to buy them because they didn't really understand the problem. Others agreed to buy them, and Gotbaum was in this predicament because he did understand the problem—so he agreed to buy them. But there was a difference. Gotbaum himself was a trustee of the retirement system, as was Feinstein [Teamsters], as was John DeLury [Sanitation]. They, as trustees, said I will vote for it. They could do that. Shanker, however, is not a trustee of the pension system. In the teachers' system there are elected members. And they said "no soap."

The sequence of events that finally resulted in the UFT's retirement trustees committing their funds to the city will be discussed later. First, it is necessary to put forward the other version of the process by which these funds were committed. This version is offered by Edward Handman of District Council 37. It should be remembered that the unions had already set a precedent for investment when they loaned the city money to rehire laid-off workers as late as July 1975. At this time, the city was prepared and actually did lay off, on June 30, 19,000 workers, including 5,000 police and 2,000 firefighters. As Seymour Mann, also of District Council 37, and Edward Handman described it:

This brought immediate response in the streets. Over the next few days, sanitation began a wildcat strike; 500 police staged a rush-hour demonstration at the City Hall end of the Brooklyn Bridge; firemen began a call-in-sick program; and a wildcat strike of highway workers tied up traffic on the Henry Hudson Parkway.[14]

This response led to a financing package with funding from new city taxing power and contributions from the city's unions. "Within two days, 2,000 laid-off policemen and 750 laid-off firemen were returned to work as were all laid-off sanitationmen."[15] The precedent of union money funding city jobs was set. Still, this money was used directly for saving jobs. Pension funds, on the other hand, would not be used for those direct purposes. Lastly, the union leaders seemed to have lost the message: worker militancy had the potential to change the course of the crisis.

Mann and Handman go on to describe the strategy concerning union pension funds allegedly first offered by Victor Gotbaum.

> Indicative of one view of the new role of unions, Victor Gotbaum . . . put forth the notion to defer wage increases to save jobs and also offered a plan for the unions to buy two-year city bonds at lower interest than the city was paying on the market, with the savings to be used for rehiring. This plan was received cooly by the other unions and MAC.[16]

Yet, with brief reprieves from bankruptcy foreshadowing future disaster, the city needed to achieve financial security. The union pension funds, along with the federal assistance program in the form of seasonal loans and with state and MAC funds, became the basis for avoiding a formal declaration of bankruptcy. By October 1, 1975, the pension funds had invested nearly $1 billion in MAC, city, and city-related securities. A partial list of pension fund investments committed during this stage of the fiscal crisis include: August 1975—$150 million; September 1975—$100 million in MAC bonds; again, September 1975—$41.5 million in MAC bonds; October 1975—another $150 million in MAC bonds; all of these totaling $441.5 million. Despite this investment, however, there were still some anxious moments over the next few months, when the city would once again face the threat of bankruptcy. With each threat came pressure to further commit pension monies both to ward off bankruptcy and to reduce the degree of austerity. By October 1, 1975, the city's fiscal situation was so bleak that it tried to secure a "crisis loan" from the city's unions. Evelyn Seinfeld, the research librarian of the Department of Research and Negotiations of District Council 37, summarized the situation this way:

> City urged to tap its pension funds for a crisis loan of up to $4 billion. But trustees for portfolios of public employees are cool to proposal.

Simultaneously word spread that bankers have told fiscal aides that the State's ability to borrow money on its own behalf—backed by its heretofore unquestioned full faith and credit—is now in serious doubt. Trustees of City pensions are wary of more City bonds, asserting that they have already $1 billion invested in MAC, City and City related securities and further loans might raise questions about their fiduciary responsibilities and might also force the funds to either borrow money or sell other securities now in their portfolios at a loss. [17]

This, then, was the city's financial status when, on October 16, 1975, the city's Teacher Retirement System was asked to invest $150 million in MAC bonds. As previously described by William Scott, the trustees answered this request with an adamant "no soap." As this scenario was being acted out, Mayor Beame announced a three-year rescue plan,

> which the unions attacked for its continued wholesale firings and for ending collective bargaining. Barry Feinstein, of [Teamster]Local 237, publicly called for a general strike, but it was apparent that the idea was not acceptable to other unions. A last minute purchase of $150 million in bonds by the Teacher's Pension Fund averted default on October 17, and the city was given two months before the next default deadline in December. [18]

Actually, this commitment was not so easily procured, and the manner in which it was procured demonstrates the enormous pressure under which the trustees made their decision. The hidden story, the one not publicly disclosed, has been told by William Scott. His version gives us a much clearer perception both of the "public" pressure brought to bear on the unions (and, by implication, *not* brought to bear on the banks) and of the lack of unity among the unions. According to Scott:

> Scott: They, the trustees, said "no soap." We have a personal liability here. We have a prudent man law that we can be held responsible for. And we're not going to do it. I met with that board. And we finally met up in the governor's office and we sat there all day and we went home at 6 o'clock. And then Shanker had been called in. But Shanker was not called in to agree to that investment. He was called in to convince his members to agree to it. Needless to say, he had a healthy influence on them. In a subsequent legal action the question was raised—the retirement board was sued and one of the questions that the federal judge insisted on having an answer to in affidavits was if Shanker ever talked to the teacher members [the trustees] before that meeting as to whether they should or should not buy those securities. And under an affidavit he said that no, he did not, and that they did not talk to him. Did they talk to him that morning? Yes, after

he had been called in by the governor and put with Dick Ravitch [land-lord, one-time chairman of the Urban Development Corporation, developer, and former chairman of the Metropolitan Transit Authority] and the governor, and in Ravitch's apartment he agreed then that even though he said that he is invading a personal responsibility that these people have, he would go down to talk to them. And he did that. Down in the governor's office. And they did come out of that. And then they sent for Felix Rohatyn and George Gould, and they got letters from them that they would never ask the retirement board to buy any more. And there were conditions that had to be met, among them a law that had to be passed in Albany before they would buy it. All of this was negotiated not with Shanker, but they negotiated this with Rohatyn and Gould.

The split within labor's ranks was most evident over this issue. While the trustees of the Teacher Retirement System resisted the $150 million investment, Victor Gotbaum quietly made it known that his union, by itself or with others, would supply the additional investment if the teachers refused to commit. We had here the case of one union leader undercutting the trustees of another union pension fund. This represented in extreme form the total lack of labor unity, without which opposition to austerity, and to the banks, was futile. Scott continued to make the coercion clear:

SCOTT: So at this time there was a question as to whether the Teacher's Retirement Board would buy or not. And it was at this point that Gotbaum's crew came forward and said if they don't buy we will buy their share at this reduced rate of interest. So it wasn't an offer to come in and buy the whole bundle at a reduced share or rate. It was an offer to come in and fill up a slack if the Teacher's Retirement Board did not vote to buy. However, they did vote it . . . All Shanker did was—together with the governor—to lean on the trustees. And the governor leaned just as heavy. Why do you think it was held in his office? It was held in his office to intimidate the trustees. Otherwise they would have had it in their own office.

The buckling under to pressure by the Teacher's Retirement Board trustees followed the last major attempt at opposing the use of pension monies to fund and underwrite the city. In late November, the city once again averted formal default and bankruptcy when the city's unions and banks agreed to renegotiate the city debt that they held; the union pension funds also agreed to an added $2.5 million investment. The financial plan arrived at allowed the city some breathing room over the length of the three-year austerity plan. The plan reached fruition on November 26, 1975, and included: new taxing authority for the city, estimated at $500 million over three years; a deferral to 1986 by both the banks and pension funds of $819,220,000 of city notes at a reduced interest rate of 6 percent; a restructuring of $1,808,323,000 of MAC bonds held by banks, pension funds, and sinking funds to save the MAC and the city $573 million of interest; and the $2.5 billion investment by the union pension funds in new long-term city bonds.

> Through June 30, 1976, $500 million had been invested by the pension funds. In addition, the pension funds agreed to reinvest in City bonds $500 to $600 million of these newly purchased bonds which were expected to mature in the second and third years of the plan period. [19]

With this package intact, President Ford approved the New York City Federal Seasonal Financing Act of 1975. The act made short-term loans of $1.3 billion, $2.3 billion, and $2.3 billion available to the city for fiscal years 1976, 1977, and 1978, respectively. This federal loan program, was not approved, however, until the city's unions had buckled under and had shown that they would not oppose the three-year austerity program. Not only would they not oppose it, we might even say that they were now integrated within it, as a major source of investment capital. They were not quite the city's bankers, for they did not have the power that accompanied that class position. But their fate was clearly now enmeshed in the financial structure of the city. On April 13, 1977, Victor Gotbaum appeared on WCBS-TV's "Newsmakers," an interview show. He was asked if the city's unions were now its bankers, given the fact that they had invested nearly $3.7 billion since the fiscal crisis. Gotbaum answered:

> GOTBAUM: Absolutely . . . I don't like to use the words—bankers. Let us say that the workers have put their future livelihoods on the line. I think we ought to put it that way, because I'm tired of being called a banker after meeting those clowns. . . . The alternative would be [instead of investing] laughing all the way to the graveyard. When you realize, when you think of what default would mean to the city, and mean to the people I represent, this was what we had to do. As it makes for a paradox, a difficulty, I don't deny it. But we got to face up to it.

Given the investments, so large and so socially profound, labor conflict might now endanger labor's pension funds and therefore the pensioners' future. Without being active participants in the reorganization of city government (for the unions were not primary or influential participants within the MAC or the EFCB or, for that matter, in the everyday managing of city services), the unions had effectively been limited in their future political options. Newfield and DuBrul summarize this point, as it relates to Victor Gotbaum and District Council 37.

> Yet in the wake of the fiscal compromises worked out by MAC and the EFCB, Gotbaum is in the unenviable position of being not only New York City's major labor leader but its biggest creditor as well. And public-employee pension funds are likely to go on being the city's fiscal crutch for at least a decade. To protect his billions in city paper, Gotbaum will continue to be asked to sacrifice his members. He walks a narrow line: a misstep in one direction means endangering the pensions; a wrong step in the other direction means new layoffs. In the event, Gotbaum has become frozen, a captive of the business elite running New York City and now effectively running his union. [20]

The extent to which the union pension funds bankrolled the city is revealed in Table 7.1, which shows the holdings of city and MAC debt as of December 31, 1977. The table has been adapted to show the percentage that each institutional investor held of the total city and MAC debt outstanding as of that date.

We can see from these data that the single major institutional creditor was the city's union pension funds, as they were responsible for holding 21 percent of the total outstanding debt. And by June of 1978, the unions' total was scheduled to increase to $3.8 billion in city and MAC securities—representing approximately 38 percent of union assets.

Table 7.1: Holdings of City and MAC Debt, December 31, 1977 ($ in Millions)

Holder	City	Mac	Total	Percent of Total
City Pension Funds	$2,111	$ 886	$2,997	21%
State Pension Funds	0	0	0	0
NY Clearinghouse Association Banks	328	1,662	1,990	14
NY State Commercial Banks	115	33	148	1
US Commercial Banks	111	12	123	1
Savings and Loan Associations	86	68	154	1
US Treasury	1,875	0	1,875	13
Other Investors	4,580	2,497	7,077	49
Total	$9,206	$5,158	$14,364	100

SOURCES: Offices of the City and State Comptrollers; adapted from the *Fiscal Observer*, the New School for Social Research, 15 June, 1978, p.7.

The contrast between the unions' commitment to invest and the commercial banks' commitment to disinvest, is a glaring one. Ken Auletta has provided us with data compiled by Senator William Proxmire, Senatorial overseer of the federal rescue plan.

Senator Proxmire revealed . . . reason to celebrate: the assets of the largest city banks jumped by 23.5 percent between September 30, 1975, and September 30, 1977. Yet their holdings of city and MAC securities dropped 3.4 percent. By the Spring of 1978, the six major banks had less than 1 percent of their assets tied up in city paper, compared to a scheduled 38 percent by the city's pension funds. If the banks simply returned to their 1975 level of investment . . . this would net New York City about $2.3 billion in long-term financing over the next four years.[21]

The unions invested, the banks disinvested. The six major New York banks—Citibank, Chase, Morgan, Bankers Trust, Manufacturers, and Chemical—had approximately 70 percent of the total assets of this country's eight largest banks. From 1975 to 1977, these banks reduced their holdings of New York City and MAC debt from $1,735 million to $1,676 million. The city's union pension funds, in contrast, increased their holdings of this same debt from approximately $1,002 million to $2,943 million, representing from 8 percent to 21 percent of all MAC and city debt. The May 4, 1978, issue of the *Fiscal Observer* summarized the data in this way:

> The city pension funds and major banks in the city are *local* resources, but they are not *city* resources. The city cannot force them to lend their capital. The city has to negotiate for it.
> In 1975, the six banks' holdings of city and MAC debt represented 0.92% of their $188 billion in assets . . . Two years later, their holdings amounted to 0.72% of their $232 billion in assets. In contrast, the city pension funds had 13% of their $7.5 billion in assets in city and MAC debt in 1975 but 32% of $9.3 billion in assets in 1977. The city pension funds—whose assets equal 4% of those of the six banks—now hold nearly twice as much city and MAC debt as do the six banks.[22]

The banks had begun their disinvestment well before the creation of the MAC. With the MAC, and with the threat of bankruptcy, the unions did indeed become the city's bankers—but without power. The austerity plans went ahead full force. Between January 1975 and May 1976, the city cut its payroll by about 15 percent. Because seniority was used to select the workers to be laid off, minorities were disproportionately affected. In the city's schools, the proportion of black and hispanic teachers dropped from approximately 11 percent to 3 percent. As a result of the budget cuts, the city lost nearly half of its hispanic workers, approximately 35 percent of its black workers. Past discrimination in hiring meant that minority workers were more likely to face the prospect of unemployment.[23]

Despite the uneven suffering—workers were laid off, the unions lost power, work rules were changed, women and low-income families lost day-care centers, mass-transit-dependent New Yorkers found themselves paying higher fares for deteriorating service, city dwellers found fewer policemen and firefighters available, and the streets grew dirtier, turning "Fun City"into "Dirt City"—Felix Rohatyn would later claim that all New Yorkers pitched in and did their part to save the city from default. Not quite true—some suffered, some disinvested, and Mr. Rohatyn found himself national fame. He would later tell David Susskind and those television viewers who were tuned in:

> ROHATYN: We raised through the MAC and the city directly, and the city's pension systems, etc., from 1975 to date [1984] about $12 billion in all in various forms. . . . We at the MAC made it a condition before we invested our money. . . . All of these investments were conditioned on other people doing their thing. They were conditioned on the city's unions freezing their wages, agreeing to lower levels of workforce, changes in work rules which would help us balance our budget. They were conditioned on the city and the state doing certain things. On the state assuming some of the costs of our higher education programs; on the city charging tuition at the City University of New York . . . the University used to be free. On the Transit Authority raising the cost of fares, in order to lower the deficit of our transit system; on the banks lowering the interest rate and extending the maturity of the bonds they were buying. So all of these pieces were conditioned on each other, and they all worked to solve this problem, to balance our budget and refinance our debt.

Nevertheless, the suffering was not equal. The unions' choice to invest in New York City restricted their future options. The choice had been made with only two options seen as politically realistic: pension fund investment or city bankruptcy. Given their outlook and political weakness, the unions chose the former. In this choice, we can see the decline of the unions' political influence; public policy, in the form of austerity, could now be instituted with the unions' full cooperation. A new class politics had been formed to the disadvantage of the city's unions and working class. At that moment of class struggle, the limitations of public sector unionism outweighed the possibilities for power that were dramatized by the militant 1960s.

Class Struggle and Corporate Unionism

Up to this point we have been concerned with describing and analyzing the city's unions as a political force. In relation to the city's power structure, we have seen the unions' impotence during the fiscal crisis, just as we had seen earlier how these very same unions had grown and gained influence prior to the fiscal crisis.

This loss of political muscle demonstrates the historical phases of class struggle that these unions passed through. First, the organizing phase, during which the city's public sector unions gained organizational and legal legitimacy. Second, the militant phase, during which these young unions gained political influence through class conflict and as a consequence of their organizational response to worker militancy. Third, the seizing of control over union influence by capital and management. This third phase occurred through an austerity policy which functioned to render the unions powerless and passive vis-a-vis management's program of "fiscal restraint." We saw that this last phase necessitated a superordinate policy body, which isolated the unions from influencing the institutionalization of austerity. This isolation, achieved through the MAC and the EFCB, eroded the unions' strength, even as it encouraged union participation in financing the city. Such participation, we saw, was based upon political weakness and, once accomplished, precluded union opposition to the city's austerity policy.

Now let us move the argument away from the political question to a more general concern. The unions represent not only a political development, exerting political influence, but also and more importantly, the social development of a class. This is clear when we consider the union as an institutional consequence of a social movement arising from and within class antagonism.

The dialectic of class society separates union from worker, public from private, and capital from society. Each of these social relations—union, public, and capital—becomes alien and hostile to the construction of an autonomous working class as class antagonism is concretely institutionalized. Its institutionalization becomes its mediation—and this serves to regulate, control, and channel worker insurgency into nonthreatening forms of struggle. As class conflict becomes routinized, alternatives to capitalism are denied. It is at this moment that unionism becomes a vehicle of control.

This holds true for public sector as well as private sector unions. These become mechanisms to channel worker insurgency away from challenges to corporatism, which are then deemed impractical. Since worker autonomy is viewed in this way, labor conflict during crisis is seen by labor leaders as irresponsible. Furthermore, the union aims to be responsible to a "community," which is, in the last instance, a corporate community. And this corporate community lives by the cold, calculating rationality of the bottom line. The bottom line, then, becomes responsible for the "difficult" decisions made during crisis.

The separation between the union and the worker results from a class relation between capital and labor. The union arises from a labor process which creates and is created by a working class and a capitalist class—defining each other in opposition. We can view the city's policies as a result of this class opposition. As the city expanded its service network during the 1960s and early 1970s to still the activism of its poor and its working class, it provided a glue to hold together, however temporarily, a city that was vitally important to capital. *The social relation then was not a fiscal one, despite analyses to the contrary, but one of class.*

We have viewed the city government and its policies as constituting *both a mediating product and a process* moving between the antagonistic needs of management and labor, capital and community. As the process of struggle continued, city expenditures increased to meet the demands of the then militant labor unions. To some, it appeared that these unions controlled city government; that is, that they exerted direct power over decision-making and city policy. However, the fiscal crisis and its resolution dispelled this appearance of control.

We saw that power was not held by these unions; in a sense, it was borrowed in much the same way that operating capital was borrowed from finance capital. It was power borrowed through struggle and returned when capital was able to turn the struggle in its favor. It is still, after all, a capitalist society.

We can now see how the unions, trapped by their ideology, failed to act forcefully to oppose austerity. It was not a policy that they needed to act against; it was the class behind the policy. And that class, the capitalist class, grows in power when capital is separated from the needs of the community, used privately, and withdrawn from the public need.

The unions leaders' response to austerity, the decision to sacrifice the jobs, wages, benefits, and working conditions of their members, effectively separated their own needs from their members' needs. The unions' needs as organizations were given priority over the needs of the city's workers. Given union passivity at the moment of crisis, the separation of union from worker effectively isolated any worker insurgency from effective opposition to austerity. The unions can therefore now argue that their strategy for survival was successful: collective bargaining still formally exists, and their members can still claim most of the benefits won prior to the fiscal crisis. Al Viani placed union strategy in this perspective:

VIANI: Unions and union leaders are very pragmatic people generally and they have to deal with the real world. They also have to look in terms of what their long-term goals are. Our [D.C. 37] goal during the fiscal crisis was to . . . recognize that there was a truly severe and real fiscal crisis and . . . that we had to deal with it. And we had to devise a strategy that would enable the employees to come out of the period with as many of their benefits intact as possible, without any long-lasting cutbacks, and to try to make the compromises—but compromises that were not going to erode the basic benefit structure. And I think we were successful in that respect. There hasn't been any of what a lot of commentators have been calliing for: a cutback in employee benefits, fringe benefits, etc., except in one area. That has been in pensions and not for active employees but for newly hired employees. Our big concern in the crisis was layoffs and cutbacks in basic salary and fringe structures. We came out of the contract negotiations [1976] without any erosion of our basic fringe benefit structure, and we came out of the negotiations with the best that I think we could possibly do in terms of the salary. The sacrifice on the wages was a deferral. It wasn't a giveup. That money is owed; it was only a one-year thing. They [a fact-finding panel that ruled that the deferral was only temporary] restored the salary rates. Our most trying period was the last contract [June 1978], where we just had these cost of living adjustments. *So that tactically I think we came out of it in good shape, even a little stronger now, I think, than [we were] prior to the crisis.* And we picked up a lot of members during the crisis, because people understood that had it not been for the union there would have been more severe layoffs and more severe cutbacks—permanent kinds of cutbacks in benefits and salaries. [Emphasis added.]

According to Viani's analysis, the city's unions actually were stronger *after* the sacrifices were made during the fiscal crisis. Nevertheless, we saw that the layoffs were not union sacrifices, but banker demands. To sacrifice implies the power to decide, and we saw that the unions did not hold such power. The unions did survive as formal organizations, but many union members did not. That Viani could make the above claim demonstrates the separation of the union from the worker.

This separation of union from worker represents, on the one hand, the concentration of power in capital, and, on the other, the mediating process of both union and government in class society. Arguing the conservative function of corporate unionism, Stanley Aronowitz writes that:

trade unionism still appears as a progressive force among the mass of working poor, such as farm and hospital workers, who labor under conditions of severe degradation. At first, unionization seems to be a kind of deliverance from bondage. But after the initial upsurge has been spent, most unions fall back into patterns of class collaboration and repression. At the point when grinding poverty has been overcome and unions have settled into their conservative groove, their bureaucratic character becomes manifest to workers.[24]

It seems that the bureaucratic character of the city's unions became dominant not due to the personal malevolence of union leaders, but rather because the needs of workers cannot be met by unions that are ideologically and organizationally committed to corporate capitalism. It is during crisis that we can see this commitment. Jerry Wurf, President of the American Federation of State, County, and Municipal Employees, pointed to this commitment as a serious flaw in the American labor movement.

> Fundamentally, the labor movement in this society accepts the social, economic, and political system unquestioningly. As a matter of fact, it is sometimes more defensive about it than our other institutions . . . Labor here is not an adversary institution . . . The American labor movement supports the economic and social status quo.[25]

In that light, given an ideological commitment to class society and the lack of power to oppose austerity effectively, the unions' strategy made sense.

Theirs were indeed limited goals, which already accepted the inevitability and necessity of austerity. The unions retreated from representing the class interests of its workers. They had withdrawn in the face of crisis, as they realized their own powerlessness. And as they retreated, they produced even more powerlessness. In crisis, the unions cooperated with an austerity policy at the expense of the city's rank and file: the need for social control dominated their organizational response.

8

The Class Basis
of Austerity

"There has been a rather complete shakeup in the financial management of the city, with outstanding businessmen like the president of the Metropolitan Life Insurance Company, Richard Shinn, and the president of the New York Telephone Company, Mr. William Ellinghaus, having a direct relation to how the city runs its fiscal affairs.

. . . New York is unique . . . we have been the receptacle for a tremendous migration in the United States with hundreds of thousands of rural poor from the South . . . The result has been an enormous welfare undertaking of some $600 million a year paid directly by the city from its own tax base . . . And a 12-percent-plus unemployment rate makes New York practically a disaster area . . .

. . . A freeze has been placed on the wages of municipal employees and a hiring freeze instituted. Subway and bus fares have been raised from 35 to 50 cents . . . 31,211 city employees have been laid off since the beginning of the year. . . ."[1]

Sen. Jacob Javitz testifying before
Senate Committee hearings on federal assistance
to New York City (9 Oct. 1975)

"I don't think there is any question we have asked more of our society than it is capable of delivering, and we have told everybody that the money is unlimited, the resources are unlimited, and we have promised more than we can deliver.

At some point those two curves cross.

In the city of New York, they have now crossed."[2]

Walter Wriston, testifying before the same committee
(18 Oct. 1975)

185

"Let me add that I am simply appalled by the supposedly liberal and compassionate attitude, that one can cut sanitation, and one can cut schools
and fire protection, and police protection, and health services—everything
can be cut, everything may be sacrificed, except debt service. That is
sacrosanct."[3]

> Martin Mayer, testifying before the same committee
> (18 Oct. 1975)

"It is cruel that it has to come out of the hide of the workers, but that's the
way it is."

> Sen. William Proxmire, speaking to Mayor Koch
> during Senate Committee hearings on aid
> to New York City (6 June 1978)

Austerity and the Relationship of Class and Power

On Thursday, October 9, 1975, Secretary of the Treasury William E.
Simon, a former specialist in municipal bonds and a former member of
the Technical Debt Advisory Committee, which advised the city on its
borrowing needs and practices, addressed the United States Senate's
Committee on Banking, Housing, and Urban Affairs. This committee
was charged with the responsibility of reviewing the city's fiscal crisis and
recommending appropriate federal action. Secretary Simon was ap-
pearing before this committee to ensure that the Ford administration's
policy toward the city and its fiscal crisis would not be superseded by a
more lenient, compassionate policy. He was there to make certain that
austerity became the foundation of any federal policy toward the city
and its fiscal crisis. In simple terms, Secretary Simon was there to prevent
a federal "bailout" of the city.

In his opening remarks to the senators on the committee, Secretary
Simon argued against the notion that a New York City default would
have far-reaching effects on the nation's banking system, on the city's
major banks, or on the municipal bond market. Nor would default
create conditions that might cause other cities and municipalities to
default. The consequences of a default could be limited to the city's
boundaries. Before submitting to the questions that the Committee members had for him, Secretary Simon concluded with the following
remarks.

SECRETARY SIMON: "If . . . default were avoided by a federal
assistance program, the reaction could be more complex. Clearly there
would be no basis for concluding that avoidance of default meant that
state and local governments were able to carry out their financial
obligations. Just the contrary would be true. Meanwhile, there would

be far more incentive for state and local governments to embark on more spending programs, irrespective of whether resources were available to finance them. The discipline built into the present system would be lost entirely.

What the federal government would do for New York, all would believe, it would necessarily do for any other jurisdiction which became unable to meet its obligations . . .

Mr. Chairman, I would like to conclude my remarks today with some purely personal observations. It has been nearly seven months to the day that the city's bankers reached the conclusion that a market no longer existed for the securities of the city. For this entire period, the citizens of the greatest city in the world—its financial, industrial, and cultural hub—have lived from crisis to crisis. As one with deep personal and professional ties to New York City, I have great compassion for the plight of the citizens of New York and I share their determination to achieve a prompt and proper end to the crisis.

Over this period much in the way of laudable progress has been made. An "untouchable" expenditure increase for fiscal year 1975–1976 was pared somewhat. The inexorable growth in the municipal payroll has been pared to some degree. The cumbersome overlay of bureaucratic structures has been partially reorganized and financial professionals are now playing an increasingly important role in the affairs of the city.

. . . There can be no doubt that Federal financial involvement at any point along the way would have stopped the reform process dead in its tracks. We need only look at what occurred when MAC was created in early June. For six weeks, virtually nothing in the way of reforms was accomplished. In late June, the need to obtain legislative approval of the city's budget caused a brief flurry of activity—announcements of layoffs, hospital and firehouse closings. But as the garbage piled up over the Fourth of July weekend, most layoffs were rescinded, and the closing orders have been largely ignored.

It was not until it became clear that MAC would be unable to borrow in August that the process of reform began anew. Each new deadline was faced with more strident demands for federal assistance. And, after such assistance was again refused, the city and the state managed to take another hesitant, painful step in the right direction. . . .

The time has come . . . to concentrate all of our efforts to restoring our greatest city to fiscal integrity . . . As we proceed through this difficult period in our history, I can only hope that the travails of New York City will have some impact on our attitudes as to the proper role of government in our society. What New York City has learned in the past seven months is a valuable lesson for us all. As we proceed with legislative consideration of the city's financial crisis, let us not ignore this important message.[4]

The message was indeed clear to all who would look. The city was being "disciplined" by the markets, by the bankers, and now, by the federal government. There would be no easy bailout from the Ford administration. Nor would there be an acceptance of the expansion of the social welfare apparatus at any level of government. The prior history of struggles by the workers and the poor, by public sector unions and community activists, was to be turned around and put in its place. Government would not pick up the pieces of a capitalism that had grown unevenly and left some cities, some regions, and the poor behind. The city would have to be disciplined, and, in the process, the gains made by the city's working classes—in city offices and in the workplace—and by its poor would have to be relinquished. What was being disciplined and changed was no less than the social arrangements between labor and management, the poor and the government, workers and capital, capital and the state, that were the basis of the American social welfare state—however weak and meager it may have been, compared to the social welfare states of northern Europe. A new state was emerging—what I have called the "austerity state."

It is instructive to look at Secretary Simon's remarks in that context. As the following exchange with Senator Tower of Texas indicates, the antilabor and, indeed, the antipoor and antisocial welfare bias behind austerity stands out:

SENATOR TOWER: I have just been noting some interesting figures, that seem to indicate rather severe discrepancies between fiscal practices in different cities. These are 1971 figures . . . the per capita outstanding debt of New York City was $1,288 compared to the next highest city, Philadelphia, $572, less than half that amount. New York's spending was at the rate of $1,207 per capita compared to the next highest city, this time being Seattle, of $446, almost three times more. The 1971 expenditures of New York City were greater than the combined expenditures of the next 24 largest cities comprising 23 million people, compared to 8 million people in New York . . .

Of course, I think we all know that New York is in the grip of the trade unions. We know that wages are inordinately high there and they are ordinarily dictated by the trade unions without regard to demand for productivity or the burden on the city or anything like that. . . .

Do you think that perhaps default on the part of New York City, perhaps a worsening of the problem, would ultimately force reform on the part of New York City so that it could act responsibly? Could it perhaps serve as an object lesson to other cities in the United States?

SECRETARY SIMON: I think that everything that's occurred thus far has already served adequate warning on other cities in the United

States . . . What I fear, Senator Tower, is that if the Federal Government steps in at this point to guarantee or insure [New York City securities], does this remove the very strict and necessary discipline of the marketplace for many other cities in this country? Does it precipitate, regardless of what the punitive costs we might put on the borrowings, the demand for more Federal funds and more fiscal laxity than now exists? . . . if the Congress in its wisdom determines that the Federal financial assistance is essential in this effort, I would urge that it not create a new bureaucracy, an RFC [Reconstructive Finance Corporation] type bureaucracy that always grows and cannot be gotten rid of to interpose itself into every facet of local affairs. . . . I would urge . . . a narrow and restrictive program that would be administered by the Secretary of the Treasury.

I would further urge that any program prohibit assistance until the Secretary is satisfied beyond every reasonable doubt that the recipient is inexorably on the road to fiscal integrity and I would finally urge again . . . that the financial terms of assistance be made so punitive, the overall experience be made so painful, that no city, no political subdivision would ever be tempted to go down the same road.[5]

Secretary Simon's testimony went on until his antiwelfare politics emerged. The continuing attempt to slash social welfare programs at local, state, and federal levels may be viewed as having been tested during the fiscal crisis. In that sense, the fiscal crisis of New York City and its austerity policy represented a major move away from the social welfare state and created an opportunity for conservatives, in and out of government, to try out their agenda. This move was accomplished, even though Felix Rohatyn was anything but a conservative of William Simon's type. Simon's reference to the RFC as being just another layer of unnecessary bureaucracy, which might not go away, was an argument against Rohatyn's political agenda, which included an RFC. This conflict is a most significant one, and indicates a split of major political and social importance within the capitalist class, to which we will return. Before continuing, however, it is important to demonstrate the kind of antiwelfare bias that the conservatives have used to institute austerity programs throughout the nation. I return to Secretary Simon's testimony:

SECRETARY SIMON: I would say that in a great many ways [New York City is a unique city] due to the fact that it is the port of entry of so many people and it has so many peculiar characteristics: but again, some of its problems as far as its welfare programs are brought upon themselves. I have a friend of mine—an acquaintance, who works in Newark, N.J., and has a very good job and he lives in New York City. I said, "My goodness, that's an unusual thing. Why don't you live in the suburbs?" He said, "Well, my wife was a government employee, and by living in New York City, she can collect large welfare payments, and so we're living there instead."

Well, I suggest that all of these encouraging factors—the welfare program that's obviously rewarding—I will not repeat here for the record what I said to this chap, but you can imagine, Senator, but I would imagine that's going on quite a bit.[6]

Welfare chiselers, union rabble, powerful and corrupt union leaders, lazy, shiftless public sector workers—all these ideological images dominated the discourse about the fiscal crisis of New York City. Despite significant union concessions, worker sacrifices, worker layoffs and attrition, the hiking of subway and bus fares (which adversely affect those who are most dependent on public transportation—the poor), the closing of day-care facilities, the imposition of tuition at the City University of New York (which had educated the city's working classes for generations), there were still claims that the city's government was owned and controlled by either the unions or the poor, or by both. An example of this muddled, but ever-so-popular, thinking was provided by Representative Jerry Solomon, a Republican congressman from Albany. Addressing the House of Representatives during a debate on aid to New York City, which he opposed, Congressman Solomon stated that: "In New York City public employee unions and welfare recipients now control the politicians. Five years after they promised me [to balance the budget] they still have a deficit of $1 billion. The politicians of that city have given it away."

If Solomon's analysis of the power structure in the city of New York had been his alone, it would not be cause for worry or even for further comment. But this analysis, so ideological and so wholly without foundation, has become the rallying cry and legitimator of austerity. His position concerning New York has become the position held throughout much of the United States. It has gained political legitimacy, especially with the onslaught against the social welfare state by the Reagan administration. We are at a new era in American politics. A new class politic has emerged.

Fiscal Crisis and Class Struggle

The preceding chapters were concerned, for the most part, with showing the relationship between class struggle and contemporary urban crisis. The main concern was with detailing and analyzing the ever-changing reciprocity of this relationship. First, labor seemed to ascend. Then, capital stripped the mystique of power from the public sector union movement. We have examined the ebb and flow of class struggle and how it impacted on and produced the fiscal crisis of New York City. This examination necessitated a detailed historical analysis of the actions of the representatives of the capitalist and working classes at the historical moment of crisis. It was argued that the representatives by historical circumstance were the city's banking and investment firms, on the one hand, and its labor unions, on the other.

The major actors involved in the production and mediation of this crisis were identified, and their actions were discussed. They were not viewed as independent actors in this dialectic, however. Their "class being" was shown, as well as their consciousness of the class character of their actions, and it was demonstrated that the actors in this crisis acted within parameters set by a larger struggle and by the history of that struggle.

The theory that the fiscal crisis was both the product and the process of class struggle was presented: that this crisis was the culmination and reorganization of twenty years of class struggle and that it was, in fact, the beginning of a turning away from a government policy of enlarging the social service priorities in fiscal politics. In James O'Connor's terms, it represented a shift away from legitimation toward support for accumulation. This shift is viewed as the development of austerity capitalism. As Alan Wolfe so ably argues, "crises, whether of population, energy, legitimacy, budgets, or politics, do not manifest themselves out of thin air; they are, in Lukacs' phrase, 'an intensification of everyday life,' a culmination, not a negation, of historical processes."[8]

The preceding analysis of the fiscal crisis of New York City showed the means by which New York City's government, in particular its budgetary processes, was transformed by the city's major banks. We saw how they forced Mayor Beame, through the Financial Community Liaison Group, the Municipal Assistance Corporation, and the Emergency Financial Control Board, to institute austerity and, by seizing control of the city's finances, to assure investor confidence. This analysis showed how the city's banks were simultaneously able to disinvest in the city's securities, thereby precipitating a "fiscal crisis," and still mobilize their forces to gain power over the redirection of the city's finances and therefore its politics. By controlling their flow of capital out of the city, the banks set the preconditions for their power. By using those preconditions, the banks seized power. The banks were able to "use" the structural conditions of crisis to realize their class aims. Jac Friedgut of Citibank and the FCLG made this point in an interview:

FRIEDGUT: We [the banks] had two advantages [over the unions]. . . . One is that since we were dealing on our home turf in terms of finances, we knew basically what we were talking about, and we knew and had a better idea what it takes to reopen the market or sell this bond or that bond. Even though our judgment was wrong in some cases, nevertheless, we were still quantum leaps ahead of the unions, because they were not in the business of selling securities . . . The second advantage is that we do have a certain noblesse oblige or tight and firm discipline. So that we could marshal our forces, and when we spoke to the city or unions we could speak as one voice. . . . Once a certain basic process has been established that's an environment in which our intellectual leadership . . . can be tolerated or recognized . . . we're able to get things effected.

And they were able to first construct an "environment" in which they could "get things effected," while avoiding any of the negative repercussions that their large and shaky New York investments might have brought.

We cannot dispute the reality or the severity of the fiscal crisis. The crisis was a result of a combination of class-related factors: the decline of the city's economy, the growth of influence of the municipal labor unions, the militancy of community organizations, and the interest that investors had in the city's increasing debt service. Certainly, as has been indicated, the pressure to increase the city's debt service came from both the banking community and from the city's poor and its working class. Each of these class "needs" pushed the city toward its fiscal crisis. Yet, this "mutuality" of class interests was short-lived. As Michel Aglietta has argued, the development of the international debt economy created a "fully-fledged international credit system, deterritorialized and beyond regulation by any national sovereign state."[9] With this changing international monetary system, the New York banks emerged as truly international banks, with Citibank leading the way. International speculation, which would later show up as the debt crises of 1984 and beyond, took finance capital away from the debt instruments that the city had so easily marketed in the past. These developments were not in the city's control. They were international in scope and part of the very process of capital accumulation. A global money market had made New York a less attractive investment. It is here that we can draw out one major conclusion to this work: Here we see the global "face" of capital, which knows no national or local boundaries. Capital is international, yet governments are geographically fixed in their jurisdictions. Furthermore, the working class is rooted in local communities and therefore at a disadvantage when faced with the hypermobility of both finance and corporate capital. In New York City, a fiscal crisis grew out of a changing international financial system, along with finance capital's new interests. The fiscal crisis was therefore the result, in this sense, of the breakdown of the mutual interests joining labor/government/capital. This was a crisis that grew out of a policy—increasing debt—that seemed to benefit and reconcile factions of otherwise conflicting classes. The overall debt grew, the bankers made a bundle, the city's workers received higher paychecks, the unions' strength grew. But the city grew more and more dependent on the banks and finance capital. Ultimately, when the banks withdrew from this triad of mutual interests, their power over city policy grew. One might suggest that this process is now being acted out on a national level—creating an "austerity state."

In New York, with the public credit market experiencing a great deal of competition from local governments that were eager to borrow, the banks began to produce and use fiscal crisis to reshape long-term city policy. In this way the crisis was both real and produced: it existed, was real, as a result of economic decline and working-class activism; it was produced by actions of New York's investment community. The banks and major institutional investors simply did not need the city in the same way as they did when they enthusiastically met the city's borrowing needs. They no longer needed the city's securities; hence, they no longer needed the "social contract" that they shared with the city's unions and its political administrations. The liberal "contract," which had encouraged the growth of social spending and of the public sector work force—to be paid for by the marketing of debt in the municipal securities market—broke down. It was no longer necessary. Finance capital was shifted elsewhere. Down came the "liberal" social welfare governing mechanisms of the post-1960s. In their place came the austerity state.

Austerity politics is a different type of politics than heretofore encountered. Its underlying basis involves a strong reliance on finance capital to underwrite government debt; yet, finance capital's needs are not fixed to the national debt. It retains, when it is able to, an independence from national "loyalty" and an ability, indeed a need, to flow where it can prosper. Yet, as the debtors increase their debts, finance capital is itself threatened. Therein lies the contradiction as well as the impetus for instability. Since the flow of finance capital involves large quantities of speculative investment, the potential for chaos and collapse is increased. Local governments are pushed toward austerity budgeting to insure their ability to secure the debt, which enhances the power of finance capital as it "negotiates" with governments at all levels. In 1974, it was New York City; in 1984, Argentina; before long, it could be the federal government of the U. S. In this uncertain world milieu, the possibilities for financial chaos are endless.

Within this realm of economic uncertainty, with speculative investing and the hypermobility of both finance and industrial capital characterizing the class politic, one thing seems certain. The capitalist state, in its national and local manifestations, has either moved or been moved toward austerity budgeting. In New York City, government had to be moved, through a coercive threat of bankruptcy. The Beame administration had built its power on years of Democratic party coalition building. It shared a particular political language and landscape with the city's unions, as well as with its working- and middle-class constituencies. The poor were kept acquiescent, even in the face of increasing poverty, as the city's economy faltered and was transformed. Given this political alignment, it made sense that Mayor Beame would try to fight the banker-led austerity. Given the constraints that were built into the city's need to borrow much of its revenue, the mayor had little ammunition with which to fight. As Jac Friedgut correctly maintained, both the unions and the mayor were fighting the bankers on the bankers' own turf. It was apparent that the redistribution of power would be effectively made in favor of both finance and corporate capital. With this came a redistribution of state favors, a flow of tax benefits, tax abatements, and economic incentives to the financial and corporate sectors. State activity and fiscal policy were redirected to spur economic growth. Yet, it was an uneven growth. It did not touch the poor. It jumped from lower and mid-Manhattan out to Scarsdale and Connecticut, skipping Harlem and the Bronx. It was a type of growth that forced the poor from their apartments and cleaned up the city by trying to clean out the poor. It was and is a type of growth that has left the subways smelling like sewers and running like snails. It is a growth that victimizes too many, for the sake of too few. It might have Donald Trump—the young, politically connected builder of concrete empires—smiling, but his smiles mask the tax abatements that his power expropriated from the city of New York. Behind this growth lies austerity and, indeed, a government policy based on scarcity.

As a consequence of the process through which the fiscal crisis was resolved, the class forces now stand in an altered relation to one another and to the state. In a very real sense, working-class struggles, by state workers and by community activists, altered the constellation of class forces vis-a-vis the state after and during the 1960s. The postwar corporate hegemony was pushed to an expanded need for legitimacy. Government helped to provide that legitimacy through socially directed state expenditures.

Through these struggles, working-class movements pushed the capitalist state toward its fiscal crisis. Fiscal crisis became a structural condition of the capitalist state. It is instructive to review James O'Connor's theory of the fiscal crisis of the state. For O'Connor, the capitalist state must serve as both a device to promote accumulation and legitimation. It must help to expand capital and, at the same time, protect capital by promoting loyalty to the system as a whole. The state also must legitimize itself, for how can it provide the legitimation of capitalism if it is not itself legitimate? But, as both Ralph Miliband and Claus Offe have noted, this leads those at the helm of the state—the political leader and the entrenched government administrator (or bureaucrat, if one wishes to be derisive)—to see state interests as their own interests. The state, then, tends to establish its own field of interests, which seems to function quite independent of the state as the mediator among factions of the capitalist class. This view may also provide an explanation in some contexts for the apparent "irrationality" of state actions concerning economic planning.

For O'Connor, the state seems to be a fixed object, whose primary purpose is tied to the capital accumulation process and its logic. Its budgetary process is therefore tied to the structure and logic of capital. Fiscal crisis is then the result of the logic of capital: its contradictions, its history. O'Connor's theory seems to be the application of capital-logic theory to the state. Lost in his analysis is an emphasis on struggle. On first appearance, O'Connor's theory seems to be anything but what has just been stated. Indeed, O'Connor claims that his work challenges capital-logic theory.[10] Giving O'Connor the credit that his theory deserves, it did move theorizing about the state beyond the issue of its staffing. Yet, to speak of social expenditures merely as a legitimation device is to lose the history of class struggle which, at times, *pushed* the state into its expanded role. As was detailed in Chapter 4 of this book, the increase in government expenditures must be understood in part as a consequence of the organized pressures applied by sustained social movements—by labor, by community activists, and by the poor. That is not to say that these expenditures did not contain a social control, therefore a legitimation function. They were both at the same time: both victories for the movements that secured them and legitimation and social control vehicles for government and capitalism.

O'Connor's theory makes the state's budget the victim of capital's imperatives, absent the working-class and class struggles. Furthermore, to say that the state is the prime vehicle of legitimation is to fail to address the question of the overall process of ideological legitimation. It is now necessary for critical theories of the state to join that theorizing with questions that do not strictly confine themselves to the question of the state. In any case, O'Connor's theorizing must be addressed within the framework of our topic in this book—the contemporary process of crisis in general and of fiscal crisis in particular. If we accept O'Connor's major point—that social welfare expenditures were legitimators for the overall expansion of capital accumulation—we must also locate the validity of this point for a particular and now limited historical time period. This analysis may have been profoundly accurate for the time period of long-term economic growth after World War II until the era of decline of the 1970s. Where that long-term growth left poverty, government could justify the expansion of the social welfare state. In the United States, the growth of these expenditures was fueled by the organized pressure of the union movement, and of the civil rights and community activism movements, as well as by the Democratic political machines of the industrial Northeast and Midwest. And, given these constituencies, such expenditures served as ideological legitimators. Here the state provided the ideology, concretely displayed in its politics, that capitalism was an enlightened system.

This begs the question, however. In a time of growth, ideological legitimacy also shifts to growth itself. Perhaps as important, the commodity itself becomes a legitimation of the system. Certainly, commodities and the consumer society provide seductive and powerful modes of legitimation—so long as they are widely available. And this mode of legitimation is not dependent on the state. Only certain segments of the population depend on the state to provide them with their major source of resources, in order to purchase commodities and an entrance into commodity happiness. Bourgeois culture thus provides its own legitimation, without state intervention. However, this is all predicated on growth. During crisis, threatening both private and state resources, we have seen that the state shifted its legitimation function away from social expenditures and, instead, toward nationalism, militarism, anti-communism, jingoistic Americanism, racism, sexism, reborn individualism, and the rebirth of religion.

Once the depth of this crisis was revealed, the state budgets were cut back, at least for the social expenditures that comprise the legitimation function to which O'Connor refers. Government cutbacks were effectively made without immediately threatening the state's or, for that matter, capitalist production's legitimacy. This study shows that a state fiscal crisis, within a broader economic crisis, itself becomes the legitimator for socially regressive policies and, especially, for austerity. Within the context of the crisis—both fiscal crisis and general economic crisis—grew a new legitimation, an altered ideology, far from the past ideologies of affluence and government expansion that economic growth had provided. The ideology of scarcity, within a language and framework of government limitations, turned the former ideologies of affluence on their heads. The language of limitation, of scarcity—which encouraged and legitimated a redirection of state fiscal policies, a turning away from social programs, and a return to an emphasis of the private sector as against the public sector—supplanted the language of growth and abundance.

Within this ideology of scarcity and its policy of austerity, the state was and is viewed as limited in resources and organizational skill. The attack against bureaucracy has become in recent years an attack against the social welfare apparatus of the modern capitalist state. Of course, both the military bureaucracy and the government bureaucracies that were designed to encourage economic growth through tax incentives and other encouragements to investment have been spared this critique of bureaucracy.[11] The state, from the federal level down to the local level of government, is now viewed as being both broke and inefficient. In a curious but powerfully effective manner, the crisis of capital became the fiscal crisis of the state. Then this fiscal crisis was used to attack the state in a renewal of a free-market ideology, which seeks a state redirected toward the accumulation of capital at *the expense of* government programs that are designed to legitimize capitalism, on the one hand, and to buy off class opposition on the other. Having weakened labor resistance, both in the private marketplace and through the internationalized division of labor, and having weakened labor through the rapid, hypermobility of capital, capital then sought to weaken both labor and the state. An antistatist ideology, coupled with an attack against the poor and the public sector workers, was effective in neutralizing any significant opposition to austerity. With the absence of a bridge between the labor "movement," such as it is, and the poor, this task—that of mobilizing sentiment against "big" government, social welfare expenditures, and public sector workers—was accomplished quite easily. State austerity was viewed as a vehicle for the restoration of capital's growth, at both national and local levels. The ideology of austerity claims that state scarcity-austerity leads to and is the precondition for the battle against economic-private scarcity. The austerity state depends on trickle-down theories and promises: state-sponsored suffering will eventually lead to private marketplace affluence. Both the state and its clients must be disciplined through austerity. Austerity is offered as an alternative public response to the overall crisis of capitalism for both the social welfare state and a corporatist-interventionist state, as favored by Felix Rohatyn.

Rohatyn's strategy—of intervention by the private sector through control boards and state financing instruments—proposes a Reconstruction Finance Corporation (RFC), modeled on his experience in New York's fiscal crisis. According to Rohatyn, the RFC would be the application of the Municipal Assistance Corporation on a national scale. First, he addresses the similarities of the United States national crisis to the New York fiscal crisis.

The situation of America today is not so different from that of New York City in 1975. The similarities are striking:
increasing deficits, internal and external, year after year, papered

over with accounting gimmicks to allow politicians to sidestep
politically difficult decisions
increasing reliance on borrowed money to finance those deficits . . .
while neglecting capital formation, with resulting deterioration of
physical plant
creating greater and greater hidden liabilities in the form of un-
funded private and public pensions, Social Security, etc.
losing private-sector jobs, driven out by high taxes and low productivity
continuing to absorb large numbers of illegal immigrants at a time of
high unemployment.[12]

In the context of nationwide crisis, industrial decline, and large-scale
technological transformation, Rohatyn proposes a national MAC. For
Rohatyn, New York's fiscal crisis was corrected by the successful uniting
of labor/capital/government. According to the architect of the city's
"rescue":

> . . . the Municipal Assistance Corporation was able to play a pivotal
> role in the bargains that had to be struck between competing con-
> stituencies; it was the linchpin between business, labor and govern-
> ment regarding those prickly issues of fairness and wealth. On a
> national scale, a similar role could be played by a modern version of
> the Reconstruction Finance Corporation (RFC) which would provide
> capital to northern cities falling into ruin and older industries unable
> to face foreign competition.
>
> The free market is inadequate to the task. Far from simply bailing
> out failing companies or politicians unwilling to face reality, the RFC
> would offer its capital only to those entities willing to make the
> sacrifices required to make them viable: corporations whose unions
> are willing to make wage and productivity concessions and rely more
> on profit-sharing; managements that will make equivalent sacrifices
> and limit price increases; stockholders who will forego dividends in or-
> der to maximize investments. The list should include cities in states
> where legislatures are willing to require the suburbs to pay for their
> fair share of city services; where budget oversight is in structures like
> the New York City Financial Control Board; where public-sector
> unions restrain wage and pension demands; and where the business
> community continues to invest and build.[13]

For Rohatyn, this kind of arrangement can work only if the class
politics of confrontation and conflict give way to a new era of labor-
business cooperation. The incentive for this cooperation is the threat of
economic decline for the private sector and a lower standard of living for
America's working and middle classes. He continually uses the fiscal
crisis of New York as his model. As he told viewers who watched his interview with David Susskind:

ROHATYN: And the point that I think is important is that the total federal involvement [in solving New York's fiscal crisis] was to guarantee a billion and a half dollars of our bonds. The guarantee cost the federal government nothing, and on which they were making money and on which they will never spend a dime. On the basis of that billion-and-a-half guarantee, we raised $12 billion and we turned the city's economy around. I think you can apply that theory and that approach to some of the problems of our older industries; to the problems of some of our cities. I think that this country can't survive without a viable industrial base. Now that doesn't mean that we have to pour money down the drain to bail out inefficient steel companies. But it means that we can invest in getting modern high technology steel and metallurgical companies, functioning automotive industries, and viable cities. I don't think we can say, well, the Koreans make steel cheaper than we do, and therefore we're going to shut down our steel capacity in order to buy Korean steel. Or the Japanese will always be able to make cheaper cars than we do, so we're going to shut down our car capacity. But we have to be competitive. We have to bring our costs down, and in order to do that the government, business, and labor have to change their adversarial relationship and try to do some things together.

SUSSKIND: You would create a super MAC, called a RFC, with the federal government giving it an initial $5 billion funding, and then it would issue bonds of about $24 billion?

ROHATYN: Possibly.

SUSSKIND: Which would be backed up by federal guarantees?

ROHATYN: Not necessarily. I don't think you need federal guarantees beyond the initial capital of the $5 billion. I think that as a matter of fact that it would be protection against wasting money to have this agency subject to the discipline of the public markets.

According to Rohatyn, the RFC could be the institutional device to provide labor peace, the incentive to lower labor costs, and, at the same time, to provide capital for the growth of high-technology industries in the United States. Furthermore, the RFC could provide funds, through low-cost loans, to municipalities to modernize their mass transit and infrastructural facilities on which the corporate sector depends. For Rohatyn, the choices and options for American industry are few. Industry's needs cannot be met by the supply-side dreams of the Reagan right. Nor is it enough to resort to traditional Keynesian incentives and deficits. A much more aggressive corporate state is necessary. As Rohatyn argues in his book of essays:

In setting an American economic and social agenda for the 1980s, the issues of regional disparities, older industries, inner-city blight and alternative energy sources must come high on the list. The RFC would have a role in each of these areas.

The current experiment in supply-side economics is a gamble, in more ways than one. In terms of pure economics, it is a gamble in that its potential for success rests on the requirement of unprecedented behavior on the part of 220 million Americans in their spending and saving patterns. It is a greater gamble in its underlying philosophy of a government with a minimal role in our social structure and an activist role almost solely limited to defense. The damage caused by excessive government regulation and interference in the 1970s will not be cured by government abdication in the 1980s. . . .

A balanced budget is not inconsistent with liberal aspirations; in many ways, those aspirations should require it, since only thus can we have lower interest rates, lower inflation and high economic activity. An RFC, higher gasoline taxes, rebuilding older cities and older industries—these are not inconsistent with conservative aims. . . . Both labor and business would have to sacrifice; freedom would be abridged. However, both fairness and wealth would ultimately benefit. . . .

Balanced budget liberalism should be the liberal economic agenda for the 1980s. It should aim at the creation of wealth and its fair distribution at every level of our society and in every part of our country as well as at a realistic view of America's security needs . . .

A predominantly free economy is a necessity; a totally free market is a myth. Conservatives will find that they cannot be partially virginal as far as the free market is concerned. As long as so-called voluntary restraints are demanded of the Japanese, we should go further and require wage restraints from the United Auto Workers and price restraint from auto industry managements. Conservatives will have to recognize that providing a $6 billion windfall to savings and loan associations neither is consistent with their philosophy nor will it solve the problem. Liberals, on the other hand, will have to learn to treat government spending as if it were their own money, because it is.

Americans do not live in a free-market economy today. The prices of energy, food and credit are not freely set. Americans live in a mixed economy, predominantly free-market oriented, but in which the government plays and must continue to play an important role. It must be an active participant, along with business and labor, in striking those bargains which are required to apportion benefits and sacrifice as evenly as possible among various constituencies.[14]

Felix Rohatyn has been quoted at length to underline the significance of both the fiscal crisis of New York City and the split within the capitalist class and government over the strategies that are necessary and desirable to "cure" both the crisis of American capitalism and the fiscal crisis of the state. In this chapter, we have seen the split between, on the one hand, the free-market economic conservatives and the supply-side advocates of the Reagan right, versus, on the other hand, the austerity government neoliberals of the Rohatyn "left." The depiction of the Rohatynites as a "left" is made, of course, to distinguish between a corporate left and a socialist left. The corporate left aims for more state planning and coordination in order to *fund* capitalism—not to alter the basic accumulation process. Nor does that left seek to provide worker-led planning. We could call this "corporate top-down planning." Its advocates seek the austerity state to protect capital and guide it through its crisis, as a vehicle for further integrating the labor unions into a capitalist state based on austerity, sacrifice, and profits. Furthermore, we see here an attempt to break down any barriers to capital accumulation that might be presented by the state itself.

This view speaks to Marxist theorists, like Claus Offe, Fred Block, and Ralph Miliband (in his current work), who argue that there is a division of labor within capitalist society between the private sector and the state. The relationship between corporate and state power is not one of total state dependence or subordination on a dominating private sector. The state sector exerts—both through its structural relationship with capital and with other classes and sectors of society and through its political institutions, in which "state managers" reside with political careers—a set of needs that are supportive of capitalism but not mere instruments of capitalists. For one thing, if the state managers do not encourage private investment and capital accumulation, masses of citizens suffer economic losses—in wages, careers, and consumption. Such losses threaten the political careers of the state managers, as well as the legitimacy of the state. Second, the state itself is dependent on resources gathered in both tax revenues and direct investment in public securities. In that way, the state itself is dependent on capital accumulation and on finance capital.

In the case study presented here, however, the relationship between capital and the government is clearly a changing one. It is not fixed within any permanent power structure. The relations between state and capital, as well as those between labor and capital and labor and government, are the outcome of class struggle; therefore, they are not permanent. They are open to struggle. They are open to change. As Nicol Poulantzas has argued, the state itself is a "strategic field" for class struggle.[15]

Given these points, it is important to view Rohatyn's suggestions as an attempt to break this division of labor, as well as the stubborness of the class struggle. Austerity, instituted through the MAC and the EFCB in New York and disciplined by the private markets and finance capital, weakened the resolve and the ability of New York's labor unions to fight back. With this austerity structure—of a mini-RFC—New York's economy rebounded for the benefit of the rentier class of landlords and real estate speculators.[16] Furthermore, labor was weakened throughout the city, and the city's government was redirected to meet capital's needs. In *Business Week's* words, the result was: "THE NEW YORK COLOSSUS—ITS SURGE TO WORLD FINANCIAL SUPREMACY MAKES IT THE CAPITAL OF 'CAPITAL.' "[17] Rohatyn wants to do for America what was done for New York—create an austerity state.

Austerity in New York: Mobilizing through Crisis

It is instructive, then, to recall the means by which the fiscal crisis was "resolved" to make the city "THE CAPITAL OF 'CAPITAL'." The methods by which the city government was pressured into austerity involved the withholding of financing and the withdrawal of credit from the city, the development and staffing of a state financing instrument (the Municipal Assistance Corporation) and a state financial control board (the Emergency Financial Control Board); and, most importantly, the establishing of social and institutional constraints to inhibit labor resistance as austerity was instituted. The city's labor unions became integrated into the austerity structure as they invested pension monies to finance the city while it was shut out of private markets. From the evidence presented in the preceding chapters, it is clear that those who developed and initiated this institutionalization of austerity were powerful members of the capitalist class and that they represented various factions of finance and corporate capital that was operative in New York. These influential actors developed the instruments through which austerity was adopted, instituted, and enforced against potential disruptions.

The most influential actor was, in fact, Felix Rohatyn, the "liberal" investment banker and later chairman of the Municipal Assistance Corporation, member of the Emergency Financial Control Board, and originator of countless strategies to "save" the city from bankruptcy. Jac Friedgut maintained in an interview in January 1979 that "by the summer of 1975 people like Felix Rohatyn were essentially making financial policy for the state and the city." Donna Shalala agreed when she was interviewed in October 1978. The fiscal crisis was "seen as a financing problem . . . Remember, the problem was credibility with the financial community . . . During that period it was Rohatyn and only Rohatyn. He, in effect, shaped the financial settlements."

During crisis periods, power structures become more visible and open to change, since they become contested terrains. New means to mediate crisis and class conflict are developed and institutionalized to replace or reform the old. This often necessitates transforming the mechanisms of government or, as Nicos Poulantzas suggested, in the formal mechanisms of government being superseded by informal ruling class power relations. In his last book—*State, Power, Socialism*—Poulantzas theorized that hegemonic fractions of a ruling class form power blocs within the state and are able to isolate the state as their mechanism of domination. This is achieved by transferring the centers of power away from the areas of the state that are accessible to influence and struggle by the dominated. For Poulantzas:

> The unity-centralization of the State, which currently favours monopoly capital, is therefore established through a complex process. The state institutions undergo changes whereby certain *dominant* mechanisms, modes, and decision making centres are made impermeable to all but monopoly interests, becoming centres for switching the rails of state policy or for bottling up measures taken "elsewhere" in the State that favour other fractions of capital. Moreover, we are talking here of a two-way causal relation: not only does the hegemonic class or fraction establish as dominant the apparatus that already crystallizes its interests, but in the long term, every dominant state apparatus . . . tends to become the privileged seat of the hegemonic fraction's interests, and to incarnate changes in the relations of hegemony. This unity of state power is established through a whole chain whereby certain apparatuses are subordinated to others, and through the domination of a particular state apparatus or branch (the military, a political party, a ministry, or whatever) which crystallizes the interests of the hegemonic fraction—domination, that is to say, exercised over other branches or apparatuses that are the resistance centres of other factions of the power bloc. The process may therefore involve multiform underdetermination or duplication of apparatuses: *shifts in function and competence, and constant divergence between real power and formal power; the establishment of a functional trans-state network rising above and short-circuiting every level of state apparatus and branch . . . and crystallizing monopoly interests by its very nature.* [Emphasis added.][18]

Poulantzas' theorizing correctly points out the process by which the city's powerful—its corporate and banking capitalists—were able to institutionalize their power by constructing austerity boards (the MAC and the EFCB), which were isolated from popular centers of resistance or opposition. Their informal power was made into a formal power, which supplanted the formal democratic processes of the liberal state. The "hegemonic fraction"—notably finance and corporate capital—was thus able to enforce its needs and its perception of the fiscal crisis from *within the state*. Even though they were part of the state apparatus, with formal legal status and authority over the city's finances, its budget, and its labor contracts, these ruling-class mechanisms were not open to the influence of those who might struggle against austerity. Capital seized the state, while labor was left to oppose capital and austerity from a position of weakness, from *outside* the state. As Poulantzas correctly points out, dominated classes exist with respect to the state "not by means of apparatuses concentrating a power of their own, but essentially in the form of centres of opposition to the power of the dominant classes."[19] Given the strength exhibited by public sector labor unions vis-a-vis city government *prior* to the fiscal crisis of New York, the crisis became the milieu for undercutting and otherwise encircling the power of the labor unions by circumventing the authority of city government. The "discipline" of the market weakened the ability of both labor and city government to oppose this maneuver. So it was that New York City's government, beset by an inability to raise operating and capital funds and influenced by militant labor unions, proved ineffectual in its response to capital's needs. As a consequence, the formal processes of city government were superseded by informal organizations representing finance capital (the Financial Community Liaison Group) at first and, later, by more formal organizations and governing bodies of financing and budgetary control (the Municipal Assistance Corporation and the Emergency Financial Control Board). One might conclude from this that the use of power by a class in part involves the transforming of formal mechanisms of government during crisis. In this case, research suggests that this process of transforming government begins with the use of informal mechanisms to pressure the existing governing bodies. These informal mechanisms are then legislated or otherwise made into more formal mechanisms for achieving class aims. These formal governing bodies consolidate the gains of the informal mechanisms. In New York City, the formal mechanisms made austerity an institutional fact, thereby consolidating the hegemony of a fraction of the capitalist class. Taking Poulantzas' analysis a bit further, the attempt by Felix Rohatyn and the neoliberals to move these austerity mechanisms, through a RFC, into national government is an extension to the federal level of the institutional framework of austerity that has already been tested and tried in municipalities across the nation. But this consolidation has found opposition from a fraction of capital, as well as from the "state managers" of the Reagan administration and the conservative wing of the Republican party. Not only is labor split but so is the capitalist class and the national policy makers within the state. So while Rohatyn warns against the lack of planning and direct state funding of capital through an RFC, the Reagan right continues its agenda of funding capital less directly through its regressive tax policies and its military build-up. At this point, the Rohatyn strategy has met strong resistance, not from labor, but from powerful fractions of the capitalist class and from those who now reside in state power. At the moment, there seems to be a lack of "unity of state power," as capital and the state continue to struggle over the means to resolve the international economic crisis, as well as the federal government's own fiscal crisis. Despite the Reagan landslide and the continuing assault on the welfare state, the battle to resolve the crisis is not over—it is still a contested terrain.

Some concluding remarks may be in order about the fiscal crisis of New York City as a contested terrain, to illustrate the importance of the continuing class struggle over the fiscal crisis of the state. In that struggle, the broader relations of class, power, and state point both to the limitations of the old strategies of labor accommodation and to the potential, as well as the need for, new strategies based on an awareness of capital's strength and of the crisis it faces. The questions here are simple: Can labor and those who suffer the onslaught of austerity find and build a new opposition, whose strategies, tactics, and organizational structure will respond to the new relations of class—that is, to the new class politics? Or will labor strike an alliance with one of the fractions of capital—with either the Rohatynites (as in N.Y.C.) or the Reaganites (as in the Teamster's case)? If labor does not do so, what are the conditions for an antiausterity alternative?

9

Labor in the Austerity State

The austerity state is now developing as a consequence of two inter-dependent processes. On the one hand, Americans are experiencing an extended period of economic decline and transformation, shattering the class compromises and arrangements of the past. On the other hand, the ideologies that have permeated the political discourse of America since the New Deal have been delegitimized in light of this decline and of the social welfare state's impotence to contain its effects. As the American economic pie no longer grows as it once did, the political and ideological discourse has shifted away from liberalism to a conservative critique of social welfare policy. Yet, no consensus has replaced liberalism; hence, the ideological terrain remains open, leaving both a threat and an opportunity for the labor movement and for other progressive forces. Both the threat and the opportunity are contained within the spectre of austerity, for both capital and labor.

It has been shown that austerity, like the crises from which it emerged, constitutes a realignment of class forces and of the structure of power within the state. These class-power arrangements are not fixed; they are fluid and open to change. As these class arrangements form, labor is presented with an historic opportunity to break away from the business unionism that characterizes its ideological framework and its strategic perspectives. An antiausterity mobilization can break the isolation of the unions from their own membership, other workers, other progressive forces, and the clients of the welfare state. All are threatened, though in different ways in the state and in the workplace, by the expansion of corporate power and the assault of the private sector. While equal sacrifice may be one of its ideological codes, austerity is the political victory of finance and corporate capital over public and private sector unionism, progressive tax policies, the income transfer and security programs that the poor and the working-middle classes expect, and the progressive agenda of the 1930s and 1960s.

Austerity is both a product and a process, in policy form, of class struggle through the state. The state and its policies have become focal points for the mobilization of corporate interests. Business unionism failed to connect its class struggles within the state with struggle at the workplace. Capital is now doing just that, with profound effects on the structural terrain of class struggle for the next decade. Nevertheless, both the state and the ideological legitimations of austerity are contested terrains; the trap door has not been slammed shut on America's progressive forces. The ideology of business unionism, however, must be challenged before unions place themselves as cooperative agents within austerity.

There is the possibility for change here. Like state policies, ideologies can shift rapidly. Crisis makes these shifts possible and perhaps likely. Crises are therefore crucial moments of opportunity for the radicalization of consciousness. Political opportunities exist within crises for strategically-organized classes. Before crises can be used in this manner, the organizations of class interest need to be politicized and ideologically prepared to take advantage of the opportunity that presents itself. Organizing against the social arrangements of the present must challenge the ideological notions of "realism," which serve to limit the ability to move toward progressive social change. The moment, and therefore the crisis, must be seized. During the fiscal crisis of New York, the city's banks and major corporations seized the moment, organized as a class against the interests and political power of other classes, and thereby altered the class arrangements that had structured city politics.

Contrasting labor's actions to capital's during the fiscal crisis, we see that labor was not prepared—ideologically or organizationally—to take advantage of the opportunities that the crisis presented. Instead, the dominant concern was to sustain an obsolete management-labor relationship. The ideologies that guided New York's unions limited their strategic perspective. They were not prepared to struggle within the new social conditions that gave rise to the austerity state. It is to this class struggle, within this new political, economic, and ideological terrain, to which we will now turn.

Class struggle ebbs and flows: at one moment capital seems to be powerful and well organized; at another moment, it appears to be labor's turn. Regardless of this chaotic rhythm, *each defines the other's power; their histories are made* together in an antagonistic unity—a unity of opposition. This point is an important one if the fiscal crisis of New York is to be understood. At times, coalitions may be forged, cutting across and forming a momentary unity between fractions of capital and labor, as well as other classes; but these coalitions are momentary. They are built on class interests which remain antagonistic—despite neoliberal illusions that "reasonable" labor leaders can unite in common cause with "reasonable" representatives of the financial and corporate class. These common causes are temporary to the extent that both labor and capital represent the class aims and class needs of their classes. It is no accident of history, nor of the stubborn personalities of labor leaders and financiers and corporate elites, that the recent gains by capital have been made at the expense of workers and the poor. It is no accident that the austerity boards—the MAC and the EFCB—were staffed and run in a manner intended to discipline labor. It is no accident that with these austerity boards in place, New York's financial and corporate sectors were able to rebuild the financial industry, and to engineer a boom in office space and luxury housing while rents for apartments have skyrocketed and wages for workers have failed to keep pace. As *Business Week* reported: "The city cut the corporate income tax in two stages from 10.05% to 9%. . . . And real-estate taxes as a percentage of the full value of real property have declined by 30%. . . . And now, New York City is offering generous, but selective, tax abatements to companies that want to locate in the city."[1] The city enthusiastically gives away tax abatements to its corporate clientele, including abatements to city-based companies that merely choose to remain in New York. As the American Express Company found out, a company merely has to threaten to leave the city, and the city jumps. Such is the power of capital in the midst of crisis.

As stated previously, this pattern of corporate and finance capital exerting its power over city government, without resistance from the city or its labor movement, characterizes the "unity" between labor/capital/government that grew during the fiscal crisis. It is not a unity of equals; nor even one where labor can coexist as a junior partner. It is a unity of domination by capital. Thus, the planning of austerity excluded effective opposition from labor or from the city government itself. The mayor's office was redirected in the Koch years to serve capital while disciplining its antagonists. The power of the new class politics was symbolically represented by the arrogance of the mayor toward those who suffered most from the decline of city services—the city's minority populations—and toward those who labor for the city—its municipal employees. These groups became the mayor's and austerity's whipping posts, the city's stepchildren. By integrating the city's labor unions into austerity for fear of bankruptcy and fear for safety of their pensions, and by limiting the authority of the mayor's office over city contracts and therefore city policy, capital was able to clear the field for the assertion of its needs over public policy. As Jac Friedgut suggested: "In a sense, the bankers did take over the city, but these were not the commercial bankers; rather, these were the Felix Rohatyns of this world." The reference here was to investment bankers. And during the fiscal crisis, there was an extraordinary degree of class unity within the investment community. "We have a certain noblesse oblige and tight and firm discipline," said Friedgut, "so that we could marshall our forces and, when we spoke to the city or to the unions, we could speak as one voice." And they opened the city—by redirecting its tax policy, by controlling its labor contracts, by changing the quality and quantity of city services—to corporate and finance capital. In this way, New York City was saved from bankruptcy. The banks were saved from huge losses. The subways constantly break down; the City University is no longer free; the poor no longer have access to quality day care; the streets have only occasional smooth surfaces between potholes; garbage litters the sidewalks in quantities that foul the air. But there is plenty of luxury housing in Manhattan. The city lives—it's just its people that are in trouble.

This was not the result of a predetermined, historically necessary development, however. This was not a solution whose rationality was beyond challenge. Austerity is not an apolitical policy, whose structure serves the interests of us all. Austerity was just one possible history that could have emerged from the fiscal crisis. To argue that it was the only possible history is to hold a mechanically applied, deterministic ideology. The ideology of austerity that holds this view weakens the potential for organizing resistance to the austerity state. It may well be that this was the political consequence of the ideological position that was adopted by the city's unions. Their ideological framework accepted austerity as the only solution to fiscal crisis, thereby inhibiting their ability and will to oppose and organize a broad-based presence against austerity.

By accepting the ideological hegemony of austerity and scarcity, the unions were unable to develop a counterhegemony. This counterhegemony could only have developed in actual resistance to austerity —in a praxis that moved the unions away from the liberal contract unionism that developed in the private sector and was in turn adopted by the public sector unions. Because of their ideology, the unions lacked the necessary class unity to resist the effective political mobilization of fractions of capital. The unions—divided by income, occupational status, and the divisions of labor within the public sector and between the public and private sectors—were unable to come together to plan effective resistance during the early and most crucial days of the fiscal crisis. Given this void, the investment community was able to enforce its definition of the crisis and its proposal for determining the relationship of financing and political control. Through its political mobilization, finance capital was able to institute austerity as government policy and establish its hegemony, however temporary it might ultimately turn out to be.

As the crisis developed, the austerity policy enveloped the unions, which, without a coalition among the threatened communities, were unable to oppose this resolution of the fiscal crisis. We saw that the unions, faced with the threat of layoffs, allowed union money to be used to forestall bankruptcy; how plans were made within the Municipal Labor Coalition to avoid strikes; how an early decision was made at the highest levels of union leadership to cooperate with the policy of fiscal austerity; how "social responsibility" was defined by union leadership to preclude radicalism. And we saw how all of these developments contributed to sealing the municipal unions into a powerless position. After investing pensions and tying them to the city's fiscal future, how could labor unions resist austerity without endangering their members' pensions?

Without the necessary class unity and an ideology of class opposition, the unions found it impractical to resist. Consequently, austerity was introduced with very little effective resistance. Workers lost their jobs; poor people saw the already low quality of their health care decline with the closing of medical facilities; students at the City University paid increased tuition to attend larger classes or dropped out for lack of tuition funds; day care centers were closed; the infrastructure of the city, its bridges, streets, and tunnels, continued to erode; and the subway system, without which labor-power cannot meet capital, continued to deteriorate, subjecting riders to discomfort at ever-higher prices per ride.

We have seen that the precrisis period was characterized by years of labor militancy. Yet, we must distinguish between offensive and defensive militancy. The precrisis activism came from a position of strength, it was offensive when the political, economic, and social conditions contributed to the clear possibility of success at achieving class aims. These very same organizations proved to be inadequate as defensive organizations. Not only were they unable to protect against the institutionalization of austerity but they were also unable to turn the fiscal crisis against the investment community. The leadership's inability to use the discontent of the rank and file to oppose austerity demonstrates the shortcomings of the public sector labor movement. These shortcomings establish the grounds for a critique of the ideological terrain in which America's business contract unionism operates. This form of unionism seeks class accommodation with capital and management in times of both growth and crisis. During crisis, however, this strategy weakens labor as an opposition force to capital. By tying itself to capital, labor gives up its potential power at the exact moment when the effective utilization of that power in the strategic sense could alter the class-power relations both at the workplace and within the state.

By following a course of collaboration, these unions find themselves turning away from, or inhibiting, rank-and-file militancy. This was the case throughout the fiscal crisis, as the rank and file made known their discontent. There were job actions by teachers, police, firefighters, sanitation workers, and hospital employees. Yet the respective union leaderships seemed to distrust the militancy of the rank and file and tended to disassociate themselves from these job actions. Instead, the union leaderships opted for a relatively conservative strategy, designed in part to control their memberships. They were, in short, afraid of losing control over their memberships in an increasingly dangerous fiscal situation. As Edward Handman stated when interviewed in December 1978: "The banks were cracking the whip." The acts of a strong membership might have brought penalties from the Emergency Financial Control Board, as was the case for the United Federation of Teachers, which was unable to persuade the EFCB to approve its contract even a year after the UFT and the city had reached agreement. As both Al Viani and Edward Handman argued, the unions could not initiate a general strike because "that's chaos." In this contract ideology, class struggle is viewed as chaos. Class collaboration is viewed as social responsibility.

This point is similar to the argument made by Stanley Aronowitz in *False Promises*, where he argues that today's private sector unions have become integrated into the control mechanisms of corporate capitalism. The data presented here suggest that the same may now be said of the public sector unions.

> The most notable feature of the present situation is that the unions are no longer in a position of leadership in workers' struggles; they are running desperately to catch up to their own membership. There are few instances in which the union heads have actually given militant voice to rank-and-file sentiment.[2]

Still, Aronowitz makes clear that the unions retain their positions as the only available organizations for worker defense. The union "remains an elementary organ of struggle, yet it has also evolved into a force for integrating the workers into the corporate capitalist system."[3] And yet, when Aronowitz wrote this in 1973, he could also state that this was not yet the case for public sector unionism. Writes Aronowitz:

> Unionism in the public sector is still somewhat raucous and unpredictable from management's standpoint. Even when labor leaders fervently desire close relations with public officials and are prepared

to cooperate in confining membership action to approved channels, the workers in hospitals, schools, post offices, and city agencies often succeed in changing the script.[4]

By the middle of the 1970s through the early 1980s the limitations of public sector unions had become similar to those in the private sector. While retaining a somewhat more politicized ideology, necessitated by its structural position in the state, the public sector unions grew less militant and more oriented to providing a comprehensive service network for their membership. In *Working Class Hero*, Aronowitz points to the success and limitation of public employee unions at the present time:

> The capacity of public employee unions to broaden their scope to include workers' aspirations on a variety of levels is the key to their success which has continued after the initial upsurge. Unlike most industrial and craft unions which have gradually abandoned not only their character as a social movement but the conception of the union as a worker's sphere and as a cultural center, many public employee unions have engaged in educational, cultural, and political activities, making the union hall a place where workers congregate even after they retire from active employment. To be sure, these activities have become more important in the 1970s and 1980s when gains at the bargaining table became more problematic. And as I have pointed out earlier, the service orientation adopted by many unions is, to some degree, a sign of the passing of the militant phase. Despite these reservations, it is also true that the typical public employee union means more to its members because they have recognized that workers' needs are not confined to better income, as important as this demand remains in the repertoire of labor's aspirations.[5]

Nevertheless, the public sector unions have turned away from their previous militancy at precisely the moment when the public sector has seen its legitimacy erode. On the one hand, the state remains the provider of last resort—of both income and services—while, on the other hand, public sector workers have been attacked as greedy, unproductive public servants. In order to diffuse this attack, union leaders have become union statesmen, showing that unionism is responsible to a community broader than its membership. Yet, this approach has failed in the light of the anti-public-sector ideology that dominates the ideological terrain of the austerity state.

This approach failed on two levels, with consequences for the unions' short-term and long-term ability to oppose austerity. First, this strategy accepted the ideological framework of austerity and the austerity state. This limited class struggle within the state against the mobilization of the corporate interests that were concretized as austerity. Underlying this approach was the liberal ideology that government and the state represent a "community" of interests which serve us all—regardless of class. This ideology masks the class character of the capitalist state—at both the national and local levels. As a consequence, the cooperative union position toward austerity fails as an immediate strategy to defend workers' interests against management and capital. It fails to show austerity's class character.

Secondly, this strategy limits the organizational impetus to unite the interests of the unions with the interests of the broader working-class, poor, and minority communities that might oppose austerity. Hence, neither an ideological nor an organizational base was developed against austerity and the assault by capital against the public sector. As one fraction of capital mobilizes for reprivatization—embodied in the Reagan policies of the 1980s—the only opposition comes from the Rohatyn wing of the capitalist class. Consequently, unions and other potentially progressive forces are forced either to take a position that opposes Reagan through a Rohatyn-type strategy, or to drift away from the policy debate altogether. The union strategy therefore fails as a long-range way to oppose the underlying basis of the austerity state in that it ends up choosing between two forms of austerity: Reaganism or Rohatynism.

In order to contest the austerity state and its reprivatization approach—embedded in antiwelfare policies, contracting out work from the public to the private sector, and regressive tax policies—the unions needed to formulate an organizational strategy which countered the ideological framework of austerity. Furthermore, a long-range strategy needs to take into account the possibility of building a mass-based movement—through the unions and other progressive allies—to protect the gains of the past within the public sector and to move forward in the light of the contemporary crisis of state and economy. The unions' strategy ignored these possibilities and embraced the ideological framework of limitations—of the public sector, of resources, of antiausterity alliances—that characterized both austerity and their own praxis. With their strategy, the unions could not develop either an immediate defense or a long-term alternative to the austerity state.

The consequences of this strategy are revealed by looking at the fiscal crisis of New York. While the municipal labor unions moved toward accommodation with austerity, their options were increasingly limited. They gave themselves little room to maneuver, thereby necessitating cooperation with a policy designed to limit their power while lowering the city's overall labor costs. Given this cooperation, a service orientation to their members might have solidified the union leadership's position within the union, despite the failure to deliver both economic benefits and a more humanized workplace. Instead of using the rank-and-file dissatisfaction with the working conditions under austerity, the unions instead epitomized the ideology—of class compromise and business unionism—that separated their organizational interests from their rank and file. Organizational interests were identified with the employer, the city of New York. The unions chose to inhibit militant action while viewing cooperation rather than conflict as the only appropriate and responsible position.[6] In an interview in December 1978, William Scott highlighted the split between the union leadership and the rank and file of the United Federation of Teachers during the 1975 teachers' strike:

> SCOTT: In 1975, that was really a strike by the membership. It was not a strike that the leadership actually wanted to lead. The leadership was aware of the financial crisis. The members felt that it fell all around them, but that it never touched them. And this they could not accept. And when the conditions in the contract that they didn't like, or when we couldn't get a settlement, they wanted a strike and strike they had. That was, I think, one of the few strikes in public areas where the leadership didn't lead them or encourage them. And in that case there was neither—not encouragement nor leadership. And it was a pretty costly strike. It cost the members.

The union leadership separated the needs of the organization from the needs that motivated its members' resistance to the austerity program that was undermining prior contract victories. It could argue later, therefore, that the municipal unions survived the fiscal crisis without suffering serious damage to their bargaining and political powers.[7] And yet, how can their political power be effective when they operate within a milieu dominated by the rationality of austerity, whose very policy it is to cut the costs of labor and services within the public sector while returning some services to the private sector? Their strategic perspectives remain dominated by a discourse of limitations concerning the ability of the public sector to deliver services efficiently and to collect the necessary resources to do so. Furthermore, while austerity dominates, with its procapital tax policies, the state's revenues will be raised through regressive tax policies; hence, the revenue payers—the working and middle classes—are prone to an anti-welfare state, anti-worker perspective, precisely because they foot the bill. With the failure of the unions to develop an independent, anticorporativist ideology, which is both prostate and antiausterity state—and, by necessity, anticapital—the unions cannot make the necessary connections between state scarcity and corporate power. For unions to be prostate is not to be statist. Rather, it allows the unions to position themselves in an alliance with the clients, workers, and progressive movements of the welfare state. Nonetheless, austerity provides the necessity for this alliance, as well as the possibility of its formation. But this can be accomplished only by strategically moving to what Stanley Aronowitz calls "class struggle unionism."[8] Without this perspective, the unions found themselves languishing in the ideological and policy terrain set by capital during the fiscal crisis. Rather than increasing their power, the unions lost power and the potential for a breakthrough in forming a progressive alliance.

There are two opposing interpretations of the fiscal crisis that should now be compared. They speak to the relative power of labor vis-a-vis management and capital. The first is given by Jack Bigel, labor consultant and, according to Jack Newfield, "power broker" for the municipal labor unions. Bigel argues that:

> I have a sense of inequality. I sense that management has more power. It is management that determines the economic fruits for its employees. We have the right to grievance. They have the right to determine people's lives. A union is a defensive instrument. [9]

According to this view, labor unions are powerless beyond the minimal gains that they might negotiate. Grievance procedures do little more than cool off labor spontaneity in the face of management intransigence. In this view, labor unions are always at a disadvantage and are therefore powerless, especially during crises.

Another view is offered by Commissioner Anthony Russo, of New York City's Office of Labor Relations. Russo states that "to a great extent, the servants have become the masters."[10] Yet, the history of the fiscal crisis belies the validity of this analysis. It was the perception of the public, and, perhaps, of city management, that the unions had consolidated their power. It has been pointed out that these unions were able to force valuable and costly concessions from city management before the fiscal crisis. But during the crisis, the unions were not negotiating with city management. The conditions under which they would labor were being decided elsewhere, and not by city management. Finance capital was demanding the rationalization of the labor process, and it was capital's rationality that was ascending. This is what Ken Auletta misunderstands when he maintains that the city's unions acquired new power as a result of their pension funds lending the city so much operating capital. Writes Auletta:

> In some way, the fiscal crisis lessens the power of the unions. They must temper their demands, worry about other audiences, including the Congress . . . forge a new partnership with the city/state/and banks to avoid bankruptcy, perform under the glare of constant

ublicity. But over the first three years of the crisis they also assumed new powers as the city's chief banker. By June 1978 the municipal employee pension funds were scheduled to have invested $3.8 billion in city and MAC securities—three times the amount invested by the banks. The unions milked this power, using it as leverage in their contract negotiations—no contract, no loan. Another indication of their power is that, strictly speaking, these are not "union" pension funds. Not only did taxpayers contribute roughly 90 percent of these funds, but public officials exercise voting control over three of the five major city pension funds, a power they prefer not to advertise since they traditionally defer to union wishes.[11]

Auletta argues that the unions became both banker and employee, thereby enhancing bargaining leverage with city management. But he neglects to add that these unions were, in a very real sense, not truly negotiating with city managers. Negotiations proceeded with eyes turned toward the Emergency Financial Control Board and Washington, where they were closely followed.

The EFCB had the final authority to pass on all of the city's major labor contracts. The EFCB, we may recall, returned the 1975 transit settlement to renegotiation because it allegedly threatened the city's three-year financial recovery (austerity) plan. With one decision, the EFCB established itself as the real negotiator of labor contracts; city management was only the first level of opposition that the unions faced. And city management had become the least important. Defeating management at the negotiating table became far less rewarding than Auletta makes it seem. And, in fact, what was negotiated was the dismantling of union influence and the reorganization of the labor conditions that had been won by these very same unions in their more militant, powerful days.

The negotiating process demonstrated the decline of power and influence that the municipal unions suffered. And as the data demonstrated, the commitment to invest pension funds was made under coercion: the coercion of bankruptcy, the coercion from the governor and from Felix Rohatyn, as well as from the federal government. Rather than proving the unions' power, these pension commitments indicate just the opposite. Furthermore, these investments tie labor's hands; to threaten the city with conflict or strike was to threaten the financial future of the unions' membership. They could no longer oppose the bottom-line rationality of capitalism, because that would now threaten their own investments. They had become integrated into the austerity structure.

It is a curious irony that the unions saw their influence fade while they were becoming the city's major institutional source of funding. As has been argued, the opposite held true for the city's major commercial and investment banks. As they disinvested in the city, they saw their influence greatly strengthened. They were able to induce the unions to take whatever risk was involved in investing in the city and in the Municipal Assistance Corporation, even as these unions saw their contracts eroding. As O'Connor argues, the functions of the government's budgetary processs depend upon the level of class organization. In this case, we can see that the legitimation functions of the state suffered as the accumulation functions were pushed by a well-organized financial sector.

The entire history of the fiscal crisis therefore calls into question the effectiveness of public sector unions as the sole source of power to oppose austerity, management, and, ultimately, the power of private capital as it influences and impacts upon the functioning of the city. This history argues against the validity of "interest group" theories, which assume that unions and fractions of capital, among other "interest" groups, can compete equally within local governments. The data here speak to the inherent strength of capital in a capitalist social system, as well as to the inherent powerlessness of a labor union detached from mass movements.

What this crisis shows is that the political process operated outside the realm of public discussion and influence, that it responded to the needs of capital—and not labor—during crisis, and that it was temporarily reorganized to mediate a crisis emerging from class struggle. Finally, the history of this fiscal crisis speaks to the weakness of public sector unions, and unions in general, when they are no longer part of a wider social movement. Without such a movement—uniting public sector workers with private sector workers, public workers with working-class communities, those with jobs with those who do not have wage labor—public employee unions have little public support with which to oppose management and capital. Ultimately, management and capital were able to use the split between public and private sector work to present the public sector unions as comprising a selfish and greedy interest group.

This brings us to the concluding points. During March 1981, the fiscal crisis was officially declared cured—six years after its official designation as a crisis. While newspapers and public officials celebrated the city's "cure," its workers, along with the working-class and poor communities, continued to feel the long-term impact of austerity. In light of the impact that austerity has had on the social, political, and economic history of this city, one ponders the hidden question of this research. What consequences did this crisis have on the political effectiveness of the public sector labor movement?

We have seen that the fiscal crisis presented the city's financial and corporate elite with the opportunity to reorganize city government. In the face of their activity, these fractions of the capitalist class met little resistance from the city's labor unions. Certainly, the city's unions did not just passively accept the bankers' plans; they did not roll over and die. Yet, they did fail to present, organize, or encourage a united opposition force, and this failure led them to cooperate with austerity in order to "cut their losses."

The impact of austerity is felt each day, as public sector workers labor within ever more strictly controlled and managed bureaucracies. These workers were the scapegoats of this crisis, allowing capital once again to shift critique away from everyday life in capitalism toward the working class itself. This ideological deflection suited capital very well and helped to strengthen management. Today, the city's workers

> are faced daily with the arrogance of those who hold power in the big public bureaucracies that supposedly serve the people. Trapped inside whole systems, the vast majority of public workers find themselves not only blamed for this cluster of failures, but, through pay cuts, lay offs, speed ups and contracting out, they are forced to pay for them as well. [12]

In view of this picture, one must challenge the contention of some union officials that they fared well during the fiscal crisis. The strategies adopted by these unions all pointed to their relative lack of power. These strategies were formulated to avoid conflict, and in that they succeeded. In their own narrow terms, the unions did survive the crisis—but in the process of surviving, the unions isolated themselves from both the city's power structure and from their own rank and file. The separation of the union leadership from the workers adds to the relative powerlessness of these unions.

During crisis, however, conflict is unavoidable if opposition forces attempt to challenge the status quo and both the rationality and power of capital. As Piven and Cloward argue in *Poor People's Movements,* "the main features of contemporary popular struggles are both a reflection of an institutionally determined logic and a challenge to that logic." [13] For opposition to be effective, in terms of broad class needs as against the unions' narrow self-interest, it must refuse the convenience of being "realistic," if that realism is formulated to inhibit resistance and social change. It has been pointed out here that this was the logic of being "realistic" during the fiscal crisis. To be realistic meant that labor had to avoid conflict, for fear of bringing about the city's bankruptcy. The labor unions backed off from challenging that logic, which thereby allowed capital to institute austerity that much more quickly.

Still, we must recognize that the unions' leadership was not "free to act without regard to the constraints imposed by their social context." [14]

Throughout the preceding chapters the argument was offered that there were powerful constraints placed upon the labor unions. Nevertheless, these constraints were constructed over a period of a full year, indicating the failure of labor to act decisively in opposition to them. It seems that the constraints only heightened the necessity of seeking labor/community unity, or just the opposite of what occurred. In analyzing the consequences of workers' and poor people's movements, Piven and Cloward forcefully make the point that these groups could not further their class interests without serious conflict and that such conflict brings backlash. The backlash itself indicates the power of the protest.

In a sense, Piven and Cloward argue as was argued here, that class struggle ebbs and flows. They argue against class collaboration as an effective means for pushing working-class interests. The unwillingness of labor unions to engage in social conflict splits the union from the activism of its membership. Piven and Cloward write that

> It is as if group or class struggles can, when carefully managed proceed without engendering conflict. Obviously, the labor struggles of the mid-thirties helped produce the corporate-led backlash that began in 1939 and culminated in the "witch-hunts" of the late forties and early fifties; and just as obviously the black struggles of the fifties and sixties helped produce the backlash of the seventies . . . But how could it have been otherwise? Important interests were at stake, and had those interests not been a profound source of contention, there would have been no need for labor insurgency in the one period nor black insurgency in the other. Put another way, the relevant question to ask is whether, on balance, the movement made gains or lost ground; whether it advanced the interests of working people or set back those interests.[15]

While this case does not involve historical conditions exactly similar to those stated by Piven and Cloward, the question remains the same. Were there political options available, "suppressed historical alternatives," as Barrington Moore terms them, that were not seized?[16] This question leads us to one final point. The fiscal crisis and its austerity solution represented a serious setback to the workers' movement, because there was an absence of a *mass movement* to protect the previously won gains of public sector workers and working-class communities. We can argue that the union leadership failed to promote such a mass movement; that it feared the loss of control over its membership; that it feared the consequences of class conflict. The union leadership chose to protect the union as an organization with decreasing political influence, instead of promoting the class needs of the rank and file. Consequently, there was no effective or sustained effort to produce a movement against austerity.

And now, with the Reagan backlash in full force, and with austere conditions facing workers, the retreat from activism pushes workers closer to the right—where easy answers promise an end to austerity through austerity.

Here, then, is our concluding point: In the absence of an antiausterity movement, uniting labor with community resistance, this fiscal crisis provided a social milieu that enabled finance capital to exercise an almost-free hand to reorganize city government to meet corporate needs. In the process, austerity became the basis of a new class politic. It became the ideological and political formula for the reassertion of power and social control by fractions of the capitalist class, as well as the basis for the reorganization of the budgetary priorities of city government. In the process, however, austerity also presented an historic opportunity for a reemergence of a worker-community movement with a mass base. Austerity does not alleviate the crisis; rather, it shifts the burden of the crisis onto the everyday lives of workers. Austerity does indicate the reassertion of control by corporate and finance capital vis-a-vis labor. Still, it is no more than a moment in the ever-changing dialectic of class struggle.

Toward an Antiausterity Movement

An austerity consciousness dominates the political discourse of the 1980s. This consciousness articulates the dominant conservative theory of the contemporary crisis, the role of the state, and the essence of what is practical and possible. This is a powerful ideology precisely because it is viewed as a common-sense framework on which to build public policy. Ideologies are most powerful precisely when they are not articulated as ideologies—when they are accepted as a matter of common sense. This acceptance gives an ideological framework the appearance of a truth—of an unquestionably logical and unchallengeable description of proper action.[17] These ideologies then assume a cultural power, which gives a particular political direction a stronger legitimacy. We come to "know" that a policy—a way of life—is necessary and/or desirable.

It has been shown that an antiausterity movement was unable to form in New York City, precisely because there was no counter ideology to the prevailing "common sense" view that there was no alternative way out of the fiscal crisis. Rohatyn's view became everyone's view: capital, labor, and eventually the mayor all shared it. This process took on an inevitability, because there was no ideological or organizational alliance connecting labor, progressive community organizations, and the minority communities that bore the brunt and pain of so much of austerity. Had these progressive interests been united, the history of the fiscal crisis might have been written differently.

Now the country faces austerity. The prior gains of minorities, the elderly, women, peace activists, environmentalists, and trade unionists are all under attack. Liberals, neoliberals, and conservatives present us with a united front on one level: they agree on the limitations of the public sector to meet the needs and demands established by the class struggles and victories of the past. How are we to defend those victories? How are we to expand those victories?

We have seen that crisis presents opportunities for progressives and reactionaries alike. These opportunities are not the same for each side: for capital and labor, rich and poor, militarists and peace activists, for instance. Nevertheless, as the capitalist state moves forward into austerity repression, there are available to progressives a number of strategic possibilities—for now and for the future. The following suggestions are meant to point to some of the possible opportunities for an antiausterity coalition. By no means do these exhaust the possibilities. Now is the time, however, to build a renewed progressive movement. To do so requires an awareness that the strategies of the past can no longer be blindly applied to the present. To accept the strategies of the past, built during the years of economic growth and/or the liberal consensus, is to find comfort in tired approaches without finding success. The movements for progressive change must come to terms with the new economic and political conditions of American capitalism and the capitalist state. Old ideological paradigms must be broken, to open the way for a new class alliance against the rationality of austerity capitalism and the austerity state.

The struggle against austerity must be and can be made on many different levels and in every political and economic sector of American society. These struggles can take form within and without the state. Within the state, these class struggles must be made at national and local levels of government. At the national level, the defense against austerity necessitates protecting while seeking to expand the economic gains of the welfare state. Here, progressive alliances can pressure liberal politicians, through electoral and other means, to choose between militarism and the human needs of the poor, the workers, the elderly, and the young. This pressure, however, necessitates active and mobilized coalitions, growing from new alliances on a local level. Furthermore, this pressure is only a temporary beginning. Struggle within the state must not be taken to exclude extraelectoral strategies. The connection between state expenditures, tax policies, corporate investment and banking policies, public works and infrastructural needs, and the austerity facing clients and workers of the public sector must all be integrated within a strategic and ideological perspective. Each impacts on the other, so struggle must be made at each point. Strategies dependent on, or primarily guided by, electoral politics run the risk of becoming integrated within austerity. These alliances cannot elect their way out of this crisis. The preconditions for class power must first be achieved. These preconditions are organizational and ideological and must be independent of the mainstream of electoral politics.

The struggle against austerity within the state necessitates new community union alliances, which will push the class struggle within and beyond the state to the centers of both the state and of corporate-financial power. This type of widened class struggle over the austerity state makes the connection between corporate-financial power and state austerity. Its ideological basis lies in debunking the ideology of limitations and scarcity that characterized labor union strategy during the fiscal crisis of New York. It challenges the rationality behind austerity by widening the discourse about the welfare state to include the issues of tax policy, capital flight, industrial policy, tax subsidization of business and real estate moguls, the militarization of the federal budget, interest owed on government debt, unemployment, underemployment, poverty, the environment, health care, day care, housing, and education. In other words, to struggle against austerity is also to challenge the hegemony of the ideology of scarcity and, therefore, the hegemony of capital. This type of widened political discourse enables progressives to move from the defense of the welfare state as it was to a more class-conscious debate over public policy affecting the poor, the working class, and capital. As a consequence, this wider ideological struggle makes clear the connection between state austerity and the narrow interests of capital.

Temporary organizational ties between unions and progressive community organizations and the movements that are geared to specific policy objectives do not necessarily provide a sufficient base to carry forward this struggle. While struggles carried forth by temporary progressive coalitions are necessary and can be made, these are not sufficient to effectively challenge the organizational and ideological strength of conservative forces and capital over the long run. Struggle over political policy is necessary, but antiausterity struggles must not be limited to temporary political coalitions, if they are to become vehicles for class struggle over the direction of both the state and the workplace.

To make such a long-term struggle, the boundaries must be broken between the union and the community of workers outside of the union's traditional organizational base and activity. If unions are to remain useful as vehicles for class struggle, and if an antiausterity movement of any consequence is to build, the tradition of the isolated union, representing its membership's economic interests in narrowly defined terms, must be broken and stretched to include extraeconomic and political functions beyond specific workplaces. Workers and union members live in both workplaces and in communities threatened by state austerity, service cutbacks, reprivatization, capital flight, and housing debilitation. Their children attend schools that lack adequate facilities and the commitment to critical reasoning. Their families fear crime. In other words, the interests of workers and unions extend well beyond the workplace and into everyday community life. The quality of life issues and the workplace issues are not exclusive of each other. Therefore, workplace and community issues provide a basis for long-term unity between unions and community organizations.

Like unions, these community organizations—organized around particular political, social, and economic issues—are essentially class organizations, since they struggle over the distribution and production of wealth and public services. Their struggles are class struggles, regardless of the conscious ideology that these organizations espouse and articulate. By struggling and organizing around specific policy objectives, these organizations seek to impact on the class process—in both the private and the public sectors. Due to the class context of austerity, this unity between unions and community organizations fighting to provide a better quality of life can be made in opposition to the privatized interests of capital.

Today, the union faces an increasingly hostile antiunion ideology and work environment. This is not a new experience in America. Nevertheless, as the number and proportion of unionized workers decline, the union itself needs to rethink its isolation, its organizational structure and principles, and its ideological framework. Both public and private sector unions are threatened by austerity and by the power of certain factions of capital to determine the structure and availability of the workplace and to influence, sometimes directly, public policy. The labor movement can find new strength, new members, and new allies by forging a nonaccommodationist position in relation to austerity and to management's power to formulate and direct public services. As these services are slashed through austerity, unions can move to formulate political and economic alternatives. For example, pension fund investments and other economic resources that are available to the unions might be used for nonprofit and low-profit but secure social investments and for community organizing. By providing economic, political, and educational services to a broader community, these unions can reverse much of the antiunion sentiment that is mistakenly presented as a new conservatism among America's working people. Unions can position themselves to use their resources to assist or provide cheaper housing, food, and medical aid. Opening up some of their benefit programs to workers who are not unionized, to the poor, and to minority communities might go a long way toward strengthening a class movement against austerity to act within the state.

There is risk here. The austerity state and its managers, as well as the corporate executives, might find it pleasing to shift the burden of social services onto the unions. Nevertheless, these services would provide the unions with progressive allies to attack the austerity state and demand a level of state spending on social services, income maintenance, education, and job training and retraining, for example, on a more humane and expanded scale. These union-community programs would not seek to replace, and thereby privatize, such services. Instead they would become an organizational, policy, and cultural basis for a new class movement. The reaching out beyond their own memberships would place unions beyond the workplace and into the community. The fragmentation of workers from other workers, workers from the unemployed, and unionized workers from the nonunionized must be broken if capital and the austerity state are to be contested. This union-community alliance could fight reprivatization, while the unions extend their bases of support beyond their traditional limitations.

The ideological hegemony of capital and the austerity state could be challenged by this new community union, which would mobilize on the human right to security, job fulfillment, and political and economic democracy. This community union could mobilize politically and could use its economic power to challenge austerity. Pension investments can be redirected away from municipalities and companies which lay off workers and toward the fulfilling of economic, political, and social goals. Where necessary, the union-community alliance must challenge the labor laws and the laws regulating pension investments. The New York State Legislature passed legislation to protect the trustees who invested millions of dollars of union pension money in New York City when it was facing bankruptcy. There is precedent. It takes power, and that is what this alliance might provide.

It seems obvious that the old progressive coalitions are weak in light of the mobilization of the corporate community behind austerity. To suggest that the welfare state of the 1960s be defended on old tactics, with old organizations, is to highlight the ideological and strategic weaknesses of the left. The liberal agenda has been delegitimized not because Americans will not support social security or Aid to Families with Dependent Children. It has been delegitimized in part because it was presented as a solution. As conservative forces grew, while economic growth slowed, left and liberal forces tried to hold on to the past without moving toward a future. In the process, the present was seized by the right.

To counter this rise, progressives must not focus entirely on specific issues, which the left is likely to do as a consequence and an affirmation of its fragmentation. There are both ideological and organizational tasks that need to be performed in order to position the left for this fight. The changes in union organization that would be required to extend mutual aid services to a broader community of workers and the poor would create a dynamic of organizational and ideological change within labor and other progressive movements.

In a sense, labor's constituency lies both within and beyond the borders of the workplace. Unions also need to organize the unorganized, the new and growing sectors of the economy, and the technical-professional-scientific workers. In addition to these constituencies, austerity creates a whole new community with economic and political interests that could provide not only new members for unions but new power for progressive change. As this new union develops, with strong organizational ties within the community, a different form of political class mobilization becomes possible. This political mobilization would come not from the top of allied organizations. Its roots and strength would extend from the bottom up, with a constituency that is already united by common struggle. Perhaps here we can see the possibility of a form of workers' community developed out of the assault of austerity and through the building of autonomy from capital and from the Democratic Party. With this type of community union, a sociocultural basis for the mobilization of class interests could take form.

These community-union alliances, building to a community union, could make successful local battles to save services, humanize public workplaces, and contest the agenda of the conservatives and neoliberals. At the same time, when givebacks by unions and giveups by communities are won by the austerity state and capital, these alliances can press for an exchange of economic losses for political service gains. As an example, if capital presses for a freeze in wages, attrition or layoffs in the public sector, the union-community alliance can press for more control over those services. In this way, a loss on one level may be parlayed into a gain elsewhere.

The union-community movement must challenge the rationality of both austerity and old alliances. While protecting the jobs of public sector workers, public sector unions must move toward a new ideology which demonstrates their commitment to a broader community. Unions must not reaffirm their image of greed, however unwarranted, while others suffer from austerity and accept the ideological baggage of austerity, sacrifice, and economic limitation. As in New York City, business unionism confirms the negative images of unions, while separating them from a broader community of support. One need only recall the arrogant Mayor Koch, leading workers who were walking to work, while pledging to be strong against the greed of the striking transit workers. Here was an illustration of the separation of unions from the broader community. For an antiausterity movement to grow, this separation must be ended, preferably by a community-union alliance that could break down the separation of union interests and community support.

While mobilizing the struggle within the state at local and national levels, particular battles for jobs, income, workplace safety, social security, public assistance to the poor, day care, clean air, and a national health care system could be made through a coordinated, sustained action, built on the strength of the local community alliances. The connection between the local and the national would thus not be ignored, and the struggle against reprivatization would continue. At the same time, the temptation to ally with the Democratic Party must be fought. Liberal Democrats, as well as the neoliberals and conservatives, have consistently become fiscal conservatives during the move toward the austerity state. Furthermore, this is a time to build a countermovement and the organizational network to make that movement possible and effective. Given the limited resources available to the left and to the progressive forces—both economic and the human resources—these resources are best not diverted to an integration within the Democratic Party. To become "the left" within the Democratic Party is to cease to be a representative of the left. Temporary coalitions with Democrats over specific policy fights are possible, but to make organizational connections and commitments is to lose the ideological and organizational autonomy on which progressives can build.

One example of both the possibilities and the limitations of progressive coalitions acting within the Democratic Party is provided by the 1981 Barbaro campaign for mayor of New York City. Frank Barbaro, an assemblyman from Brooklyn and a former longshoreman, mounted a strong challenge to Mayor Koch. Barbaro had political connections to the city's unions, which were developed while he was chairing the state assembly's Labor Committee. In order to oppose the mayor with any possibility of victory, Barbaro had to forge a progressive alliance out of the many disparate opposition community groups. Barbaro was able to forge this alliance running as the Unity candidate by mobilizing tenants, welfare rights groups, and educational and environmental groups, as well as many of the city's black political leaders. In simple terms, the Barbaro candidacy mobilized many of the city's progressive community organizations to unseat a mayor who was proclaimed by the press as being unbeatable. As the campaign progressed, the city's more liberal unions, particularly District Council 37 of the AFSCME and District 1199 of the National Hospital Union, joined the unity campaign and committed their political and organizational clout. Barbaro ultimately lost, but he went on to get approximately 36 percent of the vote by mobilizing constituencies that had often been left out of the political process and/or had been hurt by the city's austerity policy.

This case emphasizes the weakness of political-electoral strategies aimed at transforming the Democratic Party, however. Once Barbaro was defeated, the coalition ceased to exist. The unions withdrew and were not willing to continue this progressive alliance. In a sense, the unions chose to abandon the unity party, since they defined it as a temporary, short-term coalition, with one specific purpose—to challenge Mayor Koch's incumbency and his control over the party machinery. The unions refused to sustain the coalition again, demonstrating their short-term, as opposed to long-term, view of struggle. Furthermore, this case highlights the leadership's trade union ideology, which denies the validity and practicality of long-term struggle, i.e., class struggle. Here, as in national politics, unions found themselves reintegrated and dependent on the Democratic Party machinery, without an alternative and without power. Getting 36 percent of the vote was no small accomplishment. Nevertheless, the promise of progressive alternatives to the mainstream Democratic and Republican parties, and to austerity, was dashed. Once again, the limitation of this strategy was that it acted within and was confined to an electoral strategy. Hence, the alliance was a temporary one, unable to expand beyond electoral politics and into a broader-based movement.

Nevertheless, in the Barbaro campaign, the possibility of union-community alliances that go beyond electoral politics, without excluding them, was apparent. To take advantage of these possibilities means challenging corporate unionism. As union community alliances build along the directions mentioned, the possibilities of more effective political action grow, within and outside of electoral politics. As these actions become sustainable by the presence of long-term, bottom-up alliances, a party may become possible. However, that step to a party must be built from the community-union alliance. Leftist parties run the risk of being voiceless within the Democratic Party. Yet, at this point, they are superfluous to the electoral and political processes precisely because they do not have roots within the broad community of workers. One may even argue that there is no community of workers. At this point there is only the potential for community. The suggestion that austerity has provided the impetus toward community, plus union, implies the formulation of the basis of a left party. But that possibility depends on first expanding the community-union alliance.

The project of moving the political discourse to the left must be seen in historical terms. It is going to take a reexamination of the ideologies of the left. More importantly, it will take the formation of a new union ideology and organizational structure. Now is the time to regroup, rethink past positions, and reorganize labor to confront the new issues and new state. It does not seem likely that unions can go it alone. Their problem in part is that they have done too much of that. The struggles over the new workplace, over austerity, over civil rights, over women's rights, over the environment, over war and peace, world poverty, and hunger are all influenced by the political ideology of the austerity state.

To challenge the austerity state is to challenge the relations of class and state. It is to challenge the power of capital. Such challenges require a fluid strategic, ideological, and organizational movement. To challenge the class power of capital, the left must build by confronting the ideological hegemony of austerity. The possibilities are there. The battle for equal rights, the shortening of the workday, and the more equitable distribution of wealth can all be made within an antiausterity movement. The common sense on which this movement can be based is right there, within the structure of austerity itself. Where austerity emphasizes capital accumulation and belt-tightening for workers and the clients of the state, antiausterity begins with one principle: humanity first. The actual "proof" that the resources exist to provide for security, and more, is quite easy to demonstrate. For that reason, an antiausterity movement challenges the tax policies of the capitalist state and lays bare corporate power and the regressive tax system. Furthermore, by challenging the rationality of the bottom line—on which austerity is ideologically justified by the austerity-minded politician—we challenge the common sense that makes little humane sense—capital's logic.

This book points out the potential for an antiausterity, antiscarcity movement. Such a movement must be based on the common condition of suffering that austerity brings. To build this movement, we must have the ideological, organizational, and policy commitments that broaden the base of unions (especially within the public sector) and reconnect them to a constituency outside of traditional workplaces and arenas of organizing. Such a movement could not be made without the mobilization of progressive forces—in the women's movement, the civil rights movement, the peace movement, and the labor movement—to fight austerity and capital within the state and the private sector, in government, and at the workplace.

In New York City, austerity became policy because of the lack of such an alliance, and such an alliance was not formed in part because of the business unionism of the city's labor unions. If there is a lesson to be learned by the fiscal crisis of New York, it is that without a strong union-community alliance, and without an anticorporate ideology that extends beyond rhetoric and into union policy, both the unions and the progressives find themselves powerless. When that happens, and when capital and management extend their rationality and their class needs into public policy, the costs of a given crisis in the state and in the economy are borne by the working classes and the poor of America. Without a mass movement to protect and defend their class needs, both the poor and the workers, in both the public and the private sectors, find themselves without services, with less income, and with a declining quality of life. Without a mass movement, the gains of the past are threatened, while the gains of the present go to the capitalist class. If crisis does represent a structure of opportunities, as has been argued throughout this book, then it is incumbent on all of us that those opportunities empower the classes and organizations that move to humanize this society. But it is not historically inevitable that the crisis of capitalism and its social welfare state will lead either to a mass movement that will humanize it or to socialism. To assume otherwise is to be blind to the process of crisis and struggle. Capital understood that the fiscal crisis of New York constituted an opportunity to assert its class needs. Now this class struggle has moved beyond New York.

The questions remain: Can an effective antiausterity movement be organized? If so, can this movement provide a vehicle for rethinking the strategies, ideologies, and organizations of the left? As austerity deepens in postaffluent America, the opportunities grow for just such a movement. In New York City and at the national level, conservative forces were able to take advantage of this crisis, thereby making austerity national policy. Nevertheless, recent setbacks suffered by labor, workers, minorities, women, students, the disabled, and the elderly make such a reformulation of the left's organizational strategy and ideology likely. From the abyss of austerity, progressive forces find an expanded, mass base. Postaffluent America's new class politics create the structural preconditions for the rejuvenation of the left.

Notes

Chapter 1 / The Austerity State

1. Peter W. Bernstein, "David Stockman: No More Big Budget Cuts," *Fortune Magazine,* 6 February 1984, p. 56.

2. Steve Murray, "Why There's No Welfare Fat Left to Trim," *Business Week,* 26 March 1984, p. 81.

3. See Charles H. Levine and Irene Rubin, eds., *Fiscal Stress and Public Policy* (Beverly Hills: Sage Publications, 1980). Also see: Charles H. Levine, Irene S. Rubin, and George G. Wolohojian, *The Politics of Retrenchment: How Local Governments Manage Fiscal Stress* (Beverly Hills: Sage Publications, 1981); and Terry Nichols Clark and Lorna Crowley Ferguson, *City Money: Political Processes, Fiscal Strain, and Retrenchment* (New York: Columbia University Press, 1983).

4. Felix G. Rohatyn, *The Twenty-Year Century: Essays on Economics and Public Finance* (New York: Random House, 1983), p. 110.

5. Karl Marx, *The Eighteenth Brumaire of Louis Bonaparte* (New York: International Publishers, 1963), p. 15.

6. Please refer to Chapter 2 for a discussion of these and other crisis theorists.

7. *Business Week*, 23 July 1984, p. 98.

8. Linda Sandler, "U.S. Banks Prepare for Possibility of Third-World Debt Repudiation," *Wall Street Journal,* 6 July 1984, p. 17.

9. Giovanni Arrighi, "A Crisis of Hegemony," in *Dynamics of Global Crisis,* Samir Amin et al., eds. (New York: Monthly Review Press, 1982), p. 55.

10. *Business Week*, 23 July 1984, p. 99.

11. Ibid. Also see Robert Goodman, *The Last Entrepreneurs: America's Regional Wars for Jobs and Dollars* (Boston: South End Press, 1979).

12. Suzanne de Brunhoff, *The State, Capital and Economic Policy* (London: Pluto Press, 1978), p. 9.

13. Ralph Miliband, "State Power and Class Interests," in *Class Power and State Power* (London: New Left Books, 1983), p. 71.

Chapter 2/Crisis and Social Theory

1. Henri LeFebvre, *The Survival of Capitalism* (London: Allison and Busby, 1976), p. 59.

2. Stanley Aronowitz, *The Crisis in Historical Materialism: Class, Politics and Culture in Marxist Theory* (South Hadley, Mass.: Bergin and Garvey Publishers, 1981), pp. 172-73.

3. Karl Marx, *Theories of Surplus Value* 2 vols. (Moscow: Progress Publishers, 1968), Vol. 2, p. 470.

4. Immanuel Wallerstein, "Crisis as Transition," in *Dynamics of Global Crisis* (New York: Monthly Review Press, 1982), p. 15.

5. Wallerstein, *Dynamics,* p. 11.

6. Ibid., p. 13.

7. Ibid., p. 50.

8. Aronowitz, *The Crisis,* p. 170

9. See Aronowitz, *The Crisis,* for a discussion of various traditions of Marxist political economy, including the capital-logic theory. I have borrowed Aronowitz's term "capital-logic," for it best typifies the form of Marxist analysis of crisis that I have been critiquing.

10. Marx, *Theories,* Vol. 2, p. 515.

11. Karl Marx, *Capital* (New York: International Publishers, 1967), Vol. 3, 212-13.

12. Ibid., p. 241.

13. Ibid., pp. 241-42.

14. Ibid., p. 244.

15. Marx, *Theories,* Vol. 2, pp. 513-14.

16. Marx, *Capital,* Vol. 3, p. 244.

17. Ibid., pp. 244-45.

18. Ibid., pp. 249-50.

19. Ibid., p. 250.

20. Marx, *Theories,* Vol. 2, 492.

21. Ibid., p. 493.

22. Arthur Hirsh, *The French New Left: An Intellectual History from Sartre to Gorz* (Boston: South End Press, 1981), p. 165.

23. Manuel Castells, *The Economic Crisis and American Society* (Princeton: Princeton University Press, 1980), p. 11.

24. Paul M. Sweeney, "The Economic Crisis In The United States," *Monthly Review* 33 (1981):4.

25. Erik Olin Wright, *Class, Crisis and the State* (London: New Left Books, 1978), p. 28.

26. Ibid.

27. Ibid., p. 147.

28. Ibid., p. 137.

29. Ibid.

30. Castells, *The Economic Crisis,* p. 12.

Chapter 3/Causing Fiscal Crisis

1. Israel Shenker, "Urban Experts Advise, Castigate and Console the City on Its Problems," *New York Times,* 30 July 1975, as quoted in *The Fiscal Crisis of American Cities,* Roger E. Alcaly and David Mermelstein, eds. (New York: Vintage Books, 1977), p. 8. Also see: Wyndham Robertson, "Going Broke the New York Way," *Fortune Magazine,* August 1975, pp. 144-214; relevant articles in *Business Week*, October 13, 20, and November 10, 17, 1975; and Ken Auletta, *The Streets Were Paved with Gold* (New York: Vintage Books, 1979) and Charles R. Morris, *The Cost of Good Intentions* (New York: W. W. Norton, 1980).

2. "An Historical and Comparative Analysis of Expenditures in the City of New York," section 3, "Expenditure by Object," *Eighth Interim Report to the Mayor by the Temporary Commission on City Finances* (New York, 1976), p. 22.

3. William E. Simon, *A Time for Truth* (New York: Berkeley Books, 1979), pp. 147-49.

4. See, for example, "An Analysis of Public Employee Compensation Levels," *Program Planners, Inc.* (New York, 1976); also see "New York City Municipal Labor Coalition Presentation to the Honorable Senator William Proxmire," *Program Planners, Inc.* (New York, 1977).

5. Jack Newfield and Paul DuBrul, *The Abuse of Power: The Permanent Government and the Fall of New York* (New York: Viking Books, 1977), pp. 35-6.

6. Interview with Al Viani, Director of Research and Negotiations, District Council 37, AFSCME, 3 August 1978.

7. William K. Tabb, "The New York City Fiscal Crisis," in *Marxism and the Metropolis,* William K. Tabb and Larry Sawers, eds. (New York: Oxford University Press, 1978), p. 241.

8. William K. Tabb, *The Long Default: New York City and the Urban Fiscal Crisis* (New York: Monthly Review Press, 1982).

9. Congressional Budget Office, "New York City's Fiscal Crisis," in Alcaly and Mermelstein, eds., *The Fiscal Crisis,* pp. 291, 294.

10. Jurgen Habermas, *Legitimation Crisis* (Boston: Beacon Press, 1973), p. 63.

11. See Claus Offe, *Contradictions of the Welfare State,* John Keane, ed. (Cambridge, Mass.: MIT Press, 1984).

12. Ibid., p. 35.

13. Simon, *A Time for Truth,* p. 154.

14. Auletta, *The Streets,* p. 30.

15. Donna Demac and Philip Mattera, "Developing and Underdeveloping New York: The Fiscal Crisis and the Imposition of Austerity," *Zerowork* 1 (Fall 1977): 120.

16. Rohatyn, *The Twenty-Year Century,* p. 110.

17. Felix G. Rohatyn, "The Debtor Economy: A Proposal," *New York Review of Books,* 31, 8 November 1984, p. 16.

18. James O'Connor, *The Fiscal Crisis of the State* (New York: St. Martin's Press, 1973).

19. Ibid., p. 9.
20. Ibid.
21. Offe discusses the effect this has on the delegitimation of market criteria for establishing wage and productivity rates in the welfare state. Refer to Claus Offe, "Advanced Capitalism and the Welfare State," *Politics and Society,* 2 (Summer 1972); and Offe, "The Abolition of Market Control and the Problem of Legitimacy," *KAPITALISTATE,* 1 and 2, 1973.
22. See, for example, Newfield and DuBrul, *The Abuse of Power*; Frances Fox Piven and Richard A. Cloward, *Regulating the Poor: The Functions of Public Welfare* (New York: Vintage Books, 1971); Piven and Cloward, *The Politics of Turmoil: Poverty, Race and the Urban Crisis* (New York: Vintage Books, 1975); Piven and Cloward, "The Urban Crisis as an Arena for Class Mobilization," *Radical America* (January-February 1977): 3-8; Ira Katznelson, *City Trenches: Urban Politics and the Patterning of Class in the United States* (Chicago: University of Chicago Press, 1981).
23. See Alan Wolfe, *America's Impasse: The Rise and Fall of the Politics of Growth* (Boston: South End Press, 1981).
24. See Stuart Ewen, *Captains of Consciousness: Advertising and the Social Roots of the Consumer Culture* (New York: McGraw Hill, 1976); also see Stanley Aronowitz, *Food, Shelter and the American Dream* (New York: Seabury Press, 1974); Henri Lefebvre, *Everyday Life in the Modern World* (New York: Harper and Row, 1968); and, finally, the classic by Herbert Marcuse, *One-Dimensional Man* (Boston: Beacon Press, 1964).

Chapter 4/Precrisis Class Struggle

1. Securities and Exchange Commission Staff Report, Committee on Banking, Finance and Urban Affairs, *Report on Transactions in Securities of the City of New York* (Washington, D. C.: U. S. Government Printing Office, 1977), Ch. 1, p. 10.
2. Ibid., p. 12.
3. John Darnton, "Banks Rescued the City in a Similar Plight in '33," in Alcaly and Mermelstein, eds., *The Fiscal Crisis*, pp. 225-27.
4. Newfield and DuBrul, *The Abuse of Power*, p. 163.
5. O'Connor, *The Fiscal Crisis*.
6. See, for example, Alcaly and Mermelstein, *The Fiscal Crisis*; see also Tabb and Sawers, *Marxism*.
7. "The Effects of Taxation on Manufacturing in New York City," *Ninth Interim Report to the Mayor by the Temporary Commission on City Finances* (New York, 1976), p. 4. There were 35,918 manufacturing firms in 1960, employing an average of 25.8 employees, and only 22,492 in 1974, averaging 26.8 employees each; a total loss of 323,899 jobs in fifteen years.
8. Ibid., pp. 3-5.
9. John M. Goering and Eric Lichten, "The Political Economy of Cities and the Urban Crisis," in *Political Economy: A Critique of American Society,* Scott G. McNall, ed. (New York: Holt, Rinehart and Winston, 1981), pp. 300-21.
10. *The Fiscal Observer,* 15 June 1978, p. 1.

11. Piven and Cloward, in their *Regulating the Poor*, elaborate on the national causes for the expansion of welfare rolls throughout the country's cities. They argue strongly that welfare benefits expanded due both to economic factors, such as agricultural modernization, and to the militant organizing of the poor themselves. Also see Piven and Cloward, *The New Class War* (New York: Pantheon Books, 1982), for an analysis of the contemporary politics of austerity on the national level.

12. Demac and Mattera, *Developing*.

13. Adapted from the TCCF's *Eighth Interim Report*, pp. 15, 17.

14. Ibid., p. 1.

15. Ibid.

16. Piven and Cloward, *The Politics of Turmoil*, see Pt. 1: "The Public Bureaucracies and the Poor."

17. TCCF, *Eighth Interim Report*, p. 52.

18. Derek C. Bok and John T. Dunlop, *Labor and the American Community* (New York: Simon and Schuster, 1970), pp. 312-42; Aronowitz, *False Promises*; Nancy DiTomaso, "Public Employee Unions and the Urban Crisis," *Essays on the Social Relations of Work and Labor: The Insurgent Sociologist* (Fall 1978), 8: 191-205; O'Connor, *The Fiscal Crisis*.

19. Bok and Dunlop, *Labor*, p. 313.

20. O'Connor, *The Fiscal Crisis*, p. 237.

21. DiTomaso, "Public Employee Unions," p. 192.

22. Bok and Dunlop, *Labor*, p. 313.

23. O'Connor, *The Fiscal Crisis*, p. 238.

24. *Seven Days*, 11 April 1977.

25. DiTomaso, "Public Employee Unions," p. 191.

26. See, for example, Paul Johnston, "The Promise of Public-Service Unionism," *Monthly Review* (September 1978), 30: 1-17; Johnston, "Democracy, Public Work and Labor Strategy," KAPITALISTATE, no. 8 (1980), pp. 27-41; Margaret Levi, "The Political Economy of Public-Employee Unionism," *Monthly Review* (September 1980), 32: 46-54.

27. Piven and Cloward, "The Urban Crisis," pp. 10-11.

28. This is not to say that the mobilization of public employees alone accounted for this expanded social service network. Pressure by the poor, as well as incentives from the federal government in the form of the war on poverty, must be recognized as major factors behind the expanding budgets of that era. Still, I here wish to emphasize the impact of public employee unionism on the city as a background to the fiscal crisis. For a description of the federal role in the expanded service network see Morris, *The Cost of Good Intentions*, pp. 34-36.

29. Piven and Cloward, "The Urban Crisis," p. 11. Also see the two reports by the TCCF, which arrive at similar conclusions even though written as consulting tools for New York City's management.

30. TCCF, *Eighth Interim Report*, p. 4.

31. Morris, *The Cost of Good Intentions*, p. 95.

32. Ibid., p. 95.

33. Ibid., pp. 97-98.

34. Ibid., p. 97.

35. Professor Horton, quoted in Auletta, *The Streets*, p. 234.

36. Morris, *The Cost*, pp. 87-88.

37. Ibid., p. 88.

38. Ibid., pp. 88-89.

39. Ibid., p. 89.

40. Ibid., p. 90.

41. Wyndham Robertson, "Going Broke," *Fortune Magazine* (August 1975), p. 145.

42. Ibid.

43. Ibid. For an elaboration of this thesis from an opposing ideological perspective, see Richard Child Hill, "Fiscal Collapse and Political Struggle in Decaying Central Cities in the U.S.," *KAPITALISTATE,* no. 4-5 (Summer 1976); also see Tabb, in Tabb and Sawers, *Marxism*, as well as articles in Alcaly and Mermelstein, *The Fiscal Crisis*.

44. O'Connor, *The Fiscal Crisis*.

45. Aronowitz, *Food, Shelter*, p. 151.

Chapter 5/Precipitating Crisis: The Banks

1. Securities and Exchange Commission (SEC), Staff Report. See Chapters 1 and 4 for detailed, day-by-day accounts of the connections between the city and its major banks and financial underwriters.

2. SEC, chap. 1, p. 3.

3. SEC, chap. 1, p. 11.

4. Ibid.

5. SEC, chap. 1, p. 35.

6. "Several Firms Put Off Offerings as Price Cuts Continue on Old Issues," *Wall Street Journal*, 4 December 1974, p. 34.

7. The city offered three major types of short-term securities. They were Revenue Anticipation Notes (RANs), offered in anticipation of taxes (excluding real estate taxes) and monies to be collected from New York State and the federal government; Tax Anticipation Notes (TANs), offered in anticipation of real estate taxes; and, Bond Anticipation Notes (BANs), offered in anticipation of monies collected from subsequent bond offerings. Short-term securities were offered with maturities of one year and less. The city found itself, so deeply in debt, offering short-term notes to retire maturing notes. In other words, the city borrowed to pay back what it had previously borrowed.

8. SEC, chap. 4, pp. 72-73.

9. Ibid.

10. SEC, chap. 4, pp. 72-74.

11. SEC, chap. 1, p. 43.

12. SEC, chap. 1, pp. 50-51.

13. SEC, chap. 1, p. 52.

14. SEC, chap. 1, pp. 54-55.

15. SEC, chap. 1, pp. 40-41.

16. Jac Friedgut, "Perspectives on New York City's Fiscal Crisis: The Role of the Banks," *City Almanac* (June 1977), 12: 30.

17. SEC, chap. 3, p. 19.

18. Ronald Smothers, "A Chronicle of the Crucial Dates in the City's Fiscal Crisis," *New York Times*, 28 July 1975, p. 12.

19. SEC, chap. 1, p. 45.

20. SEC, chap. 3, pp. 119-20.

21. SEC, chap. 1, p. 53.

22. SEC, chap. 1, p. 56.

23. SEC, chap. 1, p. 57.

24. SEC, chap. 4, p. 16.

25. SEC, chap. 1, pp. 58-59. This speech, especially the remark about bankruptcy as an alternative, touched off angry remarks by the mayor, and statements or memorandums from some members of the financial community, suggesting that bankruptcy was not forthcoming as a feasible alternative.

26. Smothers, "A Chronicle," p. 12.

27. Seymour Z. Mann and Edward Handman, "Perspectives on New York City's Fiscal Crisis: The Role of the Municipal Unions," *City Almanac* (June 1977), 12: 9.

28. SEC, chap. 4, p. 59.

29. "New York Bankers Say They Didn't Do It," *Business Week*, 19 September 1977, p. 50.

30. The Citizen Budget Commission issued numerous reports warning of an impending fiscal crisis. These included: "On the Mayor's Executive Expense Budget for 1967-68" (May 9, 1967); "The Financial Outlook for New York City" (July 21, 1969); "Coping with Crisis" (November 9, 1970); "Facing the Fiscal Crisis" (May 19, 1972), and "New York City's Debt Problem" (July 1973).

31. SEC, chap. 4, p. 9.

32. SEC, chap. 4, pp. 7-8.

33. SEC, chap. 1, p. 102.

34. SEC, chap. 1, p. 104.

35. SEC, chap. 4, p. 51.

36. SEC, chap. 1, p. 187.

37. SEC, chap. 1, p. 189.

38. Newfield and DuBrul, *The Abuse of Power*, p. 38.

39. SEC, chap. 3, p. 21.

40. SEC, chap. 4, pp. 31-36.

41. Adapted from SEC, chap. 4, pp. 31-36.

42. SEC, chap. 4, p. 35.

43. For examples of bankers exonerating themselves and their industry, see "New York bankers say they didn't do it," *Business Week*, 1 September 1977, p. 50.

44. Ernest Mandel, *The Second Slump* (London: Verso Books, 1980), pp. 72-73.

Chapter 6/ Using Crisis: The Bankers' Coup

1. Newfield and DuBrul, *The Abuse of Power*, p. 178.

2. Ibid.

3. *Fiscal Observer*, 16 February 1978.

4. Ibid.

5. Newfield and DuBrul provide a chilling account of this meeting in *The Abuse of Power*, pp. 184-88.

6. Tabb, *The Long Default*, p. 26.

7. New York State Financial Emergency Act for the City of New York, approved by the New York State legislature, 9 September 1975, p. 2.

8. *New York Times*, 27 July 1975, pp. 1, 32.

9. Joy Cook, "A Wealth of $ Managers: Overlapping Found in Four Key Panels," *New York Post,* 17 September 1975, p. 2.

10. Ibid.

11. *New York Times*, 19 May 1976, p. 1.

12. *New York Times,* 30 March 1981, p. B4.

13. Memorandum from Alfred Brittain, III, chairman of the Board, Bankers Trust Company, to Mayor Abraham Beame, March 4, 1977.

Chapter 7/The Municipal Unions and the Fiscal Crisis

1. "Fitch Update," in SEC, chap. 1, pp. 44-46.

2. Ibid.

3. The 2,700 forced retirees are included in the estimated number of dismissals. It is not clear from the data whether these 2,700 were included in the figure of 12,700.

4. Mann and Handman, "Perspectives," p. 9.

5. Ibid.

6. Ibid.

7. Ibid.

8. Minutes of the Municipal Labor Coalition, December 9, 1974, pp. 1-2.

9. Evelyn Seinfeld, "Chronology of the New York City Fiscal Crisis: July 18, 1974 to April 4, 1977," Department of Research and Negotiations, District Council 37, American Federation of State, County and Municipal Employees, p. 4.

10. See, for example, SEC, chap. 3.

11. "Language of crisis" is used here in a conceptual manner, similar to the use developed by Lukacs (as reification), Habermas (as distorted communication), and Marcuse (as one-dimensional thought). The thread common to my concept and theirs is the technocratically distorted language that dominates bourgeois ideology. In this domination is the alienation of human communication. The reification of everyday life, best exemplified in the elevation of the commodity as the central cultural category of everyday activity, mitigates against a nondistorted, nontechnocratic, and nonreified expression of working-class needs. The language of crisis, in this case, demonstrates the technocratic quality of this alienated consciousness and, indeed, praxis. Solutions to crisis become defined by the lack of unity and powerlessness of workers vis-a-vis capital. The discussions of alternatives fails to include genuine working class and human needs. In this sense, domination by capital extends to the "ruling ideas" of crisis resolution.

12. Jeremy Rifkin and Randy Barber, *The North Will Rise Again* (Boston: Beacon Press, 1978), p. 79.

13. It is not the object of this study to argue that the fiscal crisis was not real or severe. Rather, it has been argued throughout that the crisis was symptomatic of a far deeper struggle in the social relations of production, especially as it impacts on the state sector, represented by class struggle. Furthermore, it has been shown that the fiscal crisis was used to reorganize the mechanisms of social control over this class struggle. These mechanisms of control have been conceptualized as austerity.

14. Mann and Handman, "Perspectives," p. 10.

15. Ibid.

16. Ibid.

17. Evelyn Seinfeld, "Chronology," p. 25.

18. Mann and Handman, "Perspectives," p. 11.

19. *Annual Report of the Municipal Assistance Corporation for the City of New York* (1976), p. 15.

20. Newfield and DuBrul, *The Abuse of Power*, p. 237.

21. Ken Auletta, *The Streets*, p. 290.

22. *Fiscal Observer*, 4 May 1978, p. 2.

23. See the data in Tabb, *The Long Default*.

24. Aronowitz, *False Promises: The Shaping of American Working Class Consciousness* (New York: McGraw-Hill, 1974), p. 262.

25. Henry B. Burnett, Jr., "Interview with Jerry Wurf," *Skeptic* (May-June 1976), pp. 11-12.

Chapter 8/The Class Basis of Austerity

1. "New York City Financial Crisis," Hearings before the Committee on Banking, Housing, and Urban Affairs, United States Senate, p. 76-77.

2. Ibid., p. 705.

3. Ibid., p. 712.

4. Ibid., pp. 44-45

5. Ibid., pp. 66-67

6. Ibid., p. 68.

7. *New York Daily News*, 2 May 1979.

8. Alan Wolfe, *The Limits of Legitimacy* (New York: The Free Press, 1977), p. 2. Also see Wolfe, *America's Impasse.*

9. Michel Aglietta, "World Capitalism in the Eighties," *New Left Review*, 136 (November-December 1982): p. 25. Also see Aglietta, *A Theory of Capitalist Regulation: The US Experience* (London: New Left Books, 1979).

10. See James O'Connor's critical article "The Fiscal Crisis of the State Revisited," *KAPITALISTATE,* no. 9, 1981, pp. 41-62. O'Connor presents a critique of his seminal work, *The Fiscal Crisis of the State.* For a more current and comprehensive treatment of crisis, see O'Connor, *Accumulation Crisis* (New York: Basil Blackwell, 1984).

11. See Goodman, *The Last Entrepreneurs.*

12. Rohatyn, *The Twenty-Year Century*, pp. 171-2.

13. Ibid., pp. 115-16.

14. Ibid., pp. 117-19.

15. See Fred Block, "The Ruling Class Does Not Rule," *Socialist Revolution* (1977), 7: 6-28; Also see Block, "Beyond Relative Autonomy: State Managers as

Historical Subjects," in *Socialist Register*, Ralph Miliband and John Saville, eds. (London: Merlin Press, 1980); Miliband, *Class Power and State Power* (London: New Left Books, 1983); Nicos Poulantzas, *State, Power, Socialism* (London: New Left Books, 1978); and, for an overview, see Martin Carnoy, *The State and Political Theory* (Princeton: Princeton University Press, 1984).

16. Credit for this insight goes to Stanley Aronowitz.

17. "The New York Colossus," *Business Week*, 23 July 1984, p. 98.

18. Poulantzas, *State, Power, Socialism*, p. 137.

19. Ibid., p. 142.

Chapter 9/Labor in the Austerity State

1. "The New York Colossus," *Business Week*, 23 July 1984, p. 98.

2. Aronowitz, *False Promises*, p. 214.

3. Ibid., p. 217.

4. Ibid., p. 250.

5. Stanley Aronowitz, *Working Class Hero: A New Strategy for Labor* (New York: Pilgrim Press, 1983), p. 138.

6. See DiTomaso, "Public Employee Unions," for a discussion of the attack on public sector workers and the possible responses of their unions.

7. For discussions of public sector unions, their members' militancy, and capital's "counterattack," see: John H. Mollenkopf, "The Crisis of the Public Sector in America's Cities," in Alcaly and Mermelstein, eds., *The Fiscal Crisis*, pp. 113-31.

8. Aronowitz, *Working Class Hero*, p. 179.

9. Auletta, *The Streets*, p. 188.

10. Ibid.

11. Ibid., p. 186.

12. Johnston, "Democracy," p. 30.

13. Frances Fox Piven and Richard A. Cloward, *Poor People's Movements* (New York: Vintage Books, 1979), p. x.

14. Ibid., p. xii.

15. Ibid., pp. xii-xiii.

16. Barrington Moore, *Injustice: The Social Bases of Obedience and Revolt* (New York: M. E. Sharpe, 1978), as cited by Piven and Cloward, *Poor People's Movements*, p. xiv.

17. See Henri Lefebvre, *The Survival of Capitalism*, especially chaps. 1, 2, and 4.

Bibliography

Aglietta, Michel. *A Theory of Capitalist Regulation: The US Experience*. London: New Left Books, 1979.

———. "World Capitalism in the Eighties," *New Left Review* 136 (November-December 1982): 5-41.

Alcaly, Roger, and David Mermelstein, eds. *The Fiscal Crisis of American Cities*. New York: Vintage Books, 1977.

Althusser, Louis. *For Marx*. New York: Vintage Books, 1970.

———. *Lenin and Philosophy and Other Essays*. New York: Monthly Review Press, 1971.

———. *Essays in Self Criticism*. London: New Left Books, 1976.

Amin, Samir, Giovanni Arrighi, Andre Gunder Frank, and Immanuel Wallerstein. *Dynamics of Global Crisis*. New York: Monthly Review Press, 1982.

Aronowitz, Stanley. *False Promises: The Shaping of American Working Class Consciousness*. New York: McGraw-Hill, 1973.

———. *Food, Shelter and the American Dream*. New York: Seabury Press, 1974.

———. *The Crisis in Historical Materialism: Class, Politics and Culture in Marxist Theory*. South Hadley, Mass.: Bergin and Garvey Publishers, 1981.

———. *Working Class Hero: A New Strategy for Labor*. New York: Pilgrim Press, 1983.

Arrighi, Giovanni. "A Crisis of Hegemony," in *Dynamics of Global Crisis*, Samir Amin, et. al., eds. New York: Monthly Review Press, 1982.

Auletta, Ken. *The Streets Were Paved with Gold*. New York: Vintage Books, 1979.

Bahl, Roy. *Urban Government* Finance. Beverly Hills: Sage Publications, 1981.

———. *Financing State and Local Government in the 1980s*. New York: Oxford University Press, 1984.

241

Banfield, Edward, and James Q. Wilson. *City Politics*. New York: Vintage Books, 1963.

Block, Fred. *The Origins of International Economic Disorder*. Berkeley: University of California Press, 1977.

———. "The Ruling Class Does Not Rule," *Socialist Revolution* 7 (1977): 6-28.

———. "Beyond Relative Autonomy: State Managers as Historical Subjects," in *The Socialist Register*, Ralph Miliband and John Saville, eds. London: Merlin Press, 1980.

Boggs, Vernon, Gerald Handel, and Sylvia Fava, eds. *The Apple Sliced: Sociological Studies of New York City*. South Hadley, Mass.: Bergin and Garvey Publishers, 1984.

Bok, Derek C., and John T. Dunlop. *Labor and the American Community*. New York: Simon and Schuster, 1970.

Bookchin, Murray. *The Limits of the City*. New York: Harper and Row, 1974.

Braverman, Harry. *Labor and Monopoly Capital: The Degradation of Work in the Twentieth Century*. (New York: Monthly Review Press, 1974).

Brecher, Jeremy. *Strike!* Greenwich, Conn.: Fawcett Premier Books, 1972.

Brunhoff, Suzanne de, *The State, Capital, and Economic Policy*. London: Pluto Press, 1978.

Burnett, Henry B., Jr. "Interview with Jerry Wurf," *Skeptic* 13 (May-June 1976): 10-15.

Callinicos, Alex. *Althusser's Marxism*. London: Pluto Press, 1976.

Carnoy, Martin. *The State and Political Theory*. Princeton: Princeton University Press, 1984.

Castells, Manuel. "The Wild City," *KAPITALISTATE* 4-5 (Summer 1976): 2-30.

———. *The Urban Question*. Cambridge, Mass.: MIT Press, 1977.

———. *The Economic Crisis and American Society*. Princeton: Princeton University Press, 1980.

Citizen Budget Commission. "On the Mayor's Executive Expense Budget for 1967-68" (9 May 1967).

———. "The Financial Outlook for New York City"(21 July 1969).

———. "Coping with Crisis" (9 November 1970).

———." Facing the Fiscal Crisis" (19 May 1972).

———. "New York City's Debt Problem" (July 1973).

Clarke, Simon, Terry Lovell, et al. *One-Dimensional Marxism: Althusser and the Politics of Culture*. New York: Allison and Busby, 1980.

Clark, Terry Nichols, and Lorna Crowley Ferguson. *City Money: Political Processes, Fiscal Strain, and Retrenchment*. New York: Columbia University Press, 1983.

Cleaver, Harry. *Reading Capital Politically*. Austin: University of Texas Press, 1979.

Committee on Banking, Finance, and Urban Affairs, House of Representatives. "City Needs and the Responsiveness of Federal Grant Programs," Washington, D.C.: U.S. Government Printing Office, 1978.

Committee on Banking, Housing, and Urban Affairs, United States Senate. "New York City Financial Crisis," Washington, D. C.: U. S. Government Printing Office, 1975.

Congressional Budget Office. "New York City's Fiscal Crisis," in *The Fiscal Crisis of American Cities,* Roger Alcaly and David Mermelstein, eds., New York: Vintage Books, 1977, pp. 225-27.

Cook, Joy. "A Wealth of $ Managers: Overlapping Found in Four Key Panels," *New York Post,* 17 September 1975.

Darnton, John. "Banks Rescued the City in a Similar Plight in '33," in *The Fiscal Crisis of American Cities,* Roger Alcaly and David Mermelstein, eds., New York: Vintage Books, 1977, pp. 225-27.

Demac, Donna, and Philip Mattera. "Developing and Underdeveloping New York: The Fiscal Crisis and the Imposition of Austerity," *Zerowork* (Fall 1977), 1:113-39.

Domhoff, G. William. *Who Rules America?* Englewood Cliffs, N.J.: Prentice-Hall, 1967.

———. *The Higher Circles.* New York: Vintage Books, 1970.

———. *The Bohemian Grove and Other Retreats: A Study in Ruling Class Cohesiveness.*

———. *The Powers That Be.* New York: Vintage Books, 1979.

Ecker-Racz, L.L. *The Politics and Economics of State-Local Finance.* Englewood Cliffs, N. J.: Prentice-Hall, 1970.

Ewen, Stuart. *Captains of Consciousness: Advertising and the Social Roots of the Consumer Culture.* New York: McGraw-Hill, 1976.

Fainstein, Norman I., and Susan S. Fainstein. *Urban Policy under Capitalism.* Beverly Hills: Sage Publications, 1982.

Ferretti, Fred. *The Year the Big Apple Went Bust.* New York: G. P. Putnam 1976.

Friedgut, Jac. "Perspectives on New York City's Fiscal Crisis: The Role of the Banks," *City Almanac* 12 (June 1977): 1-7.

Friedland, Roger. *Power and Crisis in the City: Corporations, Unions and Urban Policy.* New York: Schocken Books, 1983.

Friedman, Milton. *Capitalism and Freedom.* Chicago: University of Chicago Press, 1962.

———, and Rose Friedman. *Free to Choose.* New York: Harcourt Brace Jovanovich, 1980.

Goering, John M., and Eric Lichten. "The Political Economy of Cities and the Urban Crisis," in *Political Economy: A Critique of American Society,* New York: Holt, Rinehart and Winston, 1981.

Goodman, Robert. *The Last Entrepreneurs: America's Regional Wars for Jobs and Dollars.* Boston: South End Press, 1979.

Gramsci, Antonio. *Selections from the Prison Notebooks.* New York: International Publishers, 1971.

Habermas, Jurgen. *Legitimation Crisis.* Boston: Beacon Press, 1973.

Harvey, David. *Social Justice and the City.* Baltimore: Johns Hopkins University Press, 1973.

Hilferding, Rudolf. *Finance Capital: A Study of the Latest Phase of Capitalist Development.* London: Routledge and Kegal Paul, 1981.

Hill, Richard Child. "Fiscal Collapse and Political Struggle in Decaying Central Cities in the U.S.," *KAPITALISTATE* 4-5 (Summer 1976): 31-49.

Hirsh Arthur. *The French New Left: An Intellectual History from Sartre to Gorz.* Boston: South End Press, 1981.

Jessop, Bob. *The Capitalist State.* New York: New York University Press, 1982.

Johnston, Paul. "The Promise of Public-Service Unionism," *Monthly Review* 30 (September 1978): 1-17.

———. "Democracy, Public Work and Labor Strategy," *KAPITALISTATE* 8 (1980):27-42

Joint Economic Committee, Congress of the United States. "New York City's Financial Crisis: An Evaluation of its Economic Impact and of Proposed Policy Solutions," Washington, D.C.: Government Printing Office, 1975.

———. "Changing Conditions in the Market for State and Local Government Debt," Washington, D.C.: U.S. Government Printing Office, 1976.

———. "Hearings Before the Subcommittee on Fiscal and Inter-Governmental Policy," Washington, D.C.: U.S. Government Printing Office, 1979.

Katznelson, Ira. *City Trenches: Urban Politics and the Patterning of Class in the United States.* Chicago: University of Chicago Press, 1981.

Kristol, Irving. *Two Cheers for Capitalism.* New York: Mentor Books, 1978.

Kotz, David M. *Bank Control of Large Corporations in the United States.* Berkeley: University of California Press, 1978.

Lefebvre, Henri. *Everyday Life in the Modern World.* New York: Harper and Row, 1971.

———. *The Survival of Capitalism.* London: Allison and Busby, 1976.

Leinsdorf, David, and Donald Etra. *Citibank.* New York: Grossman Publishers, 1973.

Lekachman, Robert. *Greed Is Not Enough: Reaganomics.* New York: Pantheon, 1982.

Levi, Margaret. "The Political Economy of Public-Employee Unionism," *Monthly Review* Vol. 32, No. 4 (September 1980): 46-54.

Levine, Charles H. *Managing Fiscal Stress: The Crisis in the Public Sector.* Chatham, N.J.: Chatham House, 1980.

———. , and Irene Rubin, eds. *Fiscal Stress and Public Policy.* Beverly Hills: Sage Publications, 1980.

———. , and George G. Wolohojian. *The Politics of Retrenchment: How Local Governments Manage Fiscal Stress.* Beverly Hills: Sage Publications, 1981.

Lichten, Eric. "The Development of Austerity: Fiscal Crisis of New York City," in *Power Structure Research,* G. William Denhoff, ed. Beverly Hills: Sage Publications, 1980.

———. "The Fiscal Crisis of New York City and the Development of Austerity," *The Insurgent Sociologist* 9 (Fall 1979-Winter 1980): 75:92.

———. "Fiscal Crisis, Power, and Municipal Labor," in *The Apple Sliced: Sociological Studies of New York City,* Vernon Boggs, et al., eds. South Hadley: Mass.: Bergin and Garvey Publishers, 1984.

Lukacs, Georg. *History and Class Consciousness.* Cambridge: MIT Press, 1971.

Mandel, Ernest. *Late Capitalism.* London: Verso Books, 1978.

———. *The Second Slump.* London: Verso Books, 1980.

Mann, Seymour Z., and Edward Handman. "Perspectives on New York City's Fiscal Crisis: The Role of the Municipal Unions," *City Almanac* 12 (June 1977):1, 8-12.

Marcuse, Herbert. *One-Dimensional Man.* Boston: Beacon Press, 1964.

Marx, Karl. *The Eighteenth Brumaire of Louis Bonaparte.* New York: International Publishers, 1963.

———. *Capital,* 3 Vol.. New York: International Publishers, 1967.

———. *Theories of Surplus Value,* 3 Vol. Moscow: Progress Publishers, 1968.

———, and Frederick Engels. *The German Ideology.* New York: International Publishers, 1947.

Mayer, Martin. *The Bankers.* New York: Ballantine Books, 1974.

McAdam, Terry W., and Lorie Slutsky. "The New York City Fiscal Situation as of September 1976," *The New York Community Trust,* 1976.

Miliband, Ralph. *The State In Capitalist Society.* New York: Basic Books, 1969.

———. *Marxism and Politics.* New York: Oxford University Press, 1977.

———. *Class Power and State Power.* London: Verso Books, 1983.

Mills, C. Wright. *The Power Elite.* New York: Oxford University Press, 1956.

———. *The New Men of Power.* New York: Oxford University Press, 1948.

Moffitt, Michael. *The World's Money.* New York: Simon and Schuster, 1983.

Mollenkopf, John H., "The Crisis of the Public Sector in America's Cities," in *The Fiscal Crisis of American Cities,* Roger Alcaly and David Mermelstein, eds. New York: Vintage Books, 1977, pp. 113-31.

Moore, Barrington. *Injustice: The Social Bases of Obedience and Revolt.* New York: M.E. Sharpe, 1978.

Morris, Charles R. *The Cost of Good Intentions.* New York: W. W. Norton, 1980.

Municipal Assistance Corporation. *Annual Reports of the Municipal Assistance Corporation for the City of New York: 1976, 1977, 1978, 1979, 1980.* New York: Municipal Assistance Corporation.

Municipal Labor Coalition. "Minutes of the Executive Committee of the Municipal Labor Coalition" (September 1974-January 1976).

New York State Legislature. *New York State Financial Emergency Act for the City of New York* (9 September 1975).

New York State Legislative Institute. "The Cost of Savings in New York City's Fiscal Crisis—Report B: A Year of Layoffs for Civil Servants," *Survey Research Institute of New York State* (August 1976).

Newfield, Jack, and Paul DuBrul. *The Abuse of Power: The Permanent Government and the Fall of New York.* New York: Viking Books, 1977.

O'Connor, James. *The Fiscal Crisis of the State.* New York: St. Martin's Press, 1973.

———. *The Corporation and the State.* New York: Harper and Row, 1974.

———. "The Fiscal Crisis of the State Revisited," *KAPITALISTATE* 9 (1981):41-62.

———. *Accumulation Crisis.* New York: Basil Blackwell, 1984.

Offe, Claus. "Political Authority and Class Structures: An Analysis of Late Capitalist Societies," *International Journal of Sociology* 2 (Spring 1972):73-108.

———. "Advanced Capitalism and the Welfare State," *Politics and Society* 2 (Summer 1972):479-88.

———. "The Abolition of Market Control and the Problem of Legitimacy: I," *KAPITALISTATE* 1 (1973): 109-16.

———. "The Abolition of Market Control and the Problem of Legitimacy: II," *KAPITALISTATE* 2 (1973):73-75.

———. *Contradictions of the Welfare State*, John Keane ed. Cambridge: MIT Press, 1984.

Piven, Frances Fox, and Richard A. Cloward. *Regulating the Poor: The Functions of Public Welfare*. New York: Vintage Books, 1971.

———. *The Politics of Turmoil: Poverty, Race and the Urban Crisis*. New York: Vintage Books, 1975.

———. "The Urban Crisis as an Arena for Class Mobilization," *Radical America* 11 (January-February 1977):3-8.

———. *Poor People's Movements*. New York: Vintage Books, 1979.

———. *The New Class War*. New York: Pantheon, 1982.

Poulantzas, Nicos. *Political Power and Social Classes*. London: New Left Books, 1975.

———. *Classes in Contemporary Capitalism*. London: New Left Books, 1975.

———. *State, Power, Socialism*. London: New Left Books, 1978.

Program Planners. *An Analysis of Public Employee Compensation Levels*. New York: Program Planners, Inc., 1976.

———. *New York City Municipal Labor Coalition Presentation to the Honorable Senator William Proxmire,* New York: Program Planners, Inc., 1977.

Rifkin, Jeremy, and Randy Barber. *The North Will Rise Again*. Boston: Beacon Press, 1978.

Robertson, Wyndham, "Going Broke the New York Way," *Fortune Magazine* (August 1975):144-214.

Rohatyn, Felix, "Democracy's No Free Gift," *New York Times,* 7 December 1978, p. A23.

———. "The Coming Crisis and What To Do About It," *New York Review of Books,* 4 December 1980, pp. 20-25.

———. "The Disaster Facing The North," *New York Review of Books,* 22 January 1981, pp. 13-16.

———. "Re-Constructing America," *New York Review of Books,* 5 March 1981, pp. 16-20.

———. *The Twenty-Year Century: Essays on Economics and Public Finance*. New York: Random House, 1983.

———. "The Debtor Economy: A Proposal," *New York Review of Books,* 18 November 1984, p. 16.

Securities and Exchange Commission, Committee on Banking Finance, and Urban Affairs. *Report on Transactions in Securities of the City of New York*. Washington, D.C.: U. S. Government Printing Office, 1977.

Seinfeld, Evelyn. "Chronology of the New York City Fiscal Crisis: July 18, 1974, to April 4, 1977," *Department of Research and Negotiations, District Council 37 of the American Federation of State, County and Municipal Employees.*

Serrin, William. "Rohatyn, 'Going National,' Doubts Free-Market Future," *New York Times,* 21 April 1981, pp. B1, 10.

Shalala, Donna. "A State Saves a City: The New York Case," *Duke Law Journal* (1976) 6:1119-32.

Shenker, Israel. "Urban Experts Advise, Castigate and Console the City on Its Problems," in *The Fiscal Crisis of American Cities,* Roger Alcaly and David Mermelstein, eds. New York: Vintage Books, 1977, pp. 5-10.

Simmie, James. *Power, Property and Corporatism: The Political Sociology of Planning.* London: Macmillan, 1981.

Simon, William E. *A Time for Truth.* New York: Berkeley Books, 1979.

Sweezy, Paul. "The Economic Crisis in the United States," *Monthly Review* 33 (1981):1-10.

Tabb, William K. "The New York City Fiscal Crisis," in *Marxism and the Metropolis,* William K. Tabb and L. Sawers, eds. New York: Oxford University Press, 1978.

———. *The Long Default: New York City and the Urban Fiscal Crisis.* New York: Monthly Review Press, 1981.

———, and Larry Sawers, eds. *Marxism and the Metropolis.* New York: Oxford University Press, 1978.

Temporary Commission On City Finances (TCCF). "The Fiscal Impact of Retirement Benefits: Some Proposals for Reform," *Sixth Interim Report to the Mayor by the Temporary Commission On City Finances.* New York: May 1976.

———. "The Fiscal Impact of Fringe Benefits and Leave Benefits: Some Proposals for Reform," *Seventh Interim Report to the Mayor by the Temporary Commission On City Finances.* New York: June 1976.

———. "An Historical and Comparative Analysis of Expenditures in the City of New York," *Eighth Interim Report to the Mayor by the Temporary Commission On City Finances.* New York: October 1976.

———. "The Effects of Taxation on Manufacturing in New York City," *Ninth Interim Report to the Mayor by the Temporary Commission On City Finances."* New York: December 1976.

Therborn, Goran. *What Does the Ruling Class Do When It Rules?* London: New Left Books, 1978.

Thurow, Lester. *The Zero-Sum Society.* New York: Penguin Books, 1980.

Wall Street Journal. "Several Firms Put Off Offerings as Price Cuts Continue on Old Issues," 4 December 1974, p. 34.

Wallerstein, Immanuel. "Crisis as Transition," in *Dynamics of Global Crisis.* New York: Monthly Review Press, 1982, pp. 11-54.

———. *Historical Capitalism.* London: Verso, 1983.

Waniski, Jude. *The Way The World Works.* New York: Simon and Schuster, 1978.

Wright, Erik Olin. *Class, Crisis and the State.* London: New Left Books, 1978.

Wolfe, Alan. "New Directions in the Marxist Theory of Politics," *Politics and Society* (Winter 1974):131-60.

———. *The Limits of Legitimacy.* New York: The Free Press, 1977.

———. *America's Impasse: The Rise and Fall of the Politics of Growth.* Boston: South End Press, 1981.

Index

3, 49-50; in Marxist theories of crises, 30-32, 35-36; in J. O'Connor's theory of fiscal crisis, 70; in origins of N.Y. City's fiscal crisis, 74

Clearinghouse Association, 97

Clifford, Steve, 173

Cloward, Richard A., 82, 83, 219, 220

Cohen, Bart, 84

Coleman, John, 130

collective bargaining: EFCB and, 139, 142-43; by Municipal Labor Coalition, 151; Shanker on, 163; in unions' priorities, 162; won by municipal workers, 86-87

Collins, Paul, 101

commercial bankers, 133

commodities: in circuit of capital, 32; distribution of, 36

community organizations, 224

Comptroller's Technical Debt Management Committee (CTDM Committee), 96, 104-5, 115

Congressional Budget Office, 60

conservatives, 6, 200

consumer power, Marx on, 36-37

Contingency Committee on Bankruptcy, 144-46

Cook, Joy, 142

corporate unionism, 180-84

corporations, relocating out of N.Y. City, 75

Council of Business and Economic Advisors, 111

crises, 8-10; capital accumulation and, 27-29; class struggle and, 26-27, 47-48; ideological shifts during, 208; legitimation of state in, 196; Marx on, 30-40; as product of class struggle, 11-14; state regulation by, 19; theories of, 25-26, 41-47; as transformation of power, 18. *See also* fiscal crisis

Cross, William R., Jr., 115

debts, governmental, 14-21

debts, New York City's: banks' analysis of (1974), 96-97; class interests in, 192-93; encouraged by banks, 91-92; during fiscal crisis, 123, 150; leading to fiscal crisis, 73-74

debt service, by New York City (1970-75), 103, 123-24

Debt Service Fund (proposed), 146

default. *See* bankruptcy

deficits, New York City's, 128-29, 150, 157

DeLury, John, 173

Demac, Donna, 65-66, 70

Democratic Party, 227, 228

Devine, John, 96

District 1199 (National Hospital Union), 227-28

District Council 37 (AFSCME), 88, 152; in Barbaro campaign, 227-28; growth of, 79; ideology of scarcity and, 51-52; in Municipal Labor Coalition, 151; welfare workers' strike opposed by, 84

DuBrul, Paul, 56-57, 178

economy, national: crisis in, 25; decline in, 207; Rohatyn on, 200; stagnation in, 42-43

economy, New York City's: collapse of, 74-82; decline in, 93-94; uneven growth in, 194

electoral politics, 227-28

Ellinghaus, William, 130, 138, 142, 185

Emergency Financial Control Board (EFCB), 22, 106, 138-48, 191; events leading to creation of, 136-37; Horton on, 112; labor contracts approved by, 217; Newfield on, 130; Rohatyn and, 67

employment, in New York City, loss of, 67, 74-75

entitlements, Stockman on, 5

federal government, 127; aid to New York City from, 77; antiausterity movement pressure on, 222; budget of, Stockman on, 5; deficit of, 14-15; Rohatyn proposal for, 198-200; Seasonal Loan Program of, 143-44, 177; Senate hearings on New York City's fiscal crisis, 186-90

Feinstein, Barry, 173, 175

finance capital, 6, 11, 17; austerity politics and, 193; divestiture of New York City holdings by, 166; in New York City's fiscal crisis, 23, 158; operating capital of cities controlled by, 159. *See also* banks

Financial Community Liaison Group (FCLG), 107-23, 130, 133, 156, 157

Financial Control Board, 147

Fire Department, 145

firefighters, 83-84

fiscal crisis, 7-10; class struggle and, 190-202; government debts and, 14-21; J. O'Connor on, 69-72, 195; as product of class struggle, 3, 49-50;